K-9 Structure
and
Terminology

K.9

Structure & Terminology

By
E. M. GILBERT JR.
and THELMA R. BROWN

Graphic Artwork by Kathleen Banks

Based on the Original Work by
Curtis M. and Thelma R. Brown

Second Edition

DOGFOLK
ENTERPRISES

Aloha, Oregon

Dogfolk Enterprises
17195 SW Division
Aloha, Oregon 97007
(503) 642-3585

Library of Congress Cataloging-in-Publication Data
Gilbert, Edward M.
   K-9 structure and terminology/Edward M. Gilbert, Jr. and Thelma R. Brown; graphic artwork by Kathleen Banks; based on the original work by Curtis M. and Thelma R. Brown.
   Based on The art and science of judging dogs by Curtis M. and Thelma R. Brown published in 1976.
   Includes index.
   ISBN 0-9678414-1-0
   1. Dogs—Standards.   2. Dogs—Judging.   I. Brown, Thelma R.   II. Brown, Curtis M. (Curtis Maitland), 1908–
Art and science of judging dogs.   III. Title.
IV. Title: K-nine structure and terminology.
SF425.2.G54 1995   95-40908
636.7'0811—dc20   CIP

Printed in the United States of America

10 9 8 7 6 5 4 3 2

Designed by Amy Peppler Adams, designLab, Seattle

Dedicated to the memory of
Curtis M. Brown

Professor, civil engineer, businessman, author, husband, father, breeder (Opus Beagles), researcher and student of dogs.

In 1976 Curtis and Thelma Brown co-authored the book *The Art and Science of Judging Dogs* and were awarded the Gaines "Best Book" award of that year. This book is based on Curt's research and his classic work *The Art and Science of Judging Dogs*. Curtis then authored *Dog Locomotion and Gait Analysis* in 1986; it is recognized as the leading text on dog gait.

From the time of his first dog show in 1938, Curtis was interested in the how and why of dog function. As a result he took advantage of his proximity to the San Diego Zoo to study the wild dogs and other animals, in addition to his study of dogs at the shows. This research resulted in an analytical study (frame-by-frame measurements) of movie footage he took at the zoo and the shows. He established a worldwide correspondence network on this subject. His research resulted in articles in *Kennel Review, Saluki Heritage* (England), *National Dog* (Australia), *American Dachshund* and other breed publications, and several technical journals. In addition Curtis was in constant demand for seminars and symposia throughout the world.

This book is dedicated to Curtis Brown's untiring devotion to learn all he could about the structure and movement of purebred dogs. His great desire was to share this knowledge with others—that is what this book attempts to accomplish. Thank you, Curt, for communicating the results of your research for the benefit of the entire fancy: breeder, exhibitor, handler, trainer or judge.

About the Authors

Edward M. Gilbert Jr., co-author of *The Complete Afghan Hound*, (New York, Howell Book House, 1988) and winner of the Dog Writers' Association of America award, Honorable Mention, Best Dog Book of the Year, 1967. Ed has rewritten and expanded an update of Curtis and Thelma Brown's classic work *The Art and Science of Judging Dogs*. This book is called *K-9 Structure & Terminology*, released by Howell Book House in December 1995 and this Second Edition released by Dogfolk Enterprises in Winter 2001. Since 1962 Ed has written articles for the dog press in the areas of: conformation, movement, judging, breed standards, and dog legislation. Since 1963 Ed has presented both nationally and internationally seminars on dogs. Ed is included in *Who's Who in Dogs*, by Connie Vanacore. He serves as Canine Advisor on the Advisory Board for the Center for Companion Animal Health, School of Veterinary Medicine, University of California, Davis.

Ed is an approved (1969) AKC judge of Sporting, Hounds, Akitas, Dobermans, Miscellaneous and Best in Show. He has judged specialties and all-breed shows and conducted educational programs in Australia, Canada, Finland, Israel, New Zealand and judged in Hong Kong and Taiwan.

In 1978 Ed helped organize the Los Angeles Dog Judges Educational Association (LADJEA), and has been co-chairman since its inception. In October 1983 they put on their first annual 2½ day (now 3 days) seminar, open to the entire fancy, covering at least 28 breeds and five general topics, drawing between 150 and 250 attendees each year.

Thelma R. Brown is co-author, with her husband, Curtis, of *The Art and Science of Judging Dogs* (B&E Publications, Inc.), winner of the 1967 Gaines "Best Book" award. This work is the basis for *K-9 Structure & Terminology*. Thelma and Curtis Brown were involved with purebred dogs since 1967.

Thelma was an approved (1947) AKC judge of Hounds, Terriers, Toys, Non-Sporting, 8 Sporting breeds, 5 Working breeds and BIS. She has judged in Canada, Scotland, Australia, New Zealand, Mexico and South America. Thelma has retired from judging and is now an Emeritus Judge.

For two consecutive years Thelma was chosen as one of the Top Ten Judges by *Canine Chronicle*. In 1972 *The Basenji Magazine* selected Thelma as the "Best Basenji Judge of the Year."

As a leader in judges' education, Thelma was a co-organizer and panelist, in the 1960s, of the first two day symposium for dog show judges which was held in Fresno, California. She then helped organize and was in charge of the Silver Bay Judges Workshop—the first judges' workshop in the United States. This workshop was the catalyst for the Los Angeles Dog Judges Educational Association and many other regional workshops throughout the United States.

Contents

List of Illustrations xiii

Foreword by *William Bergum* xviii

Foreword by *James W. Edwards, Ph.D.* xix

Foreword (Second Edition) by *Pat Hastings* xx

Preface xxi

1   Fundamentals of Evaluating Dogs 1
    Introduction 1
    Dog Shows 2
    Evaluation and Judging Considerations 2
    The Standard of Perfection 3
    Purpose of a Breed 6
    Scientific Principles 7
    Aesthetic Appearance of Dogs 8
    Traditional Judging 8
    Type 10
    Soundness 10
    Fancy Points 10
    Behavior 12
    Anatomy 12
    History 12
    Summary 13
    Recommended Books for the Study of Evaluating Dogs 13
    Recommended Videos for the Study of Evaluating Dogs 15

2   Dog Gaits 17
    Introduction 17
    Walk 18
    Pace and Amble 19
    Trot 21
    Analysis of Lateral Instability 23
    Gallop 26

3   Muscles, Ligaments, Tendons, Joints and Levers 29

     Introduction 29

     Muscles 32

     Tendons and Ligaments 34

     Levers. 34

     Development of Muscles 35

     Joints 35

     Function of the Trapezius and Rhomboideus Muscles. 36

     Muscles Moving the Shoulder Blade 36

     Forward Pulling Muscles of the Shoulder 37

     Backward Pulling Muscles of the Shoulder 37

     Multiplying Speed of Muscle Contraction 37

     Slope of Shoulder Blade. 37

     Up and Down Motion of the Head. 38

     Elastic Rebound 38

4   Hindquarters and Feet 39

     Rear Leg Assembly 39

     Speed, Agility, Quick Turning, and Running Uphill 39

     The Pelvis and Its Slope. 44

     Croup and Croup Angle 46

     Rearing Muscle and Ischium 48

     Hip Joint 49

     Stifles. 49

     Rear Pastern or Hock 50

     Hock Angle. 51

     Sickle Hocks 52

     Feet in Motion 52

     Showing Pads 57

5   Forequarters 59

     Forequarters. 59

     Shoulder Blade Rotation 60

     Shoulder Joint. 62

     Shoulder Blade Layback/Angulation 62

     Shoulder Blade Layback for Endurance and Smooth Gait . . . 64

     Shoulder Blades for Draft. 66

     Dachshund Shoulder Blade and Upper Arm for Digging 66

Steep Shoulder Blades and Speed 67

Shoulder Blade Placement, Short Backs and Genes 68

Set of Shoulder Blades on Side of Chest 70

The Effect of the Chest on Movement 72

Angle Between Shoulder Blade and Upper Arm 74

Length of Shoulder Blade 74

Upper Arm 75

Straight and Semi-Straight Fronts 76

Pectoral Muscles 77

Other Front Leg Bones 77

Bone in the Forearm 77

Pastern 79

Hackney Action 79

Flapping 80

Paddling 81

Padding 81

6 The Head 83

Introduction 83

Nose 86

Eye Color 87

Eye Rim Color 89

Eye Placement and Size 89

Eyes and Their Purpose 90

Lower Eyelid and Haws 92

Skull or Braincase 92

Jaw and Muzzle 93

Bite 93

Fixed Bite 93

Teeth 94

Ears 95

7 Posed Examination 97

Why a Posed Examination 97

Posed Examination 97

Table Examination 97

Type 98

Symmetry or Balance 99

Attitude—Facing Off or Sparring 100

Head 100

Body Structure 101

Neck 103

Shoulder (Blade) Angle 105

Loaded Shoulders 105

Withers 106

Elbows 106

Pasterns 106

Feet 108

Back, Backline and Topline 108

Loin 112

Bottom Line 114

Ribs 114

Croup 117

Hocks 117

Stifles 117

Coat Colors 117

Coat Texture 119

Winter and Summer Coats 121

Tying Back of Hair 121

Inheritance 122

Testicles 122

Faking and Artificial Means 123

Vicious Dogs 124

8 Front and Rear Acting Together 125

Dog's Origin 125

Gaiting 126

The Legs in Action at a Trot 128

Defects Found When Front and Rear Are Out of Balance . . 129

Speed of Leg Movement 130

Single Tracking 132

Daisy Clipping/Skimming 133

Number of Joints 134

Flank and the Flex of the Back 134

Back Movement to the Side 135

Effect of Head and Neck in Motion 135

Tail 136

Endurance 136

Short and Long Bodies 136

Optical Illusions 138

Stringing Up the Dog 139

Crabbing 139

Excessive Angulation 140

Rhythm Defects in Short-Legged Dogs 141

The Roll (Old English Sheepdog) 141

Handling Tricks 141

Interfering 142

Rope Walking or Weaving 143

Lame Dogs 143

9 Application of Scientific Principles **145**

Studying Standards by Similarities 145

Arctic Breeds 145

Sighthounds 149

Terriers 154

Short-Legged Dogs 159

Mastiff Type Dogs 162

Aesthetic Breeds 166

Pointer 168

German Shepherd Dog 170

Bulldog 171

Papillon 173

10 Principles for Evaluating Dog Gaits **175**

Training Your Eye to See the Dynamics of Motion 175

A Word of Caution 176

Standard of Perfection 176

Deviations from Ideal Endurance Trot 176

Basic Principles for Judging Gait in Review 182

Summary 183

Appendix   Technical Data in Summary 185

Introduction 185

General Technical Information 185

The Dog's Front 186

The Dog's Rear 187

Odds and Ends 187

Gaits of Dogs. 187

Other Gait Features 189

Efficient Endurance Trotters 189

Efficient Gallopers 192

Pressure Plate Tests. 193

Fancy Points 195

Breed Purpose 195

Glossary   197

Index   229

Illustrations

Figure	Title	Page
1-1.	Common dog terms.	3
1-2.	The Greyhound.	5
1-3.	The black wolf.	7
1-4.	The bush dog.	8
1-5.	Keeshond head study.	9
1-6.	Fox Terrier type changes.	11
2-1.	Short stepping walk.	16
2-2.	Principles of the short stepping walk.	18
2-3.	Dog pacing.	20
2-4.	A Kerry Blue Terrier trotting.	21
2-5.	In the trot diagonals G and H, J and K are alternately on the ground.	22
2-6.	Illustration of lateral instability.	24
2-7.	Graphic representation of lateral instability.	25
2-8.	Double suspension gallop.	26
2-9.	Salukis galloping.	27
2-10.	Saluki paw stance and swing time at the gallop.	28
3-1.	Trunk—first layer of muscle under the skin.	30
3-2.	Second layer of muscle—side view.	30
3-3.	Second layer of muscle—top view.	30
3-4.	Second layer of muscle—underview of neck and chest.	31
3-5.	Muscles of the third layer—simplified.	31
3-6.	Deeper muscles of the trunk and thigh.	32
3-7.	All joints are operated by two muscles.	34
3-8.	Norwegian Elkhound.	35
4-1.	Bones of the hindquarters.	40
4-2.	Hindquarters, rear view.	41
4-3.	Muscles on inner side of left hind leg.	41
4-4.	Conformation for fast uphill travel and quick turns.	42
4-5.	Excellent uphill conformation.	43

Figure	Title	Page
4-6.	Quick turn conformation.	43
4-7.	Pelvis—top view.	44
4-8.	Normal pelvis slope provides normal back reach.	45
4-9.	Steep pelvis limits back reach.	45
4-10.	Low tail set usually indicates steep pelvis and restricted back reach.	46
4-11.	Afghan Hound with proper sloping croup.	47
4-12.	Rear propulsion.	48
4-13.	Long calcaneal process provides endurance.	50
4-14.	Bones of the forefoot.	53
4-15.	Pads and toes of the left forefoot—viewed from below.	53
4-16.	Pads and toes of the left hind foot—viewed from below.	54
4-17.	The camel has large feet for desert conditions.	55
4-18.	Cairn Terriers are diggers.	56
5-1.	Bones of the forequarters.	58
5-2.	Forequarters, front view.	60
5-3.	Muscles of outer side of right foreleg.	61
5-4.	Shoulder blade motion.	61
5-5.	Shoulder blade angles—vertical and level layback angles.	62
5-6.	Shoulder blade measurements.	63
5-7.	Maximum forward reach at a trot with a 50 degree layback angle.	64
5-8.	Trotting dogs with steep shoulder blades have reduced forward reach.	65
5-9.	The Dachshund's elbow is well above the brisket (keel).	67
5-10.	Simplified drawing illustrating layback as a function of rib cage vertebrae length.	68
5-11.	Layback with a long neck, long rib cage and a short loin.	68
5-12.	Layback with a short neck, short rib cage and medium loin.	69
5-13.	Preferred set of shoulder blades shown in (A). Shoulder blades set too far forward in (B).	71
5-14.	Giraffe shoulder blade location is far forward.	72
5-15.	Circular chest (A), oval chest (B), oval tapered chest (C).	73

Figure	Title	Page
5-16.	Short upper arm provides a straight front or terrier front.	75
5-17.	Beagle; note forequarters.	77
5-18.	Position of the horse's leg in the hackney gait.	79
5-19.	Dachshund front leg flapping.	80
6-1.	Three basic head types: (A) brachycephalic; (B) mesaticephalic; (C) dolichocephalic.	82
6-2.	Bichon Frise. Hair creates an illusion of entirely different head shape than the dog actually possesses.	84
6-3.	The skull—side view.	84
6-4.	The skull—top view.	85
6-5.	Bones and muscles of the head which primarily determine head shape.	85
6-6.	Lhasa Apso.	86
6-7.	Variations in eye shape and placement.	91
6-8.	Types of bites.	94
6-9.	Half set of teeth.	95
6-10.	Basenji ears are of benefit for hunting.	96
7-1.	Bones of the spinal column and rib cage—side view.	101
7-2.	Bones of the spinal column and rib cage—top view.	102
7-3.	Breastbone or sternum as seen from below.	103
7-4	Neck or cervical vertebrae.	104
7-5.	Arched and ewe neck.	104
7-6.	Pasterns.	107
7-7.	Back, backline and topline.	109
7-8.	Race horse backline.	109
7-9.	Chesapeake Bay Retriever.	110
7-10.	Dog toplines.	111
7-11.	Cross section of the loin, just before hip bone at sixth lumbar vertebrae.	113
7-12.	Cross section of deepest part of chest — fifth thoracic vertebrae.	115
7-13.	Rib rotation.	116
7-14.	Shih Tzu.	122
8-1.	African hunting dog.	126
8-2.	Comparison of the foot of the dog and the horse.	127

Figure	Title	Page
8-3.	Gait patterns.	127
8-4.	German Shepherd Dog in flying trot.	129
8-5.	Cheetah—reputed to be the world's fastest land mammal.	131
8-6.	Sidewise back movement.	135
8-7.	Daylight under a dog.	137
8-8.	The posed dog.	140
8-9.	Old English Sheepdog (OES) and OES Herding.	142
9-1.	Alaskan Malamute.	144
9-2.	Akita.	147
9-3.	Samoyed.	148
9-4.	Regular hock vs. Chow Chow hock.	149
9-5.	Saluki.	152
9-6.	Ibizan Hound.	154
9-7.	Pharoah Hound.	154
9-8.	Scottish Terrier.	155
9-9.	Sealyham Terrier.	156
9-10.	Welsh Terrier.	157
9-11.	Kerry Blue Terrier.	158
9-12.	Dachshund.	159
9-13.	Pembroke Welsh Corgi.	161
9-14.	Mastiff.	163
9-15.	Bullmastiff.	164
9-16.	Great Pyrenees.	165
9-17.	Rottweiler.	166
9-18.	Boston Terrier.	167
9-19.	Chinese Crested.	167
9-20.	Chinese Crested in action.	168
9-21.	Papillon.	173
10-1.	Smooth Fox Terrier.	178
10-2.	Cardigan Welsh Corgi.	179
10-3.	Bulldog.	180
10-4.	German Shepherd Dog.	181
10-5.	Pointer.	181

Figure	Title	Page
10-6.	Whippet.	182
A-1.	Alaskan Malamute all champion sled team.	184
A-2.	Alaskan Malamutes doing what they were bred for.	190
A-3.	German Shorthaired Pointer—form equals function.	194

Foreword

There is a need in the world of dogs for a comprehensive, conclusive book on canine structure and terminology. This book fills that need.

A basic introduction to the "bits and pieces" that put canines together combined with a glossary of everyday vocabulary used to describe dogs and their structure, this book takes intricate, sometimes complicated and challenging subjects and presents them in an easy-to-read, easy-to-understand format.

Written by Edward M. Gilbert Jr., award-winning co-author of *The Complete Afghan Hound*, and by Thelma Brown, who worked with her late husband Curtis M. Brown on the classic works *The Art and Science of Judging Dogs* and *Dog Locomotion and Gait Analysis*, this book expands on those authoritative publications and helps the average reader cut through scientific terms and definitions. Ed and Thelma have joined efforts to create a book that deals with complex subject matter on a level all can understand. It flows and whets the appetite for the next page and the next.

Gilbert brings to this book, *K-9 Structure and Terminology*, his experience of over forty years of participation in the dog world. He was a breeder of Sighthounds; is an American Kennel Club judge of Sporting, Hound, and Working dogs and has written for various dog publications. He has spoken extensively on anatomy, movement, conformation and dog Standards and is a true student of the sport of dogs.

Thelma Brown, with a vast background in dogs as a judge, writer and lecturer, lent to Ed Gilbert her records, knowledge and expertise to guide the formation of this book.

Reading *K-9 Structure and Terminology* has been a stimulating experience for me. I thoroughly enjoyed it and know you will as well.

William Bergum
Former Director, The American Kennel Club
Breeder and Exhibitor of Pekingese
AKC Judge—Hounds, Terriers, Toys & Non-Sporting

Foreword

The world of studying and learning canine conformation suffers from a remarkable silence if only in regard to books that meet the demands of today's concerned breeders, owners and judges. While there are classics, such as Curtis and Thelma Brown's *The Art and Science of Judging Dogs*, in only a few cases have they been revisited with two goals clearly in mind: to preserve the essence of the original and to improve it where possible.

Thelma Brown has been joined by Ed Gilbert Jr. in a transformation that meets the above criteria, and thus *K-9 Structure and Terminology* is factually and intellectually dedicated to Curtis Brown's memory and scholarship.

If you wish to begin or advance your knowledge of canine conformation, *K-9 Structure and Terminology* provides an integrated, comprehensive description of the details and concepts of canine variation. And it does so with a clear focus on the importance of establishing a common terminology that can be understood and applied.

One of the strengths of this book is the reference to principles of mammalian zoology. For example, isn't it possible to ask and answer important questions about neck length and head carriage in dogs by comparing them with these features in other mammalian species? And even if one argues that it might be misleading, doesn't the history of comparative zoology demand that such analysis occur? Well yes, with one caveat: Perhaps it is unwise without some reservation to compare natural species and their evolution with domestic breeds and the results of human selection during the last few thousand years. Of course such comparisons are interesting and probably important.

But enough rambling. Buy the book. Enjoy it, and let's talk comprehensively about canine conformation. Our world will be improved and the discussions will reach appropriate heights. Congratulations, Ed and Thelma, on a job well done.

James W. Edwards, Ph.D.
Professor of Biology, Emeritus, Salem College
American Kennel Club Director; Judging Research & Development

Foreword (Second Edition)

In 1996, I was invited to be a member of a panel of critical reviewers at the Los Angeles Dog Judges Educational Association's annual symposium. The subject up for review and discussion was the recently published book, *K-9 Structure & Terminology*, by Edward M Gilbert Jr. and Thelma R. Brown. The event marked the beginning of my deep appreciation for the educational value of this book. Every person active in the dog world can gain from its content and I encourage all to include this one in your canine library.

K-9 Structure & Terminology is based on Curtis M. and Thelma Brown's research into the structure and locomotion of animals. *The Art and Science of Judging Dogs* was published in 1978 and *Locomotion and Gait Analysis* was published in 1986. These works were the most comprehensive and insightful treatise on canine structure and movement to date. His background in engineering, combined with his fascination with animals, brought to the world a new way of looking at and analyzing structure and motion.

Ed Gilbert, in collaboration with Thelma Brown applied Brown's exceptional work to breed standards and the show ring. The results yielded a book that is easy for all of us involved in the sport of purebred dogs to read, understand, and (most importantly) learn from. Gilbert endeavors to improve the presentation, where necessary, while preserving the essence and conclusions of the original work. The addition of a comprehensive glossary of terms helps to give us an accurate, common ground vocabulary with which to continue the discussion.

All of us in the dog world should strive for perfection, if only to maintain our focus on improving the quality of purebred dogs. In this effort, we are all students. We need to train our eyes and our hands to recognize the strengths in a dog's structure and movement. This book is an excellent guide in our unending quest of applicable knowledge.

Pat Hastings
AKC Judge—Herding, Non-Sporting, Working
Lecturer
Producer—"Puppy Puzzle Video"
Author—"Tricks of the Trade—From Best Intentions to Best In Show"

Preface

Everyone involved in the sport of purebred dogs is to some degree a judge, whether they be breeder, owner, judge or exhibitor in field, obedience, or show. They all need to be able to evaluate structure to determine their dog's ability to function. This evaluation should be based on knowledge.

This book is an attempt to provide the basic knowledge, based upon fact instead of fancy. As science is continually in pursuit of new facts and the testing of theories, we would hope the reader does the same.

The potential of a dog to do certain physical tasks can, within broad limits, be predicted. A dog with a build like a Greyhound can be expected to run fast. A Labrador can be expected to swim better than a Whippet. Too little is known about the internal functions of muscles, nerves and the digestive system to allow an accurate forecast of a given dog's performance. Until such time as proof by trial is added to dog show judging, the evaluation of correct structure for performance of a given purpose will remain an opinion.

Dogs have some parts perfected for specific functions, while other parts are defective or useless. Of what benefit are dewclaws? Why a stop, or cropped ears? It would seem that the essential items should be more important than the inessential in dog judging, but this is not always so. In some breeds beauty and fancy points are weighed heavily.

It is the opinion of the authors that the mean cannot be understood *without studying the extremes*. To understand efficiency in uphill travel, the structure of goats or sheep should be analyzed. To understand how a Greyhound attains speed, the cheetah and the gazelle should be observed. For these reasons, within this book, numerous comparisons are made with other animals.

Professor Eadweard Muybridge, in the text *Animals in Motion*, was one of the first (1878) to apply photography to the study of animals in motion (including the Greyhound). Leland Stanford theorized that horses at a fast trot had all four hoofs off the ground at one time; Muybridge was employed to prove or disprove this theory. With several cameras lined up (one picture per camera), Muybridge obtained photos in series showing fast-trotting horses with all hoofs off the ground at one time. He also demonstrated that the position of horses' legs in many old paintings occurred only in the mind of the artist.

Since Muybridge's time much has been added to the volumes of knowledge about dogs and other animals. In the references listed in Chapter 1 are some of the better-known books. As time goes on we will have a better understanding and more complete knowledge of the structure and motion of dogs.

In studying this book, you should aim for at least two objectives: first, to train the mind to know what to look for in evaluating dogs; second, to begin training the subconscious mind to react quickly and recognize perfection, not imperfection, in the pictures before the eyes. Always look for quality!

The objective of this book is to point out which structure or structures best accomplish a particular work purpose. We hope that studying this book will help make you an independent thinker rather than a follower of the crowd.

The skeletal drawings in this book are based on the drawings contained in *Art Anatomy of Animals*, by Ernest Thompson Seton, 1977, and published by Running Press, Philadelphia, Pennsylvania. Graphic artwork based on these illustrations was done by Kathleen Banks. Original artwork from *The Art and Science of Judging Dogs* was lost, and Kathleen reconstructed these also. This required many long hours and much dedication. Thanks to Kathleen's professionalism for a job well done.

The authors are indebted most of all to Curtis Brown for his past research and writings on the subjects covered herein. Special thanks go to Nancy Shonbeck for the Chihuahua drawing and to the photographers and members of the fancy who provided photographs for this book. Marcy Zingler, the editor, provided many invaluable suggestions that added to the effectiveness of this book. Any errors you may uncover are solely the responsibility of Edward M. Gilbert Jr. Read, think and be challenged.

Thelma R. Brown and Edward M. Gilbert Jr.

CHAPTER 1

Fundamentals of Evaluating Dogs

Introduction

The breed Standard describes the breed, but without prior knowledge of the meaning of dog terms, the description is nebulous. New dog show exhibitors have difficulty understanding how judges evaluate dogs. When listening to others at dog shows, the novice is exposed to fads, fancies, prejudices and facts; sorting truth from bias requires insight seldom possessed.

One of the authors well remembers an early experience wherein an exhibitor vocally extolled the virtues of his pride and joy, a dog that moved with legs wide apart. Some time later the author discovered that the dog was supposed to travel with legs close together, not waddle like a duck. From this and several other exposures to faulty opinions, both authors have learned to seek verification. Since we are both students, we soon discovered that the best source of reliable dog information came from quality books. In the bibliography at the end of this chapter are classics that we believe should be read by every serious dog enthusiast.

Success in evaluating dogs requires knowledge in two areas: art and science. In one sense, selecting the best dog is an art; the dog with beauty of form, proportion, symmetry and style should win. In another sense, selecting the best dog is a science; the dog with the best structure designed to efficiently fulfill the dog's purpose in life should win. Winning dogs have both aesthetic appeal and scientifically correct structure, not just one feature.

Technical words discourage readers. For this reason, where possible here, scientific words are avoided. The parts of dogs are described by common names, not medical names. Shoulder blades are called shoulder blades, not scapulas. Scientific words are used where necessary to provide a bridge between this book and other, more technical works.

Dog Shows

The first competitive dog show was held in Newcastle, England, in 1859. The Kennel Club of Great Britain was formed in 1873; the American Kennel Club (AKC) was formed in 1884. As dog shows became more popular, people began breeding dogs for appearance rather than utility.

Most dog breeds were developed for a work purpose. With the invention of machines, the scarcity of game and changes in environment, the usefulness of dogs for work diminished. Today, Bulldogs no longer bait bulls, Dachshunds seldom hunt German badgers and Scottish Deerhounds seldom follow the almost extinct stag. Without dog shows these breeds and others like them probably would have vanished.

Many breeds not adopted by dog fanciers have disappeared. The last Pocket Beagle observed by the authors was in 1941. Although they were very popular as hunting dogs in Great Britain prior to World War I, they are probably now extinct. The English Water Spaniel, the Talbot Hound and the Large Water Dog have departed, along with many others. If these breeds had been adopted by dog fanciers, their chances of survival would have been greater.

As the work for dogs diminished, the keeping of dogs as pets and as companions increased. Breeds that evolved in size, appearance and behavior compatible with people prospered. Today, more than ever, people want dogs distinct in type, beautiful to look at and a joy to keep. Art does enter into dog evaluation and show judging.

Evaluation and Judging Considerations

At dog shows, except in the Obedience ring, the winner is selected by opinion, not trial. The Beagle is not asked to chase rabbits. The Retriever is not asked to retrieve birds. The Greyhound is not asked to run a mile to test endurance. By looking, feeling and occasionally measuring the judge selects the dog that he/she thinks best adheres to the breed Standard.

In science, things are reduced to measurements, counts, mathematical relationships or predictable outcomes. In the early days of the Royal Academy of Science, if an item could not be measured, it could not be discussed on the floor. The basis of science is measurement. If dog show judging were a science, a measuring committee would decide on the facts; no judgment or judge would be needed. Since judging in the ring is not entirely dependent upon measurements, judging is classified as an art.

This does not mean that knowledge of scientific principles cannot help judging; it can. By scientific analysis of the dog's structure it can be shown that high hocks (as on a rabbit) are better for initial speed; low hocks are better for endurance; heavy muscles are for strength and well laid-back shoulder blades produce a smooth gait. By knowing such facts a person is better able to select the dog best qualified to perform a given purpose. Knowledge of science is a necessary aid to the art of judging. Without it, judgment would indeed be poor.

When judging the quality of dogs, these points are considered:

1. The purpose of a breed
2. Scientific principles that effectuate purposes
3. The written Standard and the various interpretations of that Standard
4. Artistic or aesthetic appeal

5. Tradition (unwritten items)

6. Type

7. Soundness

8. Fancy points

9. Behavior

10. Anatomy

11. History

12. The American Kennel Club rules applicable to all dogs entered in a dog show

The numerical sequence of these items does not indicate their order of importance. All are essential, but in some breeds, one may be more important than another.

The Standard of Perfection

Every breed of dog has a written Standard of Perfection. The dog most nearly conforming to that breed's Standard should win in a show. Unfortunately, the Standard is written in English, and English words are not always exact in meaning. Is blue a color or a feeling? Experts in the dog game often argue over the exact meaning of a particular phrase or word; universal agreement does not exist. Thus, Standards have variations of interpretation. Standards are not written for novices. Figure 1-1 and the Glossary contain many of the terms.

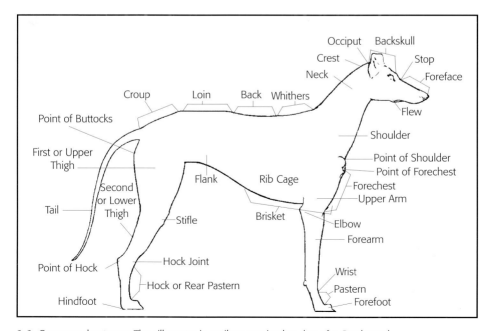

1-1. Common dog terms. The silhouette is easily recognized as that of a Greyhound.

In general, the authors of Standards assume that the reader has already acquired knowledge of:

1. Dog terms
2. Dog anatomy
3. Dog behavior
4. The dog in motion
5. The function of parts
6. Appearance (type)

Before people can claim proficiency in understanding a Standard, they must study the meaning of dog terms, go to many shows, talk to knowledgeable people, read much, keep an open mind and allow time for the true picture to sink in. It is not an overnight process. By self-proclamation, many claim to be dog experts; few are.

Below is an American Kennel Club Standard of a breed. Suppose that a complete novice read this Standard. Would he know whether the description applied to a cat, dog or some other mammal? Suppose further that the novice was told that a dog was being described. Do you think that he could tell whether a Sporting, Hound, Working, Terrier, Toy, Non-Sporting or Herding breed was described? Without looking at the answer, can you tell?

Head: *Long and narrow, fairly wide between the ears, scarcely perceptible stop, little or no development of nasal sinuses, good length of muzzle, which should be powerful without coarseness. Teeth very strong and even in front.*

Ears: *Small and fine in texture, thrown back and folded except when excited, when they are semipricked.*

Eyes: *Dark, bright, intelligent, indicating spirit.*

Neck: *Long, muscular without throatiness, slightly arched, and widening gradually into the shoulder.*

Shoulders: *Placed as obliquely as possible, muscular without being loaded.*

Forelegs: *Perfectly straight, set well into the shoulders, neither turned in nor out, pasterns strong.*

Chest: *Deep, and as wide as consistent with speed, fairly well-sprung ribs.*

Back: *Muscular and broad.*

Loins: *Good depth of muscle, well arched, well cut up in the flanks.*

Hindquarters: *Long, very muscular and powerful, wide and well let down, well-bent stifles. Hocks well bent and rather close to the ground, wide but straight fore and aft.*

Feet: *Hard and close, rather more hare than cat-feet, well knuckled up with good strong claws.*

Tail: *Long, fine and tapering with a slight upward curve.*

Coat: *Short, smooth and firm in texture.*

Color: *Immaterial.*

The weight of the dog was deliberately omitted. The missing sentence is: "*Weight— Dogs 65 to 70 pounds; bitches 60 to 65 pounds.*" With this added information a person well acquainted with dogs might conclude that the words were describing a short-haired speedster of about 65 pounds or, in other words, a Greyhound, not a Whippet or Italian Greyhound. Refer to Figure 1-2.

Without prior knowledge such a conclusion would be impossible. In the above Standard take the words, "*Shoulders—Placed as OBLIQUELY as possible,*" and "*Hocks . . . RATHER CLOSE to the ground.*" Who knows exactly what is meant by *rather close* or *obliquely*? Is *rather close* two inches, three inches or just the result of an argument that the Standard committee could not agree on? Is *oblique* 10 degrees? 20 degrees? 30 degrees? 45 degrees? 60 degrees? or what? Those displaying good judgment reason this way. What is the dog designed for? If it is speed, what oblique angle for the shoulder blade layback produces the greatest speed? 20 degrees or 30 degrees? What are the advantages of "*Hocks . . . RATHER CLOSE to the ground*"? Speed? Endurance? Do Greyhounds need endurance as well as speed? These questions need scientific analysis.

1-2. The Greyhound. The Greyhound has a long neck, long and narrow head, and rose ears. The loin is well arched. The arch is not of the roach type; the curve begins at the loin and falls away to the tail. There is no indication of a roach. *Photo by Missy Yuhl.*

If a particular point in a breed Standard is clearly defined, it is recognized and upheld as defined. But if a particular point is poorly defined, a judge must interpret the meaning of what the Standard says; most Standards require interpretation.

The American Cocker Spaniel Standard (1992) reads: "*The bony structure beneath the eyes is well chiseled with no prominence in the cheeks.*" Cocker Spaniels retrieve; a soft mouth for retrieving is desirable. Prominence in the cheeks indicates strong jaw muscles. Dogs with strong jaw muscles are apt to leave teeth marks on retrieved game. Persons knowing the reason for the Standard's words are less apt to forgive a cheeky Cocker Spaniel. Knowledge of the function of parts enables the observer to correctly interpret the Standard's words.

When we say "dog," we know it is a mammal with four legs, a "normal" set of teeth, toenails, four paws, etc. The mere fact that the Standard fails to mention that the exhibit must have four paws does not allow a dog with three paws to be eligible for consideration. We probably should think of the Standard as describing the main features of the breed, not as a document describing all details. In the above Greyhound Standard no mention is made of the number of eyes, legs, ears, toenails, teeth, or ribs. Every Standard includes much more than is written.

Purpose of a Breed

For every purpose of a dog there are specific builds that give superior performance. The wolf in Figure 1-3 has a build developed for trotting with endurance. A dog sight chasing game in open country needs to be lean, long-legged and fast (Greyhound). If the country becomes brush covered and hilly, speed combined with the ability to bound over bushes and up hilly terrain are necessities, as in the Afghan Hound. A dog that goes to ground after German badgers should be short-legged, strong and determined enough to fight a badger, fearless and capable of digging (Dachshund). The wild bush dog pictured in Figure 1-4 evolved a similar structure. A dog retrieving game from water needs to be webfooted (Chesapeake Bay Retriever). If the dog is to live in the far north, a heavy undercoat for protection from cold and big feet for footing in the snow are required. Understanding the purpose of a dog often explains how its structural parts must be built.

Not all dogs serve a working or hunting purpose. Some please people. A hackney gait in a horse pleases the eye; it does not improve working or running ability. A hackney gait in a dog (Miniature Pinscher) also pleases the eye; it does not improve efficiency of movement.

Through a correct breeding plan, dogs can become better and better adapted to a particular use. The process of developing better dogs is not confined to history. Today, by selection, many breeders are improving dog breeds to match present day needs. It can be expected that in the future, just as in the past, man will develop different types of dogs adapted to a new environment.

Many Standards of Perfection fail to mention the purpose of a breed. Those who wrote breed Standards were probably so well acquainted with their breed and its purpose that the desirability of stating the breed's purpose never occurred to them.

If a Standard is not clear in describing the dog's build, the specimen best qualified to accomplish the breed's purpose should be preferred. Knowing which build is superior for a particular purpose requires some knowledge of scientific principles.

1-3. The black wolf (Canis lupus). This is the black phase of the Mississippi Valley Red Wolf, and is probably similar to the ancestor of dogs. It has an ideal body and legs designed for trotting with endurance; it has moderate speed. All wolves will amble at times, as pictured above. Notice the angle at the hock and stifle joints. *Photo courtesy San Diego Zoo.*

Scientific Principles

Writings on the correct structure that efficiently produces motion in dogs are generally traceable to Captain M. Horace Hayes' book entitled *Points of the Horse* (7th edition, 1969). This book, first published in 1893, is still widely read by horse breeders. Authors of dog articles and dog books frequently "borrowed" ideas from this pioneer text. Some of the principles of levers, as applied to horses, are valid when applied to comparable parts in some dogs. Obviously, no horse ever dug a burrow, went to ground or baited bulls. Race horses, running at top speed, do not flex their backs like Greyhounds. Books on horses are an aid to understanding the correct structure for some dogs, but the reader must not assume that all principles applicable to horses are equally applicable to all dogs.

The difference between a scientist's view and an artist's view regarding speed is as follows: The scientist thinks, "What is the correct placement and size of bones, muscles, tendons and joints in a Greyhound that will produce the greatest speed?" The artist thinks, "What arrangement of the Greyhound's parts makes it look as though the dog is fast?" Since appearance may be an optical illusion, it is better to rely on sound scientific fact.

Those who have a good science background know that an arched neck is structurally stronger than a ewe neck. They also know that a (nearly) single tracking Sporting dog has more endurance than a dog traveling with legs spread far apart. Scientific knowledge of the function of parts is a necessary adjunct to good judgment.

1-4. The bush dog. The short legs of the bush dog, a wild animal, are similar to those found on domestic dogs; however, the two are unrelated. Short legs do occur in nature. *Photo courtesy San Diego Zoo.*

Aesthetic Appearance of Dogs

One person looks at a picture and says it is beautiful; another looks at the same picture and says it is ugly. Aesthetic opinion varies considerably, even among competent people. Whenever an item is a matter of judgment, as beauty and symmetry are, variations of opinion can be expected. At dog shows competent judges do not always select the same dog.

When judging art on visual appeal, there are no set standards; opinions vary within reasonable limits. (Refer to Figure 1-5.) For this reason, if a person wants an evaluation of a dog, several opinions should be sought.

Traditional Judging

Judging the quality of a dog by Standards that are handed down by word of mouth from one generation to another without written authority is traditional judging. This is similar to common law found in the courts. Pugs roll, but until 1991 the Standard (1883) did not say so. People knew this by tradition. The Beagle Standard (1957) says "Any true hound color." How many have seen a blue-ticked Beagle champion? Tradition and only tradition tends to follow the Beagle color pattern rather than "Any true hound color." Tradition may eventually become type.

It is probably true that no Standard covers all points taken into consideration at shows. By knowing a breed's original purpose and traditions and by knowing many

1-5. Keeshond head study. The expression of this breed is largely dependent on the distinctive characteristic called "spectacles." The small erect triangular shaped ears, foxlike expression, dark eyes, black pigmentation and lion-like ruff add to the beauty of this breed and set type. *From the portrait by Cleanthé.*

dogs, unmentioned points are evaluated. The Siberian Husky Standard (1990) neatly takes care of omitted words by stating, "*In addition to the faults already noted, the obvious structural faults common to all breeds are as undesirable in the Siberian Husky as in any other breed, even though they are not specifically mentioned herein.*"

Type

Type can be defined as "the characteristic qualities distinguishing a breed; the embodiment of a Standard's essentials." (*The Complete Dog Book.*)

Type characteristics embody structure, movement, temperament and fancy points of a given breed. Breeds have been established based on a given purpose, and function within certain environmental conditions. The breed characteristics that either met those requirements—or met the requirements in the mind of the breed founders—were in recent years incorporated into a written breed Standard.

While general type is established by the written Standard, details are best observed. Eye expression, characteristic gait and coat texture cannot be adequately described in writing, but can be fixed in the mind by looking at many outstanding specimens.

As previously stated, Standards are not always clear and often require interpretation. If type is "the characteristic qualities distinguishing a breed," and if the meaning of words in a Standard requires interpretation, it follows that type can vary, depending upon who is doing the interpreting.

Some argue that there is only one correct type for a given breed. It is probably true that there should be only one correct type, but type is not subject to count or measurement. All dog experts have fixed in their minds an image believed to correctly represent breed type. Unfortunately, that image is not always identical to the image held by others. Between experts variation of opinion does exist. (Refer to Figure 1-6.)

Soundness

The *AKC Complete Dog Book* defines soundness as: "The state of mental and physical health when all organs and faculties are complete and functioning normally, each in its rightful relation to the other." We would expand that definition to include that the dog is fit to perform whatever function it is designed to carry out. Each breed's soundness is a function of its basic original purpose as defined by the Standard.

The Bulldog has a body that is well let down between the shoulders and forelegs, giving the dog a broad, short-legged appearance. A Bulldog with this appearance is a sound Bulldog, but a Fox Terrier with this appearance is an unsound or atypical Fox Terrier. There is a subtle difference, in some cases, between a dog that is atypical or unsound and one that lacks type. A Bulldog with erect ears would lack type but could still be considered sound.

Obvious physical faults, such as lameness, blindness, deafness, etc., or temperament problems also constitute unsoundness. Unsoundness can be due to poor conformation, lack of coordination or condition, an accident, or disease. *Briefly stated, soundness is fitness to function.*

Fancy Points

As used in judging cattle, horses and other domestic animals, fancy points are arbitrary characteristics that the specimen must have in order to qualify as an acceptable member of the given breed.

Dalmatians have spots. Spots do not make the dog a better pet, a better trotter or a sounder dog, but they do set type. Dachshunds have short legs to enable them to efficiently dig and crawl through burrows; short legs exist for a purpose, *not* a fancy point. Many breed Standards require dark eyes; yellow is sometimes a disqualification.

1-6. Fox Terrier type changes. The Fox Terrier of 1806, 1895, and the present are shown. A History and Description with Reminiscences of the Fox Terrier, *Rawdon B. Lee and Horace Cox, London, 1889; bottom photo by L. F. Sosa.*

As yet no one has demonstrated that in the Arctic region or temperate zone, yellow eyes impart inferior eyesight. It is pure fancy that some Arctic dogs must have dark eyes. Some breeds require long coats, yet when hunting in certain types of brush country, the dog with a long coat is at a disadvantage; again, fancy.

Not all points required on a dog are for a structural advantage or utility purpose; many points are to set type or are for aesthetic reasons to suit the fancy. So be it. People judging dogs uphold fancy points merely because the Standard says so, not because fancy points aid utility.

Behavior

Few breed Standards adequately state what the behavior of a breed should be, yet most dog people know. A good Terrier ring can be a noisy ring; each dog may let every other dog know who is boss. Scenthounds are loving, peaceful animals used to trail in groups; they seldom fight. Bird dogs were selected for peaceful coexistence in a kennel; fighting is out of character. War dogs and guard dogs were originally selected for size and ferocity. Nowadays, within the United States, Canada and Great Britain these same breeds are selected for gentle behavior patterns. Our society and the Kennel Club rules will not tolerate mean dogs.

While few Standards clearly define the behavior of a breed, behavior is taken into consideration. A "deadhead" in the Terrier ring seldom wins. In the Group ring and for Best in Show it takes more than posed beauty to win; the dog must "ask" for the win.

It is by tradition that behavior is evaluated, even though behavior may not be specifically spelled out in the breed Standard.

Anatomy

Knowledge of canine anatomy is essential to good judging or breeding. One of the keys to understanding anatomy is knowing the terminology. The book *Canine Terminology*, by Harold Spira, provides an excellent overview with a dictionary style format and many illustrations. *Canine Terminology* attempts to explain in some detail the many technical and semi-technical phrases used both in the language of dog fanciers and throughout canine literature.

The best reference textbook on anatomy is *Anatomy of the Dog*, by Miller, Christensen and Evans. This is a highly technical work for veterinary students, but should be studied by judges as the illustrations and text are factual. *Canine Anatomy, A Systemic Study*, by Donald R. Adams, was prepared as an adjunct to *Anatomy of the Dog*. This text is far easier to read and contains excellent illustrations for use by a judge.

History

Stonehenge (John Walsh) in his writings on *The Dog in Health and Disease* in 1849 forcefully pointed out that many present day English breeds were developed from crosses using one or more of the following breeds: Greyhound, Bulldog, Bloodhound, Foxhound, Spanish Pointer and Terrier (many Terriers were crossed with a Bulldog). The Greyhound was used to improve speed, the Foxhound and Bloodhound to improve scenting, the Terrier to improve courage and the Bulldog to improve tenacity and courage. The Retriever was listed as a crossed breed, not a pure breed. The structure of the Greyhound can be detected in many Sporting breeds of English origin (small arch in the loin). Hound characteristics are sometimes penalized in Standards to eliminate unwanted traits remaining from early crosses. An interesting note in Stonehenge's book was that Deerhounds with a Bulldog cross tend to attack deer from the front, not the side, thus getting themselves impaled upon the antlers. As shown by pictures, the Bulldog has changed in type over the years. Reference to the Bulldog cross was for a more leggy dog of less massive build.

Since the above dogs were used extensively in crosses, frequent references are made to them herein. The Saluki (unlisted in Stonehenge's book) probably predates the Greyhound, but since it was not plentiful at the time of the great hunting and coursing era of the British Isles, it was not used in producing new breeds.

To understand why a particular build or structure is required for a given breed, sometimes past history must be examined. Without knowledge of earlier conditions, breeders tend to produce dogs by interpreting the Standard in the light of the present environment instead of in the light of the former environment. The profuse coat of the American Cocker Spaniel is an example; it is to please people, not an aid in hunting.

It should be clearly recognized that times change. What is wanted today may be entirely different from what was desirable in the past. Should a dog breed become extinct merely because its former purpose is no longer needed? Or should the breed be adapted to the new environment? Some breeds have changed; some are still used for their original purpose; others have vanished. It is up to the breed clubs to steer the course.

Summary

When evaluating dogs, the quality of a person's decisions depends on interpretation of the breed Standard in regard to the ability to:

1. Select dogs with a structure best suited to perform the dog's purpose in life.

2. Select dogs with the best visual appeal that matches type. In some dog breeds structural perfection is the essence of the breed; in others aesthetic appeal is the all important consideration. All around experts need perfection in both categories.

Recommended Books for the Study of Evaluating Dogs

In addition to studying the books listed below, a judge needs to read and study about specific breeds. The Parent Club Judges Education Coordinator is a source for breed specific information. Many can provide an Illustrated Standard, breed history, list of breeders who are willing to act as breed mentors, bibliography of their breed, list of upcoming Specialties and breed study groups, and other information. A list of current Parent Club Judges Education Coordinators appears in the January, April, July and October issues of *Pure-Bred Dogs American Kennel Gazette*.

The following books are recommended reading for all judges and potential judges:

American Kennel Club, *The Complete Dog Book*, New York: Howell Book House Inc.

American Kennel Club, *"Guidelines for Conformation Dog Show Judges"*, New York.

American Kennel Club, *"Rules Applying to Registration and Dog Shows"*, New York.

Berndt, Dr. Robert J., *The Science and Techniques of Judging Dogs*, Loveland, CO: Alpine Publications Inc. 2001

Brown, Curtis M., *Dog Locomotion and Gait Analysis*, Wheat Ridge, CO: Hoflin Publishing Ltd., 1986

Canadian Kennel Club, *Book of Dogs*, Toronto: General Publishing Co. Limited.

Craig, Patricia, *Born to Win*, Doral Publishing, 1997

Elliot, Rachel Page, *Dogsteps, A New Look,* 2001

Fiennes, Richard and Alice, *The Natural History of Dogs*, Garden City, New York: Natural History Press, 1968

Gilbert Jr., E. M., and Brown, Thelma, *K-9 Structure & Terminology*, Aloha, OR: Dogfolk Enterprises, 2001

Hastings, Pat, *Tricks of the Trade, From Best Intentions to Best in Show*, Aloha, OR: Dogfolk Enterprises, 2000

Hayes, Capt. Horace M., *Points of the Horse*, New York: Arco Publishing Co., 1969

Howell, A. Brazier, *Speed in Animals*, New York: Hafner Publishing Co., 1965

Little, Clarence C., *The Inheritance of Coat Color in Dogs*, New York: Howell Book House Inc., 1969

Lorenz, Konrad Z., *Man Meets Dog,* Baltimore, MD: Penquin Books, 1994

Maxwell, C. Bede, *The Truth About Sporting Dogs*, New York: Howell Book House, 1972

Miller, Malcolm E., et. al., Updated by Howard Evans, PhD, *Anatomy of the Dog*, Philadelphia, PA: W. B. Saunders Company, 1993

Muybridge, Eadweard, *Animals in Motion*, New York: Dover Publications, 1979 Reprint

Pfaffenberger, Clarence, *The New Knowledge of Dog Behavior*, New York: Howell Book House Inc., 1964

Scott, John Paul and Fuller, John L., *Dog Behavior, The Genetic Basis*, originally published as *Genetics and the Social Behavior of Dogs*, Chicago: University of Chicago Press, 1974

Spira, H. R., *Canine Terminology*, Dogwise, 2001

Tietjen, Sari Brewster, *The Dog Judge's Handbook*, New York: Howell Book House Inc., 1980

Trimberger, George W., *Dairy Cattle Judging Techniques*, Englewood Cliffs, New Jersey: Prentice Hall Inc., 1977

Recommended Videos for the Study of Evaluating Dogs

American Kennel Club Videos

Approximately 130 breed Standard videos

High on Hunting Spaniels
The AKC Hunting Tests for Flushing Spaniels

Field Testing Your Retriever
The AKC Hunting Tests for Retrievers
Pointers in the Field
The AKC Hunting Tests for Pointing Breeds
Carrying the Line
A Look at Beagle Trials
With Courage and Style
The Field Trial Retriever
Turn Them Loose
The Field Trial for Pointing Breeds

In the Ring With Mr. Wrong

AKC and the Sport of Dogs

Gait: Observing Dogs in Motion
Dogsteps—A Study of Canine Structure and Movement,
by Rachel Page Elliott

Animals Near & Far Videos (1-800-858-3169)

Salukis Around the World in 1991

The Scottish Deerhound

Origin of Lure Coursing

Waterloo Cup 1993

Dogfolk Enterprises (1-800-967-3188)

Puppy Puzzle: The Hastings Approach to Evaluating the Structural
Quality of Puppies

2-1. Short stepping walk. A Jimela Topi in a short stepping walk with all four feet supporting its weight. *Photo by F. D. Schmidt, courtesy San Diego Zoo.*

CHAPTER 2

Dog Gaits

Introduction

A given sequence of leg movements is called a gait. Horse gaits (walk, trot, pace, amble, canter, gallop and others) have been studied extensively, and horse terms are generally applied to other animals' gaits.

Using horse terms to describe dogs' gaits introduces a probability of serious misconceptions; the mind automatically thinks if the name is the same there is identity. Horses gallop and dogs gallop; therefore the best structure for galloping horses is also the best structure for galloping dogs. **Wrong!** Sighthounds arch their back in the gallop; horses do not. Structural perfection for the back of a galloping horse is quite different from that for Greyhounds.

The trotting ability of a show dog is always evaluated. From this, one might surmise that all breed Standards describe the ideal gait. Not so. Many breed Standards fail to mention gait, even though the American Kennel Club has requested that the Parent Clubs do so. Those Standards that do mention gait are vague. One can conclude that those preparing Standards could not agree upon the description of a correct gait suitable for the purpose of the breed.

To select the better moving exhibit in those breeds where the gait is not adequately described, the judge must rely on general knowledge, tradition and scientific principles. Merely because a Standard fails to describe movement does not mean that the judge may disregard movement. Those who approved the Standard and omitted movement discussion, or stated it in vague terms, left it to the judge. Each judge then must decide upon the quality of the gait best suited for the dog's purpose in life.

Before discussion of what structure produces the most efficient motion, a discussion of gaits is desirable. Common ones are: (1) walk, (2) pace, (3) amble, (4) trot, (5) single suspension gallop, (6) double suspension gallop. Other gaits will not be discussed.

Walk

The walk is the least tiring gait. Limbs move slower and more feet support the dog at one time. The dog is always supported by at least two feet, at times by three and at times by four.

It is a four-time gait; that is, each footfall occurs at about one-fourth of the time of one complete stride. The four-time sequence, prior to repeating the cycle, is: (1) RF, (2) LH, (3) LF, (4) RH (L—left, R—right, F—fore or front, H—hind or rear). In supporting the dog, legs have this sequence: (1) right pair (RF and RH); (2) right diagonal (RF and LH); (3) left pair (LF and LH); (4) left diagonal (LF and RH). When changing from one of the listed supports to the next, three or four feet are on the ground simultaneously. In the short stepping walk of Figure 2-1, the hind feet do not reach as far forward as the corresponding front footprint. In the ordinary walk the rear feet more or less cover the corresponding front footprints. In the long striding walk, the rear feet reach the front footprints.

Figure 2-1 shows the short stepping walk of the Jimela Topi, with all four feet supporting its weight. Next the rearmost leg (RH) will move forward. In this phase of the walk the legs are in a position characteristic of the pace. If the Topi were pacing (which it is not), both legs on the right side (RH, RF) would now move forward simultaneously. As with most animals that can run far and fast (cursorial), the legs are long and slim, muscles are concentrated in the upper portion of the legs, the limbs move in a single plane and the height at the withers equals the body length.

The principles of the short stepping walk can be explained by comparison with a rectangular table and weight as shown in Figure 2-2. First, if a weight is placed exactly in the center of the table and any one leg is removed, the table will fall in the direction of the missing leg. Second, if the weight is placed at one end of the table, either of the legs (not both) at the other end of the table may be removed and the table will not fall. Third, if the weight is placed on one corner of the table, the diagonally opposite leg may be removed without the table falling.

If any one of the legs of the table at the left of Figure 2-2 are removed, the table will fall. Either leg A or leg B can be removed from the table at the right and the table will continue to stand. The dog in the short stepping walk always keeps his center of gravity within the three support legs so that one leg is free to move. Assume that the table at the right in Figure 2-2 represents a dog, and the dog has shifted weight to be supported

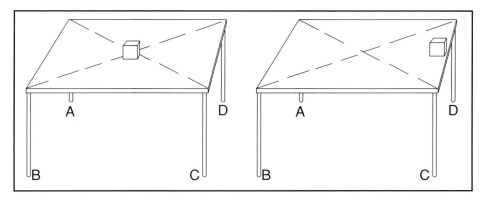

2-2. Principles of the short stepping walk. Refer to the text for the discussion of this illustration.

by legs B, C and D. Leg A is then moved forward. Next the dog shifts his weight so that legs A, B and C support the dog and then leg D is moved forward. In the short stepping walk the dog is always supported by three legs. Just prior to pointing a bird, the Pointer uses this gait.

The center of gravity of any object is at a point at which its entire weight can be considered as concentrated. In the first case, with the weight at the center of the table, the center of gravity of both the table and the weight is at the center of the table; removal of any one leg causes the table to fall. In the second and third cases the center of gravity is not in the center of the table, and the table is stable upon three support legs; the fourth leg can be removed without the table falling.

In the slow stepping walk the dog keeps its center of gravity within the triangle formed by three support legs; the fourth leg is free to move. In this gait the dog can stop in the middle of any step and not fall over. Pointers, upon moving towards a bird, use this gait; at any time they can take the three point stance without being unbalanced.

When the tempo of the walk increases, dogs can no longer keep their center of gravity within the triangle formed by the three legs. At faster speeds, as one front leg is lifted, the body will start falling towards that leg. To stop the falling motion, that leg is moved forward and set on the ground. In the faster walks there is a continual tendency for the body to fall to the right, then to the left. This side sway is called *lateral instability* or *lateral displacement*. Except for the short stepping walk, lateral instability is always present and is most pronounced in dogs that travel with their feet far apart (especially Bulldogs).

In the walk of four-footed animals, walking is falling. The hindquarters push the front forward; one front leg must swing forward to prevent falling. Up to a point, the more unbalanced the front (the further it is pushed forward), the faster the legs must move to support the front.

Pace and Amble

In the **pace** the sequence of leg movement is: (1) two right feet (RF, RH) on the ground and two left legs (LF, LH) in the air; (2) two left feet (LF, LH) on the ground and two right feet (RF, RH) in the air. (Refer to Figure 2-3.) The dog's weight is alternately supported by both right feet (called the right pair) and both left feet (called the left pair). In other words, as the dog paces both right legs move forward simultaneously, then both left legs move forward simultaneously. It is a two-time gait (two events occur before the cycle is repeated). The short stepping Topi's legs are in a position similar to that found in the pace. (Figure 2-1.) If both right legs were now to move forward simultaneously, the Topi would be pacing. To understand the pace better, try this experiment. With a partner, stand close together in single file (each facing in the same direction, with one person behind the other). Next travel forward at the same rate of speed. Since the legs are close together, the two legs on the right and then the two legs on the left must travel simultaneously; otherwise the feet will hit one another. Pairs of legs travel in unison.

During the fast pace, if there is a period of suspension of the body (airborne) between the change of pairs, the gait is called the *flying pace*. In the slow pace all four feet are on the ground at the time of changing support feet.

The word **amble** is quite variable in meaning. As used by horsemen, an amble is a slow gait that has a footfall pattern about the same as the pace. In the pace, the hoofs of

2-3. Dog pacing. The dog's right feet are moving forward simultaneously.

a pair (right or left) touch the ground at the same instant of time. In the amble, the rear foot of a pair takes off the ground just a fraction of a second sooner than the front foot. (See Figure 2-3.) Without critical observation the observer will think he is seeing the pace. Few understand this distinction; hence the word **amble** is frequently erroneously used to mean a slow pace, the regular pace, or any slow gait.

Certain of the Herding dogs (Old English Sheepdog and others) naturally amble. The Old English Sheepdog Standard (1990) states: *When trotting, movement is free and powerful . . . May amble or pace at slower speeds.*

In a camel's pace, the weight is shifted from one side to the other (lateral instability) as it paces, making the camel ride less comfortable than riding a trotting horse. It is like riding in a boat that rolls from side to side. Most horses trot; however, when tired, they will readily change to a pace or amble. Both the trot and pace are economical in the use of energy and both allow reasonable speed over long distances. A tired dog often changes from a trot to a pace (or amble); a change in gait is a relief. The extremely short-bodied giraffe has difficulty with the trot and pace. Contrary to common opinion, it normally gallops or walks. The natural period of oscillation of the long neck apparently makes the pace uncomfortable or impossible. No dog Standard approves the pace except for the Old English Sheepdog (1990); several call the pace a fault. Many Standards approve the trot, and most by inference assume that dogs are judged at the trot. There is no scientific reason for this bias; both gaits should be acceptable. Extracts from Standards are:

SAMOYED (1993)—*Gait*—*The Samoyed should trot, not pace.*

SHETLAND SHEEPDOG (1990)—*Gait*—*Faults*— . . . *Pacing gait.*

LABRADOR RETRIEVER (1994)—*Movement*— . . . *moving straight forward without pacing* . . .

GERMAN SHEPHERD DOG *(1994)—Gait—A German Shepherd Dog is a trotting dog, and its structure has been developed to meet the requirements of its work.*

BRIARD *(1992)—He is above all a trotter, single-tracking, occasionally galloping and he frequently needs to change his speed to accomplish his work.*

GIANT SCHNAUZER *(1983),* **MINIATURE SCHNAUZER** *(1991)— Gait—The trot is the gait at which movement is judged.*

In the pace a foot on one side may interfere with a leg on the other side, but two feet on the same side cannot hit each other. Both legs and feet on one side move forward at the same time.

Trot

Like the pace, the trot is also a two-time gait. Diagonals (RF and LH or LF and RH) are alternately on the ground. The two-time sequence is: (1) The right fore and left hind feet (called the right diagonals) are on the ground and the LF and RH (called the left diagonals) are in the air. Next, (2) the LF and the RH are on the ground and the RF and LH are in the air. (See Figures 2-4 and 2-5.) Stated in another way, diagonal legs move forward at the same time.

A Kerry Blue Terrier (Figure 2-4) is trotting with the LF and RH (the left diagonals) moving forward. As the LF swings forward, the pastern is bent to give ground clearance. The rearmost leg has lots of back reach (in the picture the rear leg has already started to move forward). A dog at the trot should be shown and judged with a loose lead as shown. A tight lead takes weight off the front and sometimes hides a fault; at other times it creates the illusion of a fault where none exists.

2-4. A Kerry Blue Terrier trotting.

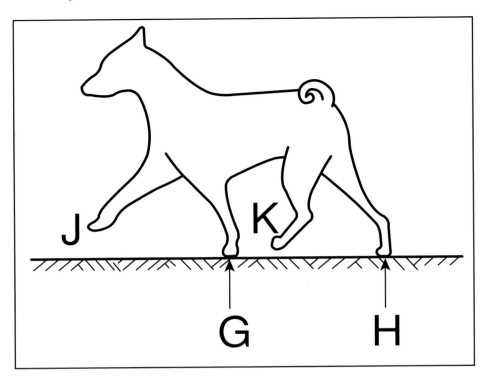

2-5. In the trot diagonals G and H, J and K are alternately on the ground.

In the trot, as the rear leg on one side is brought forward, it approaches the front foot on that side. The front foot must be raised off the ground just a fraction of a second before the rear foot touches the ground; otherwise collision (nicking) will occur.

To better understand the trot, try this experiment. With a partner, stand in single file facing the same direction and with partners' bodies a good arm's length apart. Next, place the outstretched arms of the rear person on the front person's shoulders. Now, both partners should start walking at the same time with front person starting with the right foot and rear person starting with the left foot. Continue walking with the diagonals in cadence. When walking in this manner, it will be found that on a given side the front and rear foot tend to interfere with one another. If care is not used, the rear partner will kick the front partner's foot.

A trotting dog with faulty structure often takes evasive action to prevent the rear foot from hitting the front foot. This can take the form of short steps or crabbing. In crabbing, the dog's backbone moves obliquely and one rear leg passes inside *or* outside of the front foot. That is, if the dog's spine is not pointed straight in the direction of travel, the dog is crabbing.

Since faults (especially crabbing) are more apparent in the trot than in the pace, the quality of a dog's movements is best determined at the trot.

Some dogs develop timing such that the forefoot lifts and clears a fraction of a second before the hind foot lands. This timing permits a short-backed dog to trot properly, without taking faulty evasive action. This timing is a function of the nervous system and is acceptable for the trot.

In some breeds, when the dog is moving at either a flying or fast trot, a rear leg may move inside the front leg. If the back is in a straight line in the direction of travel, the dog is not crabbing. The German Shepherd Dog Standard (1994) states:

> *The over-reach of the hindquarters usually necessitates one hind foot passing out-side and the other hind foot passing inside the track of the forefeet, and such action is not faulty unless the locomotion is crabwise with the dog's body sideways out of the normal straight line.*

The trot may be classified into three kinds: (1) the short or slow trot, in which the rear foot does not reach the front footprint; (2) the ordinary trot, in which the hind foot covers the front footprint; and (3) the flying trot, in which there is a period of suspension (airborne) when changing diagonals and the hind feet reach beyond the front footprints. If a dog predominantly trots, a long body is advantageous; the rear foot can have greater reach without the front and rear feet hitting. Most wild relatives of dogs (wolves and foxes) are long bodied.

In the trot or pace, ideally, each leg should be of equal length. Cats, rabbits and horses have front legs shorter than rear legs. At a fast trot (not the slow trot), the front legs have a shorter stride than the rear. To lengthen the front leg stride during the fast trot, the front must be suspended longer than the rear. When the front is suspended, the withers move up and down vertically. Dogs with excessive angulation and long rear legs cannot trot at faster speeds as smoothly as dogs with legs of equal striding length. Usually the trot is slightly slower than the pace and slightly less tiring.

Analysis of Lateral Instability

The force that causes the Bulldog to roll is the same as the force that causes the pacing dog to sway from side to side. To further understand this force, try this experiment. Have someone walk slowly across the room with feet spread well apart. The side-to-side movement of the shoulders (roll) is caused by the person's weight shifting (shifting the center of gravity) to overcome lateral instability. All dogs when moving have this force present; some have it more than others. The greater the roll of the dog (shoulders or rear moving from side to side), the greater will be the expenditure of energy to overcome the roll.

As a further experiment, have the same person walk across the room with feet as close together as possible. The side-to-side movement of the shoulders will be negligible. When dogs are trotting, pacing or running, lateral instability (roll) is diminished as the dog moves with feet closer together, that is, nearly *single tracking*. If all four feet could move in one absolutely straight line, no lateral instability could exist. But since one rear leg must pass the other rear leg and one front leg must pass the other front leg, it is impossible to entirely eliminate lateral instability. Some energy is always spent in overcoming the tendency to roll, but it should be reduced to a minimum.

Any dog that lasts in the field cannot afford to have a noticeable roll. Fighting lateral instability uses a tremendous amount of energy, thereby cutting down on endurance. However, some breeds of dogs, especially Bulldogs, have a purpose that requires the dogs to move with feet apart; in such breeds efficiency of travel is sacrificed in order to attain a useful objective.

The following is offered as an engineering explanation of lateral instability. (Those readers who dislike scientific explanations should skip to "GALLOP.") Refer to Figure

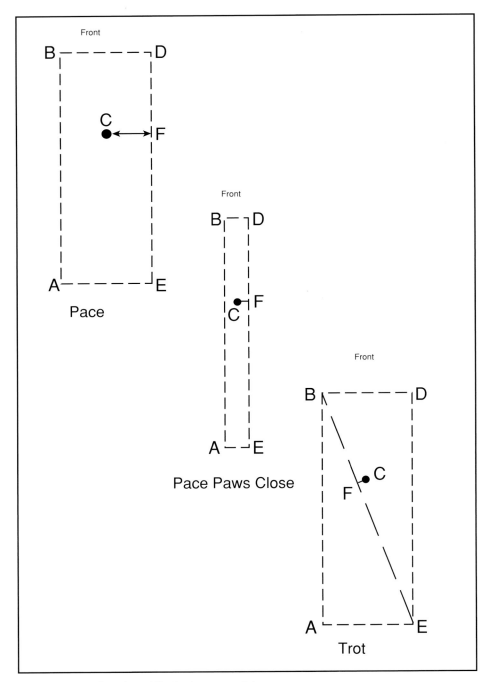

2-6. Illustration of lateral instability for the pace and the trot.

2-6. The upper part of Figure 2-6 depicts a rectangle. Assume that a dog's foot rests on each corner of the rectangle. The center of gravity (the point at which the entire weight of the dog can be considered as concentrated) of the dog is at point C. Since the front legs of the dog carry more weight than the rear legs (due to the weight of the head), the position of C is forward of the center of the rectangle. In the pace, paws A and B are off the ground while paws D and E support the dog's weight. The force arm (distance C to F in Figure 2-6 upper and middle areas) multiplied by the dog's unsupported weight is the force causing side sway. In the second half of the pace cycle, paws A and B are supporting the dog; the side sway is the same, but in the opposite direction. As the dog moves with its feet spread out, it sways to the right and then to the left. A dog moving with feet close together (Figure 2-6 middle) has less side sway (shorter force arm, C to F).

Return to the rectangle (Figure 2-6 lower) with each corner representing a dog's foot. In the trot, feet B and E support the dog while paws A and D are in the air. If the center of gravity fell exactly on the diagonal line, no lateral instability (side sway) would exist. In the trot, the center of gravity is constantly changing relative to the

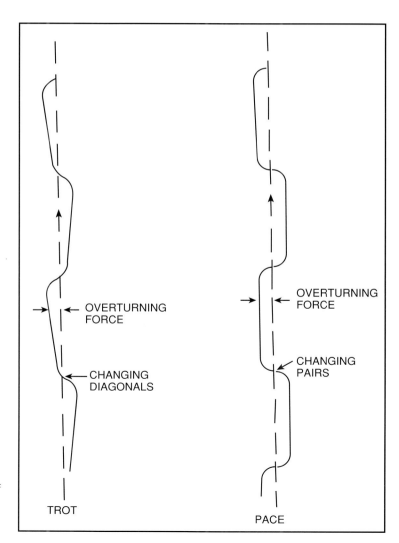

2-7. Graphic representation of lateral instability for the trot and the pace.

support feet; i.e., the distance from C to F is constantly changing. When the support diagonals (feet) are at their furthermost forward reach, the center of gravity relative to the feet is well forward.

The left side of Figure 2-7 shows a graphic representation of the side sway (lateral instability) for the trot. The dashed line represents the direction of travel. The distance between the solid line and the dashed line represents the magnitude of the swaying force. The right side of Figure 2-7 shows the side sway for the pace. As can be seen from Figure 2-7, when changing support feet, side sway is about double that of the trot. In the trot, the transition from instability to the left to instability to the right is much more gradual.

In Figure 2-7 the distance between the solid line and the dashed line represents the overturning force (side sway or roll is caused by this force). In the *trot*, at the time of changing diagonals, no overturning force exists. As the dog moves forward at a trot, the overturning force increases and reaches a maximum just before all four feet are on the ground. In the *pace*, except at the moment of changing support from one side to the other, the overturning force is greater than in the trot.

As was pointed out, if the dog single tracks there is little lateral instability for either the pace or the trot. For draft dogs, with wide rears, the trot is far less tiring than the pace. For dogs that are capable of speed and endurance, those with narrow fronts and relatively narrow rears that almost single track, the pace and the trot are about equal in energy requirements.

Gallop

The fast gaits of the dog are known as the gallop. Heavier dogs use the single suspension gallop; the Sighthounds and such dogs as the Doberman (also a few of the other breeds) use the double suspension gallop. Other gallops (the bound, the half bound of the house cat, etc.) will not be discussed. (See *The New Dogsteps* by Rachel Page Elliott [Howell Book House] and *Dog Locomotion and Gait Analysis* by Curtis M. Brown.)

2-8. Double suspension gallop. In the double suspension gallop, dogs use their backs to attain speed. *From instantaneous photographs by Muybridge.*

2-9. Salukis galloping. *Photo by Cathy Chapman.*

The word "suspension" means "airborne." In the single suspension gallop cycle the dog is airborne once; in the double suspension gallop the dog is airborne twice.

The single suspension gallop is a four-time gait; the dog's weight is supported by the feet in this unsymmetrical sequence: RF, LF, RH, LH. Suspension occurs just after taking off from the left forefoot. In this gait each forefoot must be lifted from the ground before the corresponding hind foot can be set down. If the timing is wrong, the hind foot will hit the corresponding front foot.

It is a common *myth* that the rear supplies practically all of the forward propulsion and the front merely carries weight. In the gallop, suspension occurs just after taking off from the forefoot. The front assembly must give an upward thrust and forward propulsion to cause the dog to be airborne. Both front and rear contribute to forward propulsion.

The double suspension gallop (Figure 2-8) is also a four-time gait, but the weight of the dog is not supported by the feet in the same sequence as previously described. Suspension occurs (1) just after taking off from the LH and (2) just after taking off from the RF. *This is the only gait in which the dog is fully extended,* as shown in Figures 2-8 and 2-9. The forelegs are fully extended forward and the hind legs are fully extended to the rear. Also in this gait the dog's back folds and attains maximum overreach; that is, the hind feet extend in front of the forefeet and the forefeet extend behind the hind feet. When the feet pass one another, the forefeet are *inside* the hind feet.

As shown in Figures 2-8 and 2-9, dogs use their backs to attain speed. The most flexible spot is over the loin; absence of ribs in the loin area and the tuck-up allows folding of the underpart of the body. The hind legs overreach on the outside of the forelegs. The ability to flex the back from a straight position to a well-arched position is essential for fast dogs; a permanent arch is not flexible and is therefore a serious fault.

The double suspension gallop is a leaping gait; first the hind legs propel the dog into the air, then the forelegs take their turn. Three engines are required: the muscles in the shoulder, the muscles in the "ham" and the muscles in the back. Although animals can run faster using this gait, endurance is sacrificed. Sighthounds and some cats can quickly overtake prey, but if the run is long, the prey escapes. Short-legged dogs as well as some short-legged mammals (the weasel in particular) often use this gait. Double suspension running dogs that have arched backs that will not flatten or flat backs that will not arch have serious faults.

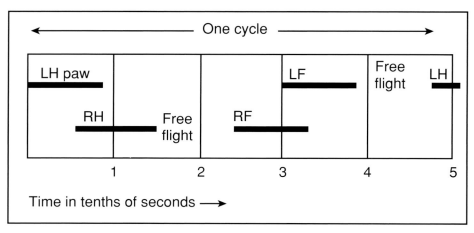

2-10. Saluki paw stance and swing time at the gallop.

The measured time for stance and swing of a Saluki during its gallop (Figure 2-9) is graphically illustrated in Figure 2-10. The time scale is shown at the bottom in tenths of seconds, and the time each paw was on the ground is shown by the bars. Each paw was on the ground about 0.09 seconds and each period of free flight lasted about 0.09 seconds. For a more detailed discussion of the double-suspension gallop, refer to *Dog Locomotion and Gait Analysis* by Curtis M. Brown.

In the United States dogs are not judged at a gallop and most fanciers have not studied these gaits. Before the structural features advantageous or disadvantageous to the gallop can be discussed, an explanation of muscles is required; this explanation is covered in Chapter 3.

CHAPTER 3

Muscles, Ligaments, Tendons, Joints and Levers

Introduction

When evaluating dogs for show and breeding, certain internal features, such as muscles, can be partially evaluated by feel or by watching the dog's gaits. Internal organs such as veins, heart and lungs cannot be seen or felt and are rarely, if ever, a judging consideration.

The musculoskeletal system provides support and movement; component parts are bone, cartilage, muscle, ligament, tendon and fascia. Bone forms the supporting and in many instances the protective framework of the body. Many bones serve as levers by which the muscles move the body.

Bones are the passive elements in motion; by themselves they are incapable of causing movement. Bones are moved by muscles and they can only do exactly what muscles dictate they do; they have no power to move themselves.

The muscle system is illustrated in Figures 3-1 through 3-6. Figure 3-1 shows the first or superficial layer of muscles after the skin is removed. Figure 3-2 shows the important muscles that can be felt, and in a sense seen, when judging. This is known as the second layer of muscles. This second layer is exposed after the skin and skin muscles are removed. Figure 3-3 shows the second layer of muscles as seen from above. Figure 3-4 shows the second layer of muscles from an underview of the chest and the neck. Figure 3-5 shows most of the muscles of the third layer. Figure 3-6 shows the deeper muscles of the trunk and thigh.

A dog's locomotion results from power developed in muscles. An electrical impulse, carried along nerves, causes stored energy in a muscle cell to contract the cell. The contracting muscle pulls tendons which in turn pull bones and set limbs in motion. The judge's eye sees legs, neck, tail and body moving. The efficiency and

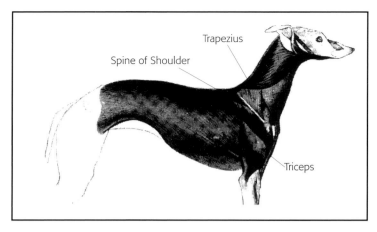

3-1. Trunk—first layer of muscle under the skin.

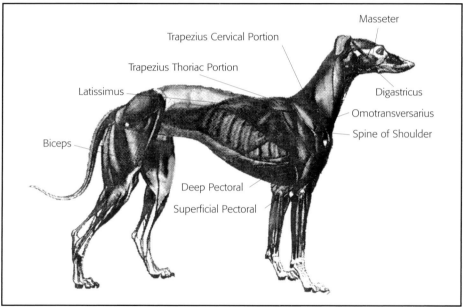

3-2. Second layer of muscle—side view.

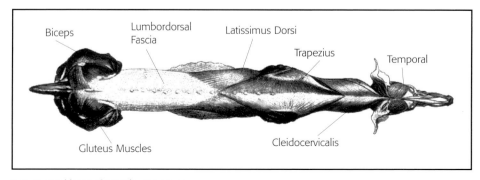

3-3. Second layer of muscle—top view.

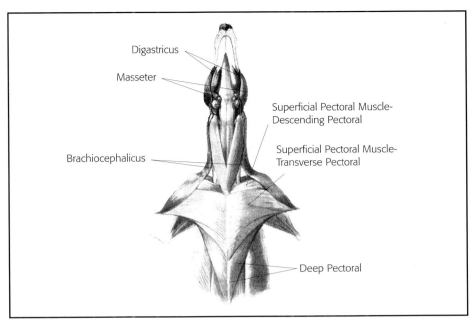

3-4. Second layer of muscle—underview of neck and chest.

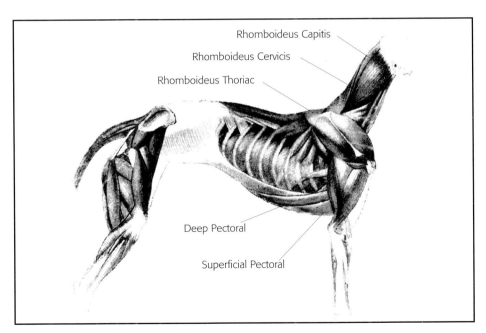

3-5. Muscles of the third layer—simplified.

coordination of the system are judged by external appearance. To evaluate motion, some knowledge of internal functions, anatomy and physical laws (pendulums and levers) is needed.

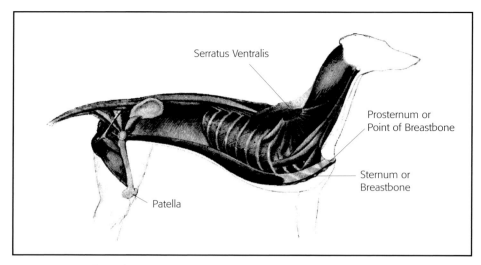

Serratus Ventralis

Prosternum or
Point of Breastbone

Sternum or
Breastbone

Patella

3-6. Deeper muscles of the trunk and thigh.

Kinesiology is the study of movement. For the student, the book by MacConaill and Basmajian, *Muscles and Movements: A Basis for Human Kinesiology*, gives a scientific analysis of the subject.

Muscles

Conformation of the dog is determined by the size, shape, condition and distribution of the muscles in conjunction with the skeleton. Dogs' muscles are composed of several bundles of fibers of very small diameter. Each fiber is connected to the brain by a nerve cell. At rest, fibers are soft and pliable, but on a signal from the brain via the nerve cells, a fiber contracts and becomes hard. The fully contracted fiber is about half the length of a fully expanded fiber.

Let us suppose that a dog wishes to have a leg move at a walk. The brain sends a signal for a bundle of fibers to contract. The contracting fibers pull a tendon, which in turn pulls a bone that sets a leg in motion. If the dog wishes to move faster, a signal is sent to contract more bundles of fibers. More fibers apply a greater force and cause the leg to move faster.

Although each muscle fiber has a corresponding nerve cell, the cells of several fibers join in a bundle. One impulse from the brain controls the whole bundle. Leg muscles, which require power rather than delicacy of movement, have large numbers of fibers per bundle. Eye muscles have few fibers per bundle. Whereas muscle *fibers* are able to contract to half their expanded length, whole muscles are unable to do so. The arrangement of fibers is such that the contraction of one fiber is not additive to another.

Tissue separates bundles of fibers, and surrounding each muscle is a sheath of tissue. Fibers are attached to tendons and the tendons extend through a muscle to attach to a bone.

The weight of the entire dog, either standing or moving, is supported by the forequarters and the hindquarters. The weight loads put stress on the limbs. This stress is greatly increased during running, when the hindquarters push against the ground and when the forequarters catch and cushion the fall of the forward-moving body after each hindquarter thrust.

An animal running at full speed needs only force sufficient to move its own weight. Any unnecessary muscles beyond those required to work the legs tend to reduce speed because of extra weight. Also, heavier muscles (larger in cross-section area) contract more slowly than lighter muscles. The term "musclebound" describes an animal that is slow to react because of excess cross-section area muscle. A speedster in proper flesh has sufficient muscle to move its weight, but no excess (it is not musclebound). Trainers recognize a fine line of distinction between over- and under-muscled dogs.

For heavy work in pulling sledges or carts, well muscled draft animals are desirable; the slower rate at which heavy muscles contract becomes an advantage. Strength, not speed, is wanted, as in the Alaskan Malamute, for example.

A muscle's speed in contracting is not wholly dependent upon the weight of the muscle; some individuals have quicker reflexes than others. If all individuals of comparable build had the same rate of muscle contraction, all would run at the same speed, but the rate of muscle contraction varies with the individual; therefore this assumption is far from true.

The speed of muscle contraction is also dependent upon breed characteristics; some breeds have "nervous," quick reflexes. The Cairn Terrier has reflexes about twice as quick as those of the Standard Poodle.

The speed of muscle contraction is also related to white and dark muscle. Turkeys have dark muscle in the legs and white muscle in the breast. The white muscle has faster contraction with less endurance; the darker muscle contracts slower but has greater endurance. Cats have a larger percentage of white muscle, and therefore have good initial speed and poor endurance.

Muscles (with minor exceptions) exist and work in pairs. If one muscle pulls a leg forward, there must be another to pull it back. One set of muscles closes the mouth and another opens it. Muscles cannot push the mouth closed; they must pull it closed. One muscle of a pair may be stronger than the other. The muscles that close a jaw are much stronger than the muscles that open the jaw.

The length of a muscle does not necessarily determine how far a muscle will contract; it is the length of the *fibers* within the muscle that determines contraction. A long muscle with short fibers may contract less than a short muscle with long fibers. Long-necked dogs (Greyhound) with long muscles are not able to move their shoulder blades faster than the extremely short-necked cheetah.

Muscles act in combination with a number of other muscles. The direction of pull on the skeletal part is due to the sum total of the forces applied by individual muscles. There are more than fifty-three muscles that act upon the foreleg, and their interactions are quite complex. As a result, we do not discuss the various muscles in detail.

The characteristics of muscles are:

1. Long muscle fibers produce greater action (the length of a muscle fiber tends to be proportionate to the extent of movement it is able to produce).

2. Thin muscles have quicker reflexes.

3. Heavy muscles produce greater strength but slower reflexes (the thickness of a muscle tends to be proportionate to its power).

4. Reflexes vary in individuals.

5. Thin muscles in proper condition give greater endurance for running (not for heavy work).

6. Muscles do useful work when contracting.

Tendons and Ligaments

Tendons (sinew) transmit the pull of muscles to the bone. Except for the cervical (neck) ligament and some other minor exceptions, tendons do not expand or contract. They transmit pull, not push (tension, not compression). They are like the strings that move a puppet. Ligaments hold joints together; tendons pull bones to create motion. Though tendons and ligaments are important to the dog, their quality can hardly be determined by an external observation.

Levers

Running is accomplished by a system of levers. To illustrate how levers work, Figure 3-7 shows the triceps and biceps muscles of the human arm and the stylized bones (humerus, radius, and ulna). When the arm is lifted, a signal from the brain contracts the fibers of the biceps. The contracting muscle pulls the arm upwards. When the arm is lowered, a signal causes the fibers of the triceps to contract; the upward pull of the rearward extension of the radius causes the arm to move downward. In simple terms, the process of moving a dog's leg consists of one muscle contracting and one muscle relaxing.

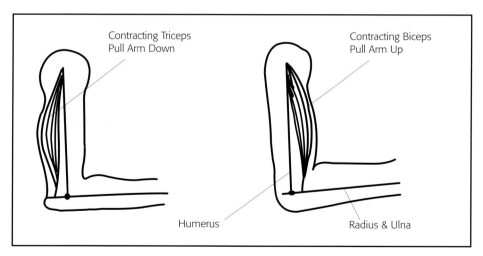

Contracting Triceps
Pull Arm Down

Contracting Biceps
Pull Arm Up

Humerus

Radius & Ulna

3-7. All joints are operated by two muscles. Muscles can pull and move a bone; they cannot push. In the human arm contracting, the triceps muscle causes the arm to move down; contracting the biceps causes the arm to move up.

The muscle that *bends* a joint (Biceps in Figure 3-7) is called a *flexor* and the muscle that *straightens* bone alignment is called an *extensor*. Flexion and extension are the primary movements necessary for locomotion. The pattern of movement resulting from muscle contractions, even for apparently simple movements, is brought about by the complex interactions of many muscles.

3-8. Norwegian Elkhound. *Photo by Smolley.*

Development of Muscles

To a limited extent, muscles can be developed by usage. It is a well known fact that weightlifters can increase muscle size by correct exercise. A slim person cannot develop a weightlifter's physique nor can a weightlifter develop the slim figure of a distance runner. Each can approach the other by correct exercise.

Great dogs in the show ring are usually trained to develop trotting muscles to perfection. Ch. Vin-Melca's Vagabond (Figure 3-8), owned by John and Pat Craige, was trained by a 2-mile daily trot behind a bicycle. We trained our own dogs by a several-mile daily fast walk. Sometimes we used a person on the tailgate of a station wagon to lead a dog around a parking lot at a fast trot.

Joints

Dogs have five general types of attachments that allow movements. These are:

1. A sliding joint (the shoulder blade muscular attachment)

2. A ball and socket joint (hip joint and shoulder blade—upper arm joint)

3. A hinge joint (elbow joint, with movement restricted to a single plane like a door)

4. Rotation movement (similar to the rotation of the human forearm)

5. Movement without bones as the tongue

The first four general types of attachments will be discussed in detail as the rear and front assemblies are explained in their respective chapters.

Function of the Trapezius and Rhomboideus Muscles

Refer to Figures 3-1, 3-2, and 3-3. The upper end of the scapula spine is attached to the backbone by the trapezius muscle. The trapezius is divided into two halves by the scapula spine and it extends from the third cervical vertebra to the ninth thoracic vertebra. The rear half is attached from the third thoracic vertebra spire to the eighth or ninth thoracic vertebra. The trapezius muscle's primary function is to hold the shoulder blade on the side of the dog; it assists motion slightly. The front half of the trapezius is partly attached to the neck or nuchal ligament. Underneath the trapezius muscle is the rhomboideus muscle (Figure 3-5), of similar location, except that it connects to the top of the shoulder blade rather than the spine.

The shoulder blade moves back and forth, as is shown in Figure 5-4. While the shoulder blade does slide up and down as well as forward and back to a small degree, it is obvious that the main function of the trapezius and rhomboideus muscles is to attach the shoulder blade to the body. If the trapezius assists in rotating the shoulder blade, it is a minor amount. The action of the trapezius is to elevate the limb and draw it forward while the paw is off the ground. The trapezius does not contribute significantly to shoulder blade motion.

The rhomboideus muscle is covered by the trapezius muscle and the action of the rhomboideus is to elevate the limb; to pull the limb and shoulder forward or backward; and to draw the shoulder blade against the trunk.

Muscles Moving the Shoulder Blade

The principal muscles responsible for moving the shoulder blade back and forth are the omotransversus (Figure 3-2), latissimus dorsi (Figures 3-2 and 3-3), pectorals (Figures 3-2 and 3-5) and brachicephalicus (Figure 3-4). There are other muscles that aid (serratus ventralis, etc.); however, the four shown are sufficient to illustrate the action.

Please note that three of them are attached to the upper arm (humerus) and only the omotransversus is attached to the shoulder blade. The other three are attached to the upper arm, not the shoulder blade.

- Holding the head high puts tension on the brachicephalicus muscle and causes high leg action.

- The two forward-pulling muscles, omotransversus and brachicephalicus, operate at a nearly constant rate regardless of gait.

- The rearward-pulling muscles can vary speed from zero to a maximum of about 40 miles per hour.

- The serratus ventralis (Figure 3-6) is a broad muscle (spanning about 150 degrees) located under the scapula; while its main function is to hold the shoulder blade to the body (stop it from sliding up), it also adds to forward and backward scapula motion.

Forward Pulling Muscles of the Shoulder

In order to understand the function of the forward pulling muscles, paw velocities during gaits must be described. The time it takes to pick up and set down a paw is nearly constant for all gaits (walk, trot, pace or gallop). In both dogs and horses it takes about 0.32 seconds; the cheetah takes 0.23 seconds. The forward pulling shoulder blade muscles operate at a nearly constant speed, and that speed for dogs, according to our observations, is in the vicinity of 12 miles per hour, relative to the dog, of course. This is not very fast. When the dog's forward speed reaches a critical point, there must be a period of suspension (all four feet off the ground at the same time) in order to get the 0.32 seconds of needed time. When the dog changes from the regular trot to the flying trot, the critical speed has been exceeded.

Cats' muscles contain a white protein that is much quicker in action than a dog's. Domestic cats, cheetahs, etc., require about 0.23 seconds in the paw pickup and setdown, whereas dogs, with their dark protein, require about 0.32 seconds.

Backward Pulling Muscles of the Shoulder

The rearward (backward) velocity of the paw can vary the dog's speed from 0 to 40 miles per hour; the muscles responsible for the motion can vary the forces causing paw velocity. The exact method the dog uses to vary the paw's rearward speed is not known for sure. It can be accomplished by the intensity of the electrical impulse that activates the muscles, but it is more likely to be the dog's control center's ability to select a few of many muscle fibers when the electrical impulse is sent.

Multiplying Speed of Muscle Contraction

The muscles that activate the leg all tend to contract at the same rate, and that rate is much less than the speed of paw movement. Obviously, there must be a lever system that multiplies speed of muscle contraction. This can be done by length of leg (most commonly used), by the arrangement of joints and muscles, and by the way muscles act. Taking into consideration the scapula only, two methods are used to increase speed of muscle contraction:

1. The length of the lever arm
2. The direction and arrangement of muscle pull

The lever arm of the shoulder extends from the center of rotation (near the top of the blade) to the point of attachment of muscle in the upper arm.

Slope of Shoulder Blade

The shoulder blade is free-floating on the side of the dog; the rest position is determined by the tension in the muscles holding it in place. The slope can be altered by the position of the paw under the dog, the height the head is held and the character of muscles.

The brachicephalicus extends from the upper arm to the dog's head (Figure 3-4). By raising the head, the tension in the muscle is increased and the blade is rotated forward. If the paw is moved forward from its normal rest position, the blade is also rotated forward. If the muscles pulling the blade towards the rear are unusually tense, the blade is rotated towards the rear. For a galloping dog it is desirable to have the rearward pulling muscles tense.

Up and Down Motion of the Head

During the gallop of a dog, the head moves down when the front paw is off the ground (the swing phase); the head moves up when the paw is on the ground in the stand phase. In theory, it would seem that the head should move up during the swing phase to assist the forward motion of the front leg, but as can be observed in slow-motion movies, it does not. To date, the reason for the reversal of the expected result is unknown.

When a dog or horse tires in a race, the head commences to bob up and down excessively to try to relieve tired muscles that operate the shoulder blade. It is possible that the timing of the up and down motion is related to elastic rebound, the next subject.

Elastic Rebound

If you drop a ball on the ground, it will bounce back. If you stretch a rubber band and let it loose, it will return to its original shape. Each has elastic rebound. Some tendons have remarkable elastic rebound. During the gallop of a Greyhound, the pastern will be flat on the ground and the tendon in the pastern will be stretched to the limit. As the paw passes back under the dog, the stored-up tension will help the dog rebound upward.

Shoulder blade muscles have some elastic rebound. After the paw leaves the ground, the paw's motion is stopped by stretching the forward pulling muscles. Whenever a muscle is fully stretched, it is ready for maximum pull in the opposite direction. In other words, the stored energy of stretched muscles is used to pull the leg in the opposite direction. If it were not for elastic rebound (recycling of energy), animals would have very little endurance.

CHAPTER 4

Hindquarters and Feet

Rear Leg Assembly

The hindquarters are made up of the pelvis; the first or upper thigh, articulating with the pelvic bones at the hip joint; the second or lower thigh, articulating with the femur at the stifle or knee joint; the hock or rear pastern, consisting of the hock or ankle joint, containing seven tarsal bones, and the metatarsus, which consists of five metatarsals; and the hind foot, consisting of the phalanges or toes. Dogs have five metatarsal bones, but in many dogs the first metatarsal bone is often quite rudimentary (for practical purposes it is missing). The first metatarsal bone is the rear dewclaw, which, when present, is situated on the inner surface of each hind leg.

The rear leg assembly of dogs (bones, tendons, ligaments, tissue, muscle, nerves and blood vessels) extends from the pelvis to the toenails. This assembly is a lever system activated by muscles that pull bones. The common names associated with the rear legs are given in Figures 4-1 and 4-2.

The stifle joint contains the patella or kneecap, shown in Figure 4-1, which slides in a notch in the lower end of the femur. In some breeds there is a tendency for the patella to be pulled upwards out of the notch; this condition is called a "slipped stifle."

The point of hock or calcaneal process, shown in Figures 4-1 and 4-2, serves as the anchor point for the calcaneal tendon insertion. This tendon is equivalent to the Achilles tendon in the human.

Figure 4-3 illustrates the muscles on the inner side of the left hind leg. The hindquarter muscles are for the purpose of propulsion. These muscles can be developed through exercise, but quite quickly become soft and flabby through lack of exercise.

Speed, Agility, Quick Turning and Running Uphill

The importance of follow-through is known by all sports enthusiasts. The golf club is not stopped the moment the club hits the ball; the arms and club follow through. The swing of the dog's leg is not stopped the instant the foot leaves the ground; the leg follows through. The back reach or back stroke of the leg (swing of the leg behind the

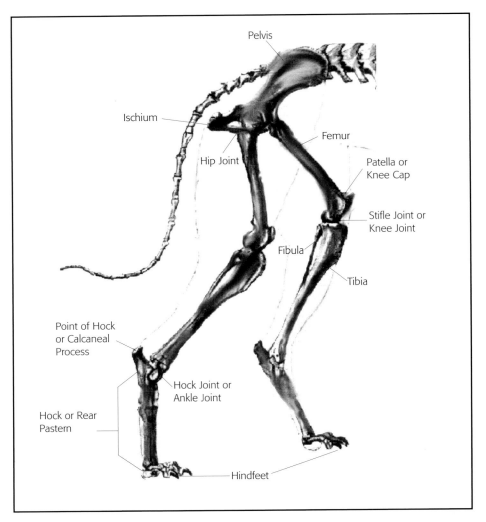

4-1. Bones of the hindquarters.

dog after the foot leaves the ground) is an important consideration for evaluating trotting and galloping dogs.

If a dog's body is moving forward at ten miles per hour, the paws on the ground must be moving backwards relative to the body at ten miles per hour. If they are not, the paws will become a brake and slow the dog. At the instant the paw is lifted from the ground, backward momentum continues until stopped by muscles. Usually, the faster the speed, the more follow-through; however, excessive follow-through can be a waste of energy.

Not all dogs are designed exclusively for running efficiency; some need quick turning and agile movements. Follow-through is not important to the Bulldog or the Bull Terrier, but good stability and the ability to turn on the hindquarters are.

If dogs are to turn quickly and run in the opposite direction, they must turn on the hindquarters, not the forequarters. Dogs that dig the rear feet into the ground, raise their fronts, then spin around on their hindquarters and take off running, will be much

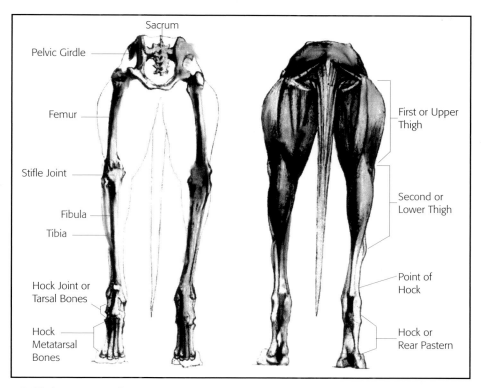

Sacrum

Pelvic Girdle

Femur

Stifle Joint

Fibula

Tibia

Hock Joint or
Tarsal Bones

Hock
Metatarsal
Bones

First or Upper
Thigh

Second or
Lower Thigh

Point of
Hock

Hock or
Rear Pastern

4-2. Hindquarters, rear view.

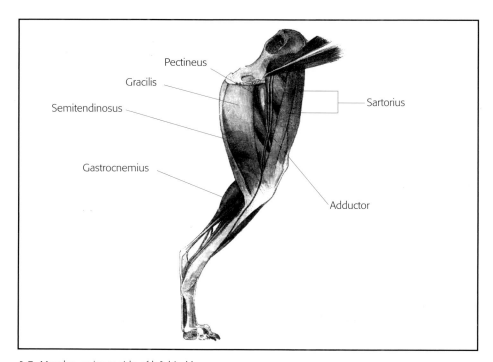

Pectineus

Gracilis

Semitendinosus

Gastrocnemius

Sartorius

Adductor

4-3. Muscles on inner side of left hind leg.

faster in the turn than dogs that plant the front feet on the ground and walk the hind feet around the front feet. In the turn-around movement, the backward reach (rear legs extended well behind) of the hind legs is not important. Only the forward reach (ability of the rear leg to extend forward) of the rear legs and the rear's ability to lift the front are important.

The ability to run uphill is closely related to the quick-turning motion. Both motions require the rear assembly to propel the dog upward as well as forward. The upward push of the rear quarters occurs when a paw is under the loin, *not* behind the rump. The structure needed to excel in the upward thrust is quite different from that needed to excel in running on the level. The wolf can outrun the goat on flat land; the goat can outrun the wolf up a steep hill.

The Standard for the Scottish Deerhound (1935) is quite specific in describing the back for uphill work:

> *The loin well arched and drooping to the tail. A straight back is not desirable, this formation being unsuited for uphill work, and very unsightly.*

Three types of action have been described:

1. Good reach (both forward and back) for speed and endurance

2. Quick turning

3. Running uphill

The angle of the pelvic bone is an indicator of the efficiency of these movements.

4-4. Conformation for fast uphill travel and quick turns. The Uganda kob, an antelope, has a flat back, steep croup and legs well under. *Photo by Ron Garrison, courtesy San Diego Zoo.*

4-5. Excellent uphill conformation. Rocky Mountain bighorn sheep have a steep croup, as is characteristic of Afghan Hounds and other animals that excel in running uphill. *Courtesy San Diego Zoo.*

4-6. Quick turn conformation. Damara zebra with foal. Note the low tail set. *Photo by Ron Garrison, courtesy San Diego Zoo.*

The antelope in Figure 4-4 has a steep pelvis and low tail set; the Topi in Figure 2-1 has a relatively flat croup and high tail set. The antelope has a flat back, steep croup and legs well under; compare this with the proper croup of the Afghan Hound in Figure 4-11. The antelope should travel fast uphill and should be capable of quick turns. The steepness of the croup is accentuated by the lack of development of the muscles above the pelvis.

Rocky Mountain bighorn sheep, as shown in Figure 4-5, have a steep croup, as is characteristic of Afghan Hounds and other animals that excel in running uphill. The rear legs are well angulated and the height at withers nearly equals the body length.

Refer to Figure 4-6. Zebras, when facing a lion, quickly spin on their hindquarters and take off. In a standing positon they have a steep pelvis. The polo pony, like the zebra, should also spin fast and be off in another direction; it also has a steep pelvis and low tail set (goose rump). The angle of the pelvis indicates turnaround efficiency. Zebras do not have great speed, probably due to poor backward reach. The length of the leg from the stifle to the ground is almost the same for mother and foal. The foal's short body plus long legs give sufficient speed and endurance to enable the youngster to escape predators. The Basenji (Figure 6-10) is high-stationed, but not as extreme as this baby zebra.

The Pelvis and Its Slope

The pelvis is made of six major bones, three on each side, that are fused together during development. (Refer to Figure 4-7.) These bones are joined to the three fused sacrum vertebrae through a rigid joint: the sacroiliac. The spine continues to the tail vertebrae. The hip socket is a weight bearing joint through which the rear thrust is applied. The head of the femur fits into this ball and socket joint.

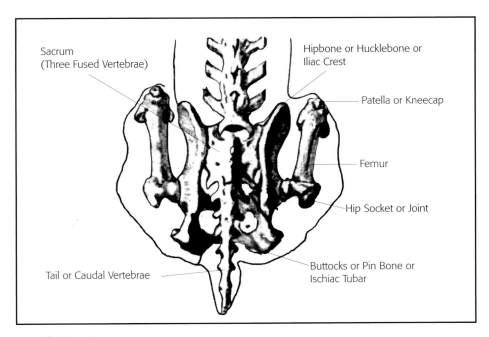

Sacrum (Three Fused Vertebrae)

Hipbone or Hucklebone or Iliac Crest

Patella or Kneecap

Femur

Hip Socket or Joint

Tail or Caudal Vertebrae

Buttocks or Pin Bone or Ischiac Tubar

4-7. Pelvis—top view.

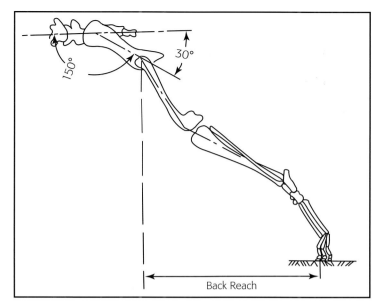

4-8. Normal pelvis slope provides normal back reach. A normal pelvis slope is 30 degrees off the horizontal or 150 degrees off spine as shown.

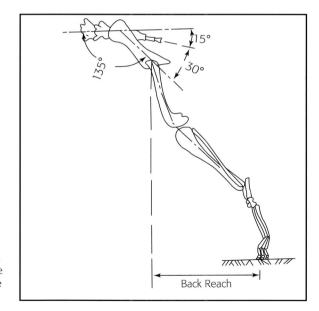

4-9. Steep pelvis limits back reach. A steep pelvis is 45 degrees off the horizontal or 135 degrees off spine as shown.

The pelvis is fused to the backbone—the three fused sacrum vertebrae. Each rear leg is attached to the pelvis by a ball and socket joint. Since the pelvis is rigidly attached to the spine, it acts similarly to a teeter-totter. If the right side of the rear drops in elevation and the spine stays at the same elevation, the left side must elevate.

At the front end of the dog, by contrast, each leg is independently suspended by muscles; no rigid bone attaches one leg to the other. The rear legs are joined by a solid crossbar (pelvis); the front legs are joined by flexible muscles. The two assemblies can be compared to an automobile with each front wheel independently supported by a spring and with the rear wheels cross-tied by the rear axle. The front legs can paddle; the rear ones cannot.

The slope of the pelvis from the horizontal helps determine rear angulation and is a major factor in rear movement. For dogs moving with good reach, the slope of the pelvis is about 30 degrees (refer to Figure 4-8). The upper thigh is limited in backward motion just as the human elbow can be straightened but not bent backwards.

The maximum angle between the pelvis and the upper thigh varies; for most dogs with good rear reach it is about 150 degrees, as shown in Figure 4-8. Figure 4-9 shows the effect of steeper pelvis placement. These figures illustrate the reason for the following principles:

1. A normal pelvis often indicates a balanced back reach (Figure 4-8).

2. A steep pelvis often indicates a short back reach (Figure 4-9).

3. A level or flat pelvis often indicates an extended back reach (not illustrated).

4. The slope of the pelvis determines backward reach or extension, while the croup angle only determines tail set.

A dog whose hind feet move with short, choppy steps probably has a steep pelvis. For some purposes, such as quick turning, heavy draft or running uphill, a steep pelvis is advantageous. For most purposes, such as speed or endurance on level ground, it is a disadvantage.

The steepness of the pelvis bone for a given dog may be judged by observing the backward reach (stroke) of the hind legs while the dog is in motion.

Croup and Croup Angle

The croup angle is determined by the slope of the sacrum vertebrae and the first two tail vertebrae with the horizontal. The croup angle only determines tail set. Remember that the slope of the sacrum vertebrae is determined by the slope of the pelvis and the angle of the fused sacrum vertebrae in respect to the pelvis.

The dog's tail at the base forms a nearly 30 degree angle with the pelvis. If the base of the dog's tail comes off the back in a straight line (Figure 4-10), the croup angle is flat. If the base of the tail has a dip (goose rump) the croup angle is steep.

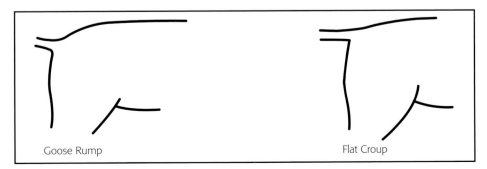

Goose Rump   Flat Croup

4-10. Low tail set usually indicates steep pelvis and restricted back reach. When a dog has a low tail set (goose rump), the back reach of the hind legs should be checked as the dog moves.

One of the keys to good judging is close observation of the tail set! Handlers are expert at trimming hair to make the tail set appear level with the back (especially with Terriers). The tail set on trimmed dogs and some long-haired dogs must be judged by feel as well as sight.

The following breeds have Standards which directly or indirectly call for a **flat croup**:

> **COCKER SPANIEL** (1992)—*The docked tail is set on and carried on a line with the topline of the back, or slightly higher.*

> **BASENJI** (1990)—*Tail is set high on topline . . .*

> **DACHSHUND** (1992)—*Croup—Long, rounded and full, sinking slightly toward the tail. Tail—Set in continuation of the spine.*

> **MINIATURE PINSCHER** (1990)—*Tail—Set high . . .*

> **AIREDALE TERRIER** (1959)—*The root of the tail should be set well up on the back.*

> **KERRY BLUE TERRIER** (1992)—*Tail should be set on high . . .*

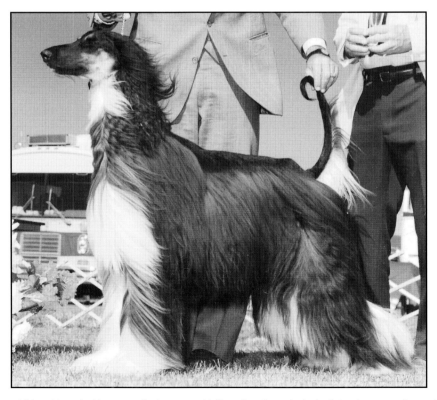

4-11. Afghan Hound with proper sloping croup. Unlike other dogs, the lack of development of muscles (or fat) on top of the pelvis bone causes an illusion; the pelvis is less steep than it appears. Goats, sheep and some antelope (Figure 4-4) with similar pelvis formation are adapted to hilly or mountain terrain. *Photo by Carl Lindemaier.*

Because of the tail set the following Standards call for **steep croup**. Also these breeds' purposes in life indicate that the pelvis should be normal to steep.

> **AFGHAN HOUND** (1948)—*Strong and powerful loin and slightly arched, falling away towards the stern with the hipbones very prominent . . . Tail set not too high on the body* (Figure 4-11).

> **BULL TERRIER** (1974)—*Tail—* . . . *set on low* . . .

> **STAFFORDSHIRE BULL TERRIER** (1990)—*The tail is* . . . *low set* . . .

> **WELSH CORGI, CARDIGAN** (1991)—*Tail set fairly low on body line* . . .

Some of the Sighthounds (Borzoi, Greyhound, Italian Greyhound, Irish Wolfhound, Scottish Deerhound and Whippet) have a downward arch in the loin, when posed, to steepen the pelvis. Since these dogs are designed for coursing or chasing game, agility or the ability to maneuver with game is of prime importance. Racing Greyhounds have a flat loin; this improves speed on the flat but sacrifices agility.

Rearing Muscle and Ischium

The extremity of the pelvis (ischium—see Figure 4-12), if it extends well to the rear, gives greater area for attachment of the rearing muscle (A-B). On dogs the ischium itself is not visible; muscles hide it. The enlarged size of the "ham" is visible. Very few Standards mention the length of the pelvis.

> **BELGIAN SHEEPDOG** (1991)—*The croup is medium long.*

> **BOXER** (1989)—*Pelvis long and in females especially broad.*

In Figure 4-12, if the rearing muscle (A-B) is contracted, the ischium is pulled down and the front of the dog is elevated. This muscle, more than any other, allows the rear to propel the front upward in the gallop. Animals with poorly developed rearing

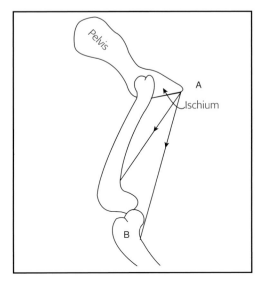

4-12. Rear propulsion. By contracting muscle A-B the ischium is pulled downward and the front of the dog is elevated.

muscles (camels) are poor gallopers and jumpers. The Afghan Hound, as a good leaper, should be well developed in this area.

Hip Joint

The upper thigh bone is connected with (articulates with) the pelvis by a ball and socket joint. Unlike other rear leg joints (hinge type), the hip joint has the ability, within limits, to rotate in all directions. Hip dysplasia is the result of: (a) malformation of one or both hip joint components, (b) increased joint laxity, or a combination of a and b; the ball does not sit correctly in the socket. A common symptom of hip dysplasia is limping, especially when turning square corners.

In recent times it has been discovered that severing the pectineal muscle relieves the tension on the joint and allows almost normal leg action. However, *the cause of hip dysplasia has not been determined*. It is not known whether the excess tension in the pectineus is due to a disease or genetic condition, or, in part, the dog's environment. One thing is certain: Hip dysplasia is more common to larger dogs, especially the heavy working type (not Greyhounds).

Stifles

The stifle joint (the joint between the upper and lower thighs) is a hinge, and can be straight or well bent depending upon the purpose of the dog. Sledge or cart dogs (especially the Arctic dogs) often have straighter stifles to aid pushing (dogs push against the ground; the harness pulls the load).

Dogs with entirely straight stifles (Chow Chow) move with a characteristic stilted motion. The rear legs do not fold under the dog as much as in dogs with well bent stifles. Leg motion with the joints flexing freely is more appealing to the eye. While it is remembered that straight legs are an advantage to certain breeds, the functional purpose, *not* artistic appeal, should be the basis of judgment. Jumping is hindered by straight stifles; most Chow Chows can be kept inside a three-foot-high fence.

A dog with well bent stifles normally has longer rear reach. Well bent stifles give flexibility to the leg; it is needed for *speed* (cheetah, pronged antelope and Greyhound), the *flying trot* (German Shepherd), *jumping* (Afghan Hound) and for *going to ground* (Dachshund). As with all parts of dogs, the stifles must be judged in the light of a breed's function. The Dachshund needs well bent stifles to fold the legs under while crawling through badger holes.

> **BORZOI** (1972)—*Hindquarters—Long, very muscular and powerful with well bent stifles.*
>
> **GERMAN SHORTHAIRED POINTER** (1992)—*Stifles are well bent.*
>
> **NORWEGIAN ELKHOUND** (1989)—*Moderate angulation at stifle and hock.*
>
> **DACHSHUND** (1992)—*The pelvis, the thigh, the second thigh, and the metatarsus are ideally the same length and form a series of right angles.*
>
> **MINIATURE PINSCHER** (1990)—*Hindquarters— . . . From the side, well angulated . . . Stifles well defined.*

PAPILLON (1991)—*Hindquarters—Well developed and well angulated.*

GERMAN SHEPHERD DOG (1994)—*Hindquarters—The whole assembly of the thigh, viewed from the side, is broad, with both upper and lower thigh well muscled, forming as nearly as possible a right angle.*

In the above Standards (except the Elkhound) several methods were used to express "Stifles well bent." When a Standard is silent on the bend of stifle, the description of the gait may explain what the stifle angle should be.

Rear Pastern or Hock

The hock joint is between the lower thigh and the tarsal bones. The point of hock is the calcaneal process. The calcaneal process has been referred to as the os calcis. "Os calcis" is the term for the human heel, which is the corresponding bone in human anatomy to the calcaneal process in the dog. Many Standards refer to the hock, while the correct term is "rear pastern." This book uses the term "hock" as this is common usage in breed Standards.

When the dog is in motion, muscles pulling on tendons (Achilles) attached to the calcaneal process give snap to the hock and foot. Muscle A in Figure 4-13 pulls the calcaneal process; the hock joint acts as a fulcrum and the foot pushes back on the ground. The shorter the calcaneal process bone and the higher the hock joint is from the ground, the greater the action (speed of movement of the foot). However, excess energy is required to get that action. The rabbit has high (long) hocks and quick initial speed, but poor endurance.

There are numerous combinations of calcaneal process and hock height. One of the world's fastest animals, the pronged antelope, has high hocks and a long calcaneal process. Cats are high on the hock and have high initial speed with poor endurance. Dogs with low (short) hocks have endurance. The pronged antelope has good speed and endurance; the longer calcaneal process compensates for higher hocks.

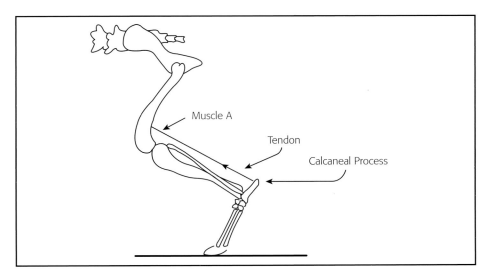

4-13. Long calcaneal process provides endurance. Muscle A pulling on the calcaneal process puts the paw in motion. A long calcaneal process as compared to the height of the hock gives endurance. A short calcaneal process as compared to the hock height gives action but requires more power.

Greyhounds and Whippets are best for a study of the calcaneal process. The lack of long hair and the thin skin at the hock joint clearly reveal this bone and the tendon that pulls it.

GREYHOUND (No Date)—*Hocks . . . wide . . .*

A hock is wide when the calcaneal process bone is long.

A person evaluating dogs should take into account the purpose of the dog prior to forming an opinion as to whether the relative height of the hock and calcaneal process are right or not. Draft animals (sledge dogs and cart dogs) certainly do not need quick initial speed; they need endurance and power. The principles determining the design of a dog's hocks are:

High hocks go with high initial speed; low hocks are for endurance.

Hock Angle

Many Standards call for a well bent hock, an angulated hock, or infer that the hock should be angular. Where the purpose of the dog is to produce a smooth trotting gait, the hock should be well bent. But if the purpose of the dog is heavy draft, agility or fighting, the hocks should be straight or moderately bent. A dog going to ground needs well bent hocks to enable him to lower his body as he travels through burrows. A straight-hocked dog would get stuck in the burrow.

The following Standards call for **well bent hocks**:

GREYHOUND (No Date)—*Hocks well bent and rather close to ground.*

AFGHAN HOUND (1947)—*Hocks are well let down; good angulation of both stifle and hock.*

DACHSHUND (1992)—*Metatarsus—Short and strong, perpendicular to the second thigh bone.*

Standards calling for moderately bent hocks:

ALASKAN MALAMUTE (1994)—*Hock joints are moderately bent and well let down.*

BEAGLE (1957)—*Hocks firm, symmetrical and moderately bent.*

BELGIAN TERVUREN (1990)—*Hocks moderately bent.*

NORWEGIAN ELKHOUND (1989)—*Moderate angulation at stifle and hock.*

Standards calling for **straight or almost straight hocks:**

CHOW CHOW (1990)—*Viewed from the side, the hind legs have little apparent angulation and the hock joint and metatarsals are directly beneath the hip joint.*

Hindquarters— . . . Hock joint . . . appears almost straight.

BULLDOG (1990)—*Hocks should be slightly bent . . .*

Where the Standard is silent on the hock angle, judgment should be based on what hock angle best suits the original purpose of the dog. The Samoyed Standard (1993) calls for "*Hocks should be well developed, sharply defined and set at approximately 30 percent of hip height.*" The Standard does not say "well bent." From the purpose of the dog (sled dogs in snow country and hunting) it can be concluded that hocks should not be as well bent as the fast moving dogs, but they should be sharply defined as called for in the Standard.

Principles of rear angulation are:

1. Well angulated dogs (both stifle and hock) have an advantage in jumping, traveling in burrows and long reach.

2. Dogs with straight hindquarters have an advantage in heavy draft.

3. Moderate angulation is seen on most wild dogs.

Sickle Hocks

A sickle hock is one where the hock is bent at more than 90 degrees to the ground when viewed from the side. This curved hock gives the appearance of a sickle used to cut grain, therefore the name "sickle hock." Often this over-angulated hock cannot be flexed in action. The hock angle does not change while the leg is moving or the dog is unable to use the joint; therefore, a sickle hock is of no benefit.

Feet in Motion

The types of feet found on dogs are:

1. Cat feet

2. Oval feet

3. Hare feet

4. Webbed feet

5. Large feet for snow or sand

Figures 4-14 through 4-16 illustrate the anatomy of the Greyhound foot.

Cat feet are round and compact with short third digital bones. *Oval feet* are intermediate between cat and hare feet and have slightly longer third digital bones. *Hare feet* have long third digital bones and require greater energy but produce greater action (speed). In general, dogs requiring endurance should not have hare feet, but dogs needing quick initial speed or bounding gait should have hare feet. *Webbed feet* are required for either swimming or for work in the snow.

When judging dogs that have hare feet, it is quite important to observe whether the feet are being properly used. Flat, splayed or broken-down feet should be severely penalized. To improve footing and leaping the Afghan Hound has large modified hare feet that are rather flat. Although this dog does appear to be somewhat flat-footed, the arched toes are capable of giving a spring to the dog's gait. The camel (Figure 4-17) has large, flat feet adapted to the desert.

For swimming, the CHESAPEAKE BAY RETRIEVER (1993) has *"Well-webbed hare feet . . . of good size . . . "* All dogs, to some extent, have webbed feet, but the Chesapeake Bay Retriever has better developed webbing. Ideally, feet for swimming should be large and with excess skin between the toes. As the dog paddles the toes spread so as to have greater area for pushing against the water. This greater area is also required for going through the tidewater mud flats. The IRISH WATER SPANIEL Standard (1990) states: *"Forefeet are large, thick and somewhat spreading; well clothed with hair both over and between the toes."*

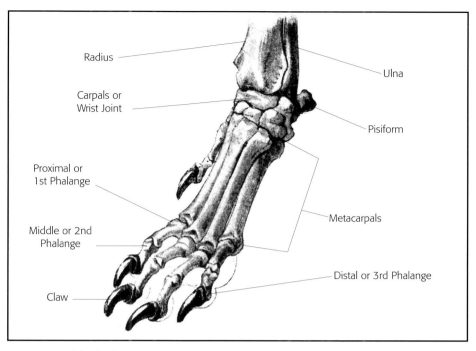

Radius

Ulna

Carpals or
Wrist Joint

Pisiform

Proximal or
1st Phalange

Metacarpals

Middle or 2nd
Phalange

Distal or 3rd Phalange

Claw

4-14. Bones of the forefoot.

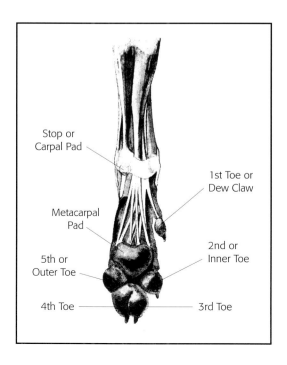

Stop or
Carpal Pad

1st Toe or
Dew Claw

Metacarpal
Pad

2nd or
Inner Toe

5th or
Outer Toe

4th Toe

3rd Toe

4-15. Pads and toes of the left forefoot—
viewed from below.

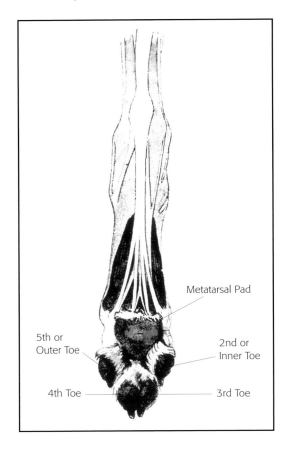

5th or
Outer Toe

Metatarsal Pad

2nd or
Inner Toe

4th Toe

3rd Toe

4-16. Pads and toes of the left hind foot—viewed from below.

For snow conditions, the SAMOYED (1993) has "*Large, long, flattish—a hare-foot, slightly spread but not splayed; toes arched; pads thick and tough, with protective growth of hair between the toes.*" If Samoyeds were unable to flex their feet, they would be of little benefit.

In rocky, mountainous regions sheep have small hoofs to cling onto cracks or small projections. Large feet are not suited for climbing steep, rocky slopes. The Cairn Terrier (Figure 4-18), as the name implies, hunts rodents on rocky slopes; and they are diggers. The Standard (1938) states: "*Forefeet larger than hind feet.*" As with many Standards, size is left to tradition.

Since the front feet of a dog carry more weight than the rear, most dogs have larger front feet. Not many Standards say so.

SHETLAND SHEEPDOG (1990)—*Feet (front and hind)—Feet should be oval and compact with the toes well arched and fitting tightly together. Pads deep and tough, nails hard and strong. Faults—Feet turned in or out. Splay feet. Hare feet. Cat feet.*

DOBERMAN PINSCHER (1990)—*Feet well arched, compact, and catlike, turning neither in nor out.*

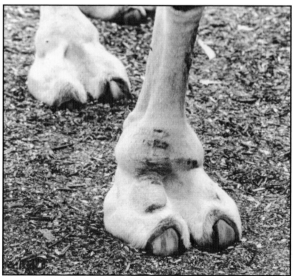

4-17. The camel has large feet for desert conditions. The hindquarters are poorly developed. The rearing muscles are not strong enough to lift the front end; a camel does not gallop efficiently (it paces). Although the rearing muscles are not strong, the camel can carry heavier loads than a horse can. *Photo by Ron Garrison, courtesy San Diego Zoo.*

PAPILLON (1991)—*Feet thin and elongated (hare-like), pointing neither in nor out.*

ALASKAN MALAMUTE (1994)—*The feet are large, toes tight fitting and well arched. There is a protective growth of hair between the toes. The pads are thick and tough; toenails short and strong.*

4-18. Cairn Terriers are diggers, forefeet are larger than hind feet.

PORTUGUESE WATER DOG (1991)—*Feet are round and rather flat. Toes neither knuckled up or too long. Webbing between the toes is of soft skin, well covered with hair, and reaches the toe tips. Central pad is very thick, others normal. Nails held up slightly off the ground. Black, brown, white and striped nails allowed.*

WEIMARANER (1971)—*Feet—Firm and compact, webbed, toes well arched, pads closed and thick, nails short and gray or amber in color. Dewclaws—Should be removed.*

The principles pertaining to feet are:

1. Cat feet are advantageous for endurance.

2. Hare feet are advantageous for high initial speed and jumping but are poor for endurance.

3. Oval feet are a compromise between endurance and high initial speed and jumping ability.

4. Large feet are advantageous for snow and sand footing; large webbed feet are advantageous for swimming.

5. In rocky regions, small feet allow the dog to cling to small cracks or crevices. On hard ground small feet are superior.

Greyhound feet (*"rather more hare than cat feet"*) were studied at Purina Dog Care Center. (Pegram, Louis, "Flat Feet In Purebred Dogs," *Popular Dogs*, Dec. 1972.) Greyhounds raised on concrete runs developed flat feet, whereas those on sand and clay runs developed normal feet. Once knuckles of the toes flattened (straightened) during the teething period, little could be done to correct the problem. Flat feet may be due to:

1. Heredity
2. Lack of exercise (mostly in youth)
3. Improper nutrition
4. Improper kennel footing during growth

Smaller breeds (Beagles and smaller) did not seem to develop flat feet on concrete (asphalt was poorer than concrete), whereas the larger breeds almost always did. The dog show judge evaluates dogs as they are presented on the day. Since flat feet in a dog may be based on heredity, and since the judge has no way of knowing whether the flat feet are due to heredity or not, he must penalize flat feet.

Showing Pads

A dog with good or excessive backward reach of the rear legs will show pads when moving away from the observer. Many times the judge, when judging a particular breed, has been heard to say, "I like to see the pads as the dog moves away." Because of flexible pasterns, the front pads often show more than the rear.

Like most rules of judging, showing the pads applies to certain breeds but not to others. Dogs described by their Standard as "straight" (such as the Chow Chow) rather than "angulated" usually do not show their pads (especially the rear pads). The German Shepherd, even though well angulated, is supposed to keep its paws close to the ground on the back reach. Its Standard (1994) reads: *"the stroke of the hind leg finishing with the foot still close to the ground in a smooth follow-through."* The Standard in describing the croup states: *"Croup long and gradually sloping."* The tail set (and pelvis) is then slightly low and the paw is not high on the rearward stroke of the hind leg.

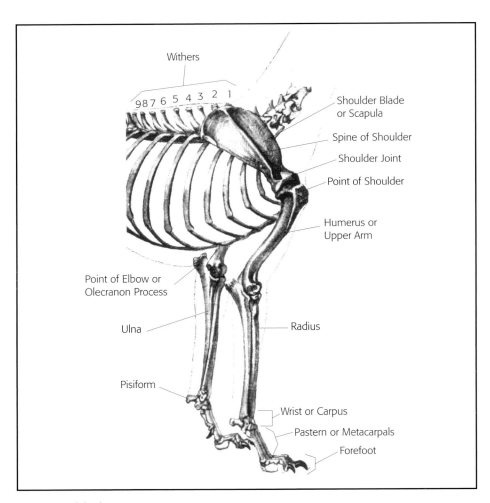

Withers

9 8 7 6 5 4 3 2 1

Shoulder Blade
or Scapula

Spine of Shoulder

Shoulder Joint

Point of Shoulder

Humerus or
Upper Arm

Point of Elbow or
Olecranon Process

Ulna

Radius

Pisiform

Wrist or Carpus

Pastern or Metacarpals

Forefoot

5-1. Bones of the forequarters.

CHAPTER 5

Forequarters

Forequarters

The forequarters of dogs are lever systems designed to carry more than half of the weight of the dog and to assist in propulsion and movement. The common names associated with the forequarters are shown in Figures 5-1 and 5-2. The forequarters are attached to the body by muscle, whereas the hindquarters are attached directly with a ball and socket joint. To a limited extent the shoulder blade can slide in any direction more or less parallel with the rib cage. If the dog has poor muscle attachment, the forequarters may move in undesirable directions. Figure 5-3 illustrates the muscles of the outer side of the right foreleg.

The forequarter is made up of the shoulder blade, which articulates with the upper arm at the shoulder joint; the upper arm, which articulates with the forearm; the forearm, which consists of the radius and ulna; the wrist, consisting of seven carpal bones; the pastern, consisting of five metacarpal bones; and the forefoot.

The upper end of the shoulder blade is joined to the backbone (thoracic vertebrae) by a portion of the trapezius muscle attached at the third through the ninth thoracic vertebrae.

The area from the first to the ninth thoracic vertebrae is called the withers. The highest part of the shoulder blade lies just below the level of the first and second vertebrae. The spine on the shoulder blade points to the highest part of the shoulder blade.

The head of the upper arm fits into the cavity on the lower end of the shoulder blade. The upper arm is the **humerus** and is the largest bone in the forequarters. It is longer than the shoulder blade. The lower end of the humerus articulates (joins) with the radius and ulna, or forearm, at the elbow joint.

The **radius** is the main weight bearing bone in the forequarters. The ulna is joined to the radius along its length so the two bones act as one. At the top of the ulna is the olecranon process, which is referred to as the point of elbow. The bottom end of the forearm joins with the top row of seven carpal bones at the wrist joint.

The **carpal bones** join the top of the metacarpal bones. The five **metacarpal bones** comprise the pastern. The lower ends of the metacarpi join to the forefoot.

Shoulder Blade Rotation

The primary function of the shoulder blade is to oscillate back and forth, thus aiding the front legs to swing back and forth. The oscillating motion of the shoulder blade is created by muscle E of Figure 5-4 relaxing, then pulling muscle H, which relaxes when muscle E is pulling. For the average shoulder blade, according to most authors, the muscles are capable of rotating the blade about 30 degrees (15 degrees in each direction from the stationary position). Approximate measurements on a Standard Poodle indicate this to be reasonably true. However, the 30 degrees is an "educated eye measurement" at best since it is almost impossible to measure the shoulder blade angle when the dog is in motion. If a dog is lying on its side and the blade is manually moved, a fair idea of the extent of motion can be obtained.

Figure 5-4 is based on fluoroscope x-ray motion pictures, taken by Dr. Jenkins of Harvard University, of dogs walking on a treadmill. The motion pictures indicate that the shoulder blade oscillates about a pivot point as shown. X-ray motion pictures at the trot show differences such as some up-and-down sliding of the shoulder blade. The oscillation of the shoulder blade allows absorption of shock as the feet touch the ground; it assists in lifting the feet off the ground on the forward motion of the leg; it increases reach; and it adds to forward propulsion.

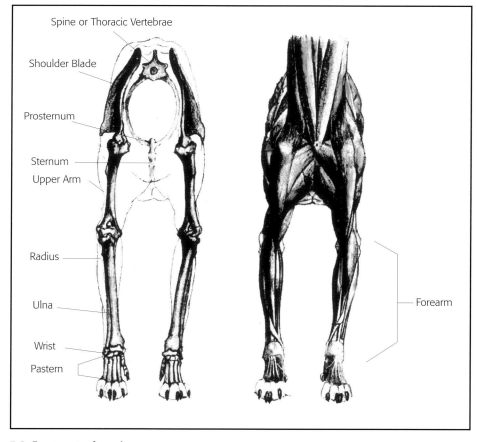

5-2. Forequarters, front view.

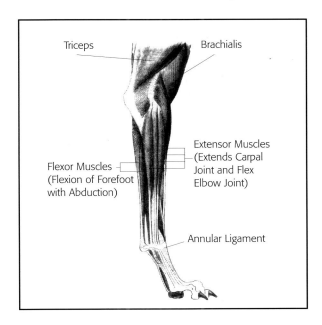

5-3. Muscles of outer side of right foreleg.

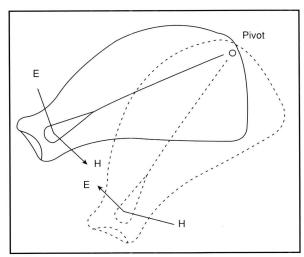

5-4. Shoulder blade motion.

Muscles other than those indicated in Figure 5-4 also assist in rotating and supporting the shoulder blade; the figure only illustrates the principle involved.

As stated above, the shoulder blade is capable of rotating 15 degrees in each direction (total 30 degrees) from a resting position. This is a reasonably good guess for the walk and trot gaits. A human hand can rotate the scapula about the same amount when the dog is lying on its side. Movies taken of lean, galloping Sighthounds show considerably more rotation. At full speed, the scapula rotates as much as 70 degrees, more than double the often quoted 30 degrees. This magnitude of rotation benefits elastic rebound.

Cats depend upon shoulder blades sliding up and down to take up concussion. At the time the cat's front paw is on the ground, the shoulder blade noticeably slides above the height of the withers. The trapezius muscles of the dog are more firmly attached at the withers and do not allow extreme vertical motion.

Shoulder Joint

The shoulder joint, like the hip joint, is a ball and socket. The point of the shoulder blade has a socket (glenoid cavity) that receives the head (articular head) of the humerus. Although the joint can move in all directions, muscles along with the form of the cavity allow greater motion in the fore and aft plane. Other joints in the foreleg are hinges—they more or less restrict motion to fore and aft.

Because of the ball and socket shoulder joint, the front, unlike the rear, may have faults such as paddling, weaving and out at the elbows.

Shoulder Blade Layback/Angulation

Since dogs are bred for various purposes, it follows that different types of shoulder blades and different placement of blades in shoulder rest position are needed for different breeds. *The shoulder blade is bone and has no means of creating motion by itself; muscles move the blade and dictate where it will come to rest.*

Instruments are utilized to make actual measurements of shoulder blade layback by measuring the spine of the shoulder blade, as this is a precisely fixed location. The shoulder layback (angle) can be quoted from the vertical or the horizontal (level). (Refer to Figure 5-5.) The layback angle is the angle the blade's spine measures off the vertical at the time the dog is standing in a rest position with the forelegs and rear pasterns vertical. The layback angle measured from the level is the difference between the vertical layback angle and 90 degrees. When the vertical layback angle is 30 degrees, the level layback angle is 60 degrees. When the layback angle is off the vertical, the smaller the angle is, the steeper the shoulder will be; when the layback angle is off the level, the larger the angle is, the steeper the shoulder will be.

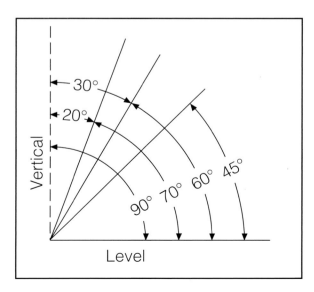

5-5. Shoulder blade angles—vertical and level layback angles.

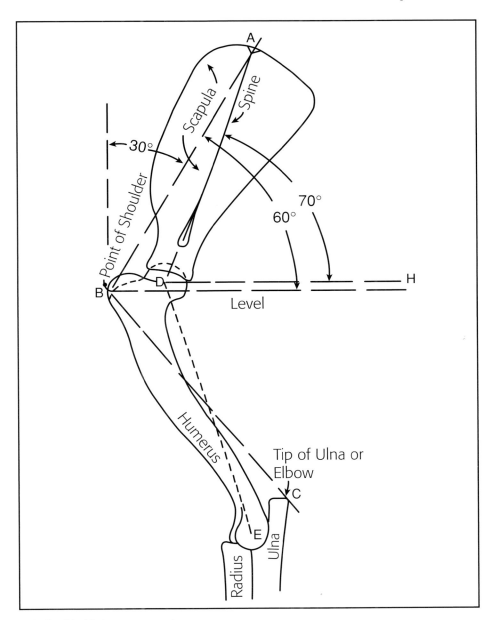

5-6. Shoulder blade measurements.

As breeders and judges we do not use instruments to measure layback angle; we utilize our hands and eyes. We measure from the top of the shoulder blade to the point of shoulder. This is done by placing one finger on top of the shoulder blade and another at the point of shoulder, and estimating the layback angle—generally in reference to the ground. (Refer to Figure 5-6.) The difference between the instrument measured layback and the estimated layback varies between 5 and 10 degrees; the esti-mate depends upon where on the top of the shoulder blade the finger is placed. The percentage of error and the repeatability of measurement on the spine is quite low; the percentage of error and repeatability of estimating is quite large. In general, shoulder blade layback measured on the spine varies from 20 to 32 degrees (70 to 58 degrees from the level); these same shoulders will be estimated between the range of 30 to 40 degrees (60 to 50 degrees from the level).

Unless otherwise stated, this book uses a layback angle as estimated by hand in reference to the level.

Anatomical considerations affect the shoulder (blade) layback. First, the blades are attached to the body by muscle, not by bone joints. Genetically, in all dogs the muscles tend to attach to vertebrae so the spine of the shoulder blade points to the top of the second or third thoracic vertebra (rarely to the first or fourth). Second, the point of shoulder is located close to the front tip of the breastbone. A blood vessel from inside the chest (at the lower part of the first rib) travels around the outside of the first rib into the leg just above the point of shoulder. Back and forth motion of the lower part of the shoulder blade is somewhat restricted by muscles to prevent the blood vessel from being ruptured. Nerves entering the same shoulder blade impose limits on blade movement. These limit the amount of layback to about 50 degrees for longer-legged dogs.

Shoulder Blade Layback for Endurance and Smooth Gait

Well laid-back shoulder blades on a deep chest are considered best for dogs that move smoothly at a trot. The layback for a well laid-back shoulder is in the range of 60 to 50 degrees. This measurement is from the point of the shoulder to a point on top of the shoulder blade, as estimated in the showring. The optimum angle has not been determined by measurements.

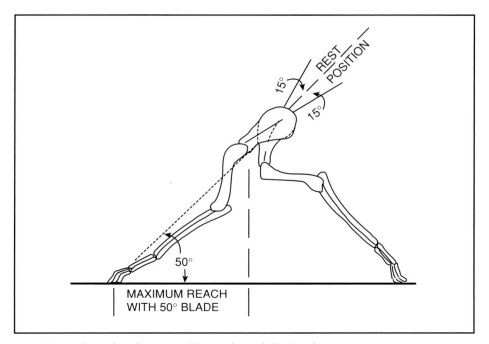

5-7. Maximum forward reach at a trot with a 50 degree layback angle.

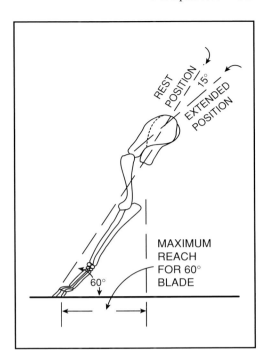

MAXIMUM
REACH
FOR 60°
BLADE

60°

REST
POSITION
15°
EXTENDED
POSITION

5-8. Trotting dogs with steep shoulder blades have reduced forward reach.

When the dog is in motion and reaches forward, the shoulder blade rotates forward about 15 degrees. Since the elbow joint and the shoulder/upper arm joint cannot completely straighten, the forward reach is about the same as the angle of the shoulder blade at rest. Therefore, the long-legged dog has a maximum forward reach of about 50 degrees, as shown in Figure 5-7.

The effect of a steep shoulder on a trotting dog is illustrated in Figure 5-8. The forward reach is approximately the angle of the blade when stationary. With steep shoulder blades, the dog either moves with short choppy steps or the dog's rearing muscles lift the front off the ground to lengthen the stride. This results in an up-and-down motion at the withers. Dogs with steep shoulders tend to trot with such a motion. A clue to steep shoulder blades is to watch the dog trot. Does the back at the withers glide or bounce up and down?

One secondary effect of a steep shoulder is to elevate the front of the dog; the topline slopes downward to the rear. This can be seen in many of the showring Irish Setters. A sloping topline may be required in the Standard for some breeds, but if well laid-back shoulders are also required, the sloping topline should not be attained at the expense of shoulder layback.

Many of the dog Standards are not specific in defining shoulder blade placement; general terms are used. If the angle is given in general terms, such as "sloping well back," it can be presumed that the most efficient shoulder layback for the original function of the dog is wanted. While several breeds of dogs call for a layback angle of 45 degrees, 45 degrees is nonexistent in practically all breeds. A 50 to 60 degree layback is well laid-back. It seems strange that some breed Standards call for a 45 degree layback, yet exhibits have never had 45 degrees by actual measurement. The following dog breeds are capable of the endurance trot:

GOLDEN RETRIEVER (1990)—*Shoulder blades long and well laid back with upper tips fairly close together at withers.*

ENGLISH SPRINGER SPANIEL (1994)—*Efficient movement in front calls for proper forequarter assembly. The shoulder blades are flat and fairly close together at the tips, molding smoothly into the contour of the body. Ideally, when measured from the top of the withers to the point of the shoulder to the elbow, the shoulder blade and upper arm are of apparent equal length, forming an angle of nearly 90 degrees; this sets the front legs well under the body and places the elbows directly beneath the tips of the shoulder blade.*

DALMATIAN (1989)—*The shoulders are smoothly muscled and well laid back.*

BEARDED COLLIE (1978)—*The shoulders are well laid back at an angle of approximately 45 degrees; a line drawn from the highest point of the shoulder blade to the forward point of articulation approximates a right angle with a line from the forward point of articulation to the point of the elbow.*

BELGIAN MALINOIS (1990)—*The shoulder is long and oblique, laid flat against the body, forming a sharp angle with the upper arm.*

COLLIE (1977)— . . . *well-sloped shoulders* . . .

SHETLAND SHEEPDOG (1990)—*From the withers the shoulder blades should slope at a 45-degree angle forward and downward to the shoulder joints.*

Shoulder Blades for Draft

Heavy horses pulling loads often have steep shoulder blades. Oxen, pound for pound, can outpull horses; oxen have very steep shoulder blades. Consider the statement in the Alaskan Malamute Standard (1994): *"The shoulders are moderately sloping . . . "* However, the Siberian Husky Standard (1990) states: *"The shoulder blade is well laid back."* Siberians were designed for pulling sleds with speed and endurance, not heavy work.

Dachshund Shoulder Blade and Upper Arm for Digging

When a dog digs, it is important that the weight of the body rests on the ground and not the elbows. The Dachshund's front assembly is reduced in size as compared to its body. Since the Dachshund's elbows are above the keel line (Figure 5-9A), the weight of the dog rests on the breastbone and the entire front is free to dig. The dog can dig while resting on its keel and can travel through burrows with ease. The extreme angulation ensures maximum reach for this reduced leg length. Leg joints are at about one-third positions to enable the compact folding of legs in burrows.

When moving through a burrow, a Dachshund's legs need to fold as compactly as possible. For any given length of forequarter the minimum length of folded forequarter is attained when all three parts (shoulder blade, upper arm and forearm with pastern) are of equal length. The same is true for the rear quarters.

Short legs (Figure 5-9B) give Dachshunds the added advantage of positioning their teeth where they can protect the front feet from rodent bites. To attain all of these advantages, something had to be sacrificed: speed in running.

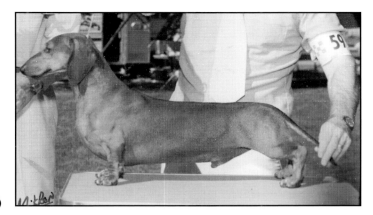

(A)

(B)

5-9. The dachshund's elbow is well above the brisket (keel). *Top photo by MikRon photo.*

Steep Shoulder Blades and Speed

From personal observations, oblique shoulder blades are essential for endurance and for smooth running. For sprinting, a properly muscled dog or cat with steep blades can run fast. The maned wolf of South America (*Chrysocyon brachyurus*) is long-legged and very cow-hocked with vertical shoulder blades, and very fast in short sprints. Some deer and antelope, noted for speed, have comparatively steep or vertical shoulder blades. The lion and cheetah have vertical blades. Never can it be said that steep blades reduce speed.

Wild dogs with well laid-back shoulders are not noted for speed. Wolves and jackals cannot catch healthy grazing animals; they catch unhealthy or old specimens. Wolves are noted for endurance and endurance requires well laid-back shoulder blades.

Measurements on Sighthounds prove that they have about 10 degrees steeper layback than do good trotting dogs. Sighthound layback is between 70 and 60 degrees.

Sighthounds use the double suspension gallop, which utilizes the flexibility of the back to obtain reach. (Refer to Brown, Curtis M., *Dog Locomotion and Gait Analysis*, Wheat Ridge, Colo.: Hoflin Publishing Ltd., 1986, for an in-depth discussion of the double suspension gallop.)

Shoulder Blade Placement, Short Backs and Genes

When judging dogs, the following relationships are usually found:

1. Dogs with short necks or short rib cages or both usually have steep shoulder blades and lack a forechest.

2. Dogs with long necks often have long rib cages and well laid-back shoulder blades.

An explanation of these statements requires knowledge of vertebrae. Practically all mammals (including all dog breeds) have the same number of vertebrae in each segment of the body: seven in the neck, thirteen in the rib cage, seven in the loin, three in the pelvis and an irregular number in the tail. Genetically, in all dogs the shoulder blade muscle attaches to the same vertebrae. Usually, the longer the rib cage, the further back the shoulder blade is attached and the further it is laid back.

Three factors associated with the vertebrae which affect shoulder layback are width of vertebrae, length of vertebrae spires and slope of spires. In order to simplify the

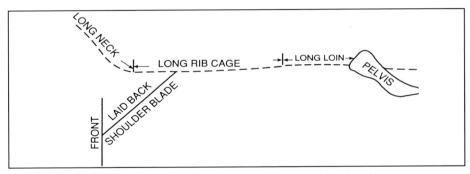

5-10. Simplified drawing illustrating layback as a function of rib cage vertebrae length.

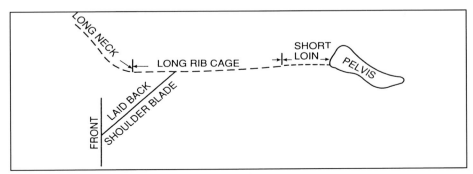

5-11. Layback with a long neck, long rib cage and short loin.

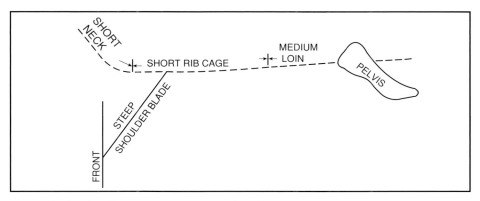

5-12. Layback with a short neck, short rib cage and medium loin.

following discussion, the term "length of vertebrae" is used to group all three factors into one entity.

In Figures 5-10, 5-11 and 5-12, each dash represents the length of a vertebra, and each line marked "front" represents the front of the rib cage. The length of the shoulder blade in all three figures is identical. The trapezius muscle on each side attaches the spine of the scapula to both the neck vertebrae (fourth through seventh) and the tips of the thoracic (rib cage) vertebrae (third through ninth). Therefore, the shoulder blade is anchored to the tips of the third through ninth vertebrae *regardless* of the length of the rib cage. The spine of the blade points to the second or third vertebra. To simplify the drawings and to make it easier to understand the principles involved, the shoulder blade is represented by a single line attached to the fourth rib cage vertebra. See Figures 5-11 and 5-12 for different vertebra lengths.

It is axiomatic that if the rib cage is long, the vertebrae are long and the shoulder blade is attached further back. Likewise if the rib cage is short, the shoulder blade is attached further forward.

Figure 5-11 represents a dog with a long rib cage; there is plenty of room for the shoulder blade to slant forward to 50 degrees without extending beyond the front of the rib cage. Figure 5-12 represents a dog with a short rib cage. The shoulder blade must either be steep as shown or it must project beyond the front of the dog. A hollow forechest causes paddling problems; the steep shoulder blade is the usual problem.

Individual vertebrae within a dog can vary in length. The giraffe has seven vertebrae in the neck and twenty-three in the back, yet the neck is longer than the back. In most mammals (including dogs), if one vertebra is long, the adjoining one tends to be long. If the front of the dog's rib cage has long vertebrae, the neck tends to have long vertebrae. Genetically it is difficult to get a short neck and long rib cage or to get a long neck and short rib cage. It then follows that a long rib cage, a long neck and well laid-back shoulder blades tend to go together.

Figure 5-11 shows a dog with a long neck, a long rib cage and a short loin (close coupled). Genetically, this type of structure is easier to breed since *vertebrae gradually reduce in length as they progress along the neck and through the rib cage to the loin.* Several dog Standards describe this build. It is probably the only practical way to attain square dogs with well laid-back shoulder blades and a forechest.

BOXER (1989)—*Neck—of ample length . . . The ribs extending far to the rear, are well arched but not barrel shaped. The back is short, straight and muscular and firmly connects the withers to the hindquarters. The loins are short and muscular.*

STANDARD SCHNAUZER (1991)—*square-built . . . Body . . . short-coupled.*

German Shepherd Dogs, with their ribbing carried well back and the relatively short loin, usually have well laid-back shoulders. Scottish Terriers, with their moderately short necks and their moderately short bodies, usually have steep shoulder blades.

The Basenji (1990), like other short-backed dogs, has a problem with steep shoulder blades. Its neck is of *"good length"* and *"well set into shoulders,"* and it is *"short-coupled,"* with *"shoulders moderately laid back."* The Basenji Standard prior to 1990 stated *"laid back shoulders,"* which was interpreted by some to mean "well laid-back shoulders"—the 1990 change brought the interpretation into conformity with the reality of genetics.

Dogs with brachycephalic heads (Pug type) normally have short necks. Some of these Standards call for well laid-back shoulders (a contradiction of the usual facts of nature).

Many Standards require a neck to merge smoothly into the body. The Vizsla Standard (1983) states: *"Neck . . . broadening nicely into shoulders."* The Great Dane Standard (1990) states: *"The neck . . . From the nape, it should gradually broaden and flow smoothly into the withers."* If the front edge of a shoulder blade is too far forward, the skin of the neck will suddenly flare out at the point of contact with the blade. A rough transition occurs between the neck and body with steep shoulder blades. A Standard calling for a smooth transition from neck to body also describes shoulders laid back.

A summary of the principles developed for shoulders is as follows:

1. At the trot, a well laid-back shoulder (blade about 50 degrees) increases reach, decreases jouncing at the withers, decreases pounding and increases endurance.

2. Steep shoulders are advantageous for heavy draft, but at the trot cause up-and-down motions at the withers with loss of endurance.

3. Fast, sprinting animals often have steep shoulders.

4. Dogs with short ribcages genetically tend to have steeper shoulders than those with long ribcages.

5. Dogs with long necks tend to have long ribcages and well laid-back shoulders.

6. Dogs with short legs and well laid-back shoulders can efficiently fold their legs to enable them to travel through burrows.

Set of Shoulder on Side of Chest (When Viewed from the Side)

As you look down on a dog from above, the front of the chest rounds off as shown in Figure 5-13. In Figure 5-13A the shoulder blade is shown flat on the side of the chest; this is the preferred set. The blades of Figure 5-13B, set too far forward, cause "out at the elbows" and "toeing in." When moving, these faults are very noticeable to a trained

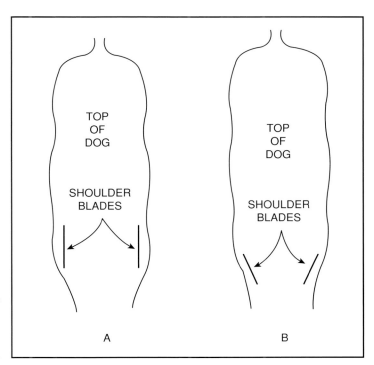

TOP
OF
DOG

SHOULDER
BLADES

A

TOP
OF
DOG

SHOULDER
BLADES

B

5-13. Preferred set of shoulder blades shown in (A). Shoulder blades set too far forward in (B).

eye. In the short-legged breeds, where all of the leg bones have been reduced in size, this fault occurs more frequently.

The forward set of the shoulders shown in Figure 5-13B causes the blades to point towards one another, thereby causing the elbows to stick out and the toes to point in. Dogs with reduced leg bone length (Dachshunds, Skye Terriers, Scotties, etc.) more frequently have this fault since their smaller shoulder blades can fit on the forward portion of the chest.

The front of a giraffe is shown in Figure 5-14. The point of the shoulder blade projects well beyond the ribcage. There is a hollow between the two blade points so there is no forechest here. Part of the shoulder blade rotates on the ribcage; part rotates in space. If the part of the shoulder blade that rotates is firmly anchored with muscles, the points of the shoulders can be held steady enough to prevent paddling (a loose front).

When this structure occurs on a dog, the muscles holding the shoulder blade in place usually have insufficient strength to prevent paddling or to prevent the legs from swinging loosely. This fault is more prevalent in short-backed dogs and in straight-front dogs such as Terriers, Foxhounds and Beagles. When judging long-coated dogs, the judge's hand should always be placed between the dog's front legs to determine whether projecting blades exist (especially on the Afghan Hound). Most dog breeds have a forechest, and the shoulder blades are located further back.

The giraffe has a short body; the shoulder blade must project well forward as shown in Figure 5-14. There is a hollow between the points of the blades; the fronts of the blades are working in space (not on a flattened side of a ribcage). When a dog has its blades too far forward and there is no forechest (only a hollow), the blades are loose in front and tend to produce dogs that paddle. Even though this structural fault for dogs is not mentioned in many Standards, it is undesirable.

5-14. Giraffe shoulder blade location is far forward. *Photo by Ron Garrison, courtesy San Diego Zoo.*

The Effect of the Chest on Movement

In theory, the shape of the chest in the area of the shoulder blade can vary, as shown in Figure 5-15. The circle has the greatest area inside its perimeter of any shape. Any other shape with equal perimeter decreases the volume of the chest cavity. Why the circular shape in many animals?

1. The ribs are structurally stronger.

2. Body surface per pound of weight is less, resulting in less heat loss through the skin, an extremely important point for small mammals.

3. There is maximum chest capacity.

The disadvantage of the circular chest is that the shoulder blade must move up and down on a curved surface. A flat surface is far more efficient. When a dog is moving fast, with the most efficient locomotion, the legs converge and nearly single-track. To single-track, the legs must taper toward a point under the body or keel. The *oval, tapered* chest gives this effect. Speedsters have a deep, narrow chest with flattened sides. The greater motion efficiency obtainable by the flatter chest more than compensates for the loss in strength of the rib structure. The cheetah is narrow in the chest.

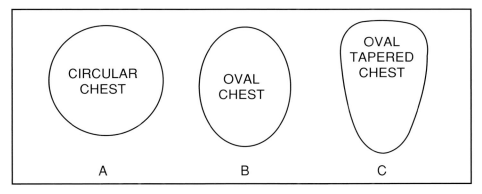

5-15. Circular chest (A) is structurally the strongest, has greatest volume with least surface area. Oval chest (B) provides flat surface for shoulder blade movement. Oval tapered chest (C) provides flat surface for shoulder blade movement and permits leg convergence.

The chests on some breeds are similar to the German Shorthaired Pointer's. The GSP Standard (1992) states: "*The chest in general gives the impression of depth rather than breadth; . . . The chest reaches down to the elbows, the ribs forming the thorax immediately show a rib spring and are not flat or slabsided; they are not perfectly round or barrel-shaped. The back ribs reach well down. The circumference of the thorax immediately behind elbows is smaller than that of the thorax about a hand's-breadth behind elbows, so that the upper arm has room for movement.*" This conformation maximizes the heart and lung room, while permitting efficiency of forequarter movement.

But what about the Bulldog? The Standard (1990) states: "*Body—The brisket and body should be very capacious, with full sides, well-rounded ribs . . . It should be well let down between the shoulders and forelegs, giving the dog a broad, low, short-legged appearance . . . The shoulders should be muscular, very heavy, widespread and slanting outward, giving stability and great power.*" If the shoulder slants outward, the chest must be round.

1. The circular chest for a given weight of dog has the largest volume for storage of heart and lungs. It also has the least surface area for a given volume (less heat loss per pound of body weight—an advantage for Arctic breeds or small dogs).

2. The shoulder blade oscillates more efficiently on the flat-sided chest of the Sighthound. Flat-sided chests have more surface area per pound of weight—an advantage in hot climates.

3. Shoulder blades too far forward on a chest cause paddling.

4. A circular chest spreads the front legs and prevents overturning (as on a Bulldog).

5. A reduction in size of the chest immediately behind the elbows and then the chest expanding to full volume maximizes heart and lung room, while permitting efficiency of forequarter movement.

Angle Between Shoulder Blade and Upper Arm

The desired angle between shoulder blade and upper arm is not and cannot be the same for all functions of a dog. For example, when digging, maximum force required is probably needed when the paw is in front of the dog. Well laid-back shoulders should aid this function, though no scientific data exist to prove it.

A given angle between shoulder blade and upper arm measured with the dog standing at rest is not desirable for all functions. The most efficient angle between the shoulder blade and the upper arm for trotting with endurance is between 100 and 120 degrees (measured in the posed position with feet under the center of the shoulder blade). For specialized fronts, such as those of the sledge dogs, the angle is greater. For digging dogs, this angle is probably between 90 and 100 degrees. The angle for Sighthounds is between 120 and 140 degrees.

> **GOLDEN RETRIEVER** (1990)—*Shoulder blades long and well laid back . . . Upper arms appear about the same length as the blades, setting the elbows back beneath the upper tip of the blades.*

> **ALASKAN MALAMUTE** (1994)—*The shoulders are moderately sloping . . .*

> **DACHSHUND** (1992)—*Shoulder Blades—Long, broad, well laid-back . . . Upper Arm—Ideally the same length as the shoulder blade and at right angles to the latter.*

Length of Shoulder Blade

In dog Standards the length of the shoulder blade is usually given in terms of the upper arm (humerus); frequently both are specified to be of equal length. Except for short-legged dogs, the actual shoulder blade and upper arm are not of equal length; the upper arm is always longer to some degree. As the leg length shortens, the upper arm approaches the shoulder blade in length. This relationship is true for Terriers. In fact, long-legged Terriers do not have short upper arms, but they have an *apparently* short upper arm. Examining or judging dogs is performed on the external surface of the dog; when measuring the length of the upper arm by hand, the length of shoulder blade includes the *point* of shoulder, which is actually a portion of the upper arm (Figure 5-1). Except in short-legged dogs, the shoulder blade is shorter than the upper arm.

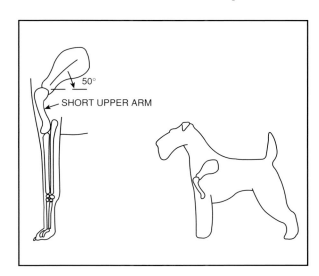

5-16. Short upper arm provides a straight front or Terrier front.

Upper Arm

Long upper arms increase reach. Sometimes the upper arm on racing fronts extends below the keel (brisket).

Many Terriers, especially the short-legged ones, go to ground. As previously stated, it is an advantage for dogs to rest on their keel while digging. This is accomplished by decreasing the size of all the bones, as is done in the Dachshund and short-legged Terriers. It can also be accomplished by a normal-size shoulder blade and having a short upper arm. This "short upper arm" is still longer than the shoulder blade.

The Fox Terrier's short upper arm developed for a different reason; it was more coincidence that the short upper arm has advantages in burrows. The Fox Terrier Standard (1991) states: *"The Terrier's legs should be carried straight forward while traveling, the forelegs hanging perpendicular and swinging parallel to the sides, like the pendulum of a clock."* A short upper arm with little bend at the elbow makes this possible, as shown in Figure 5-16.

The chest of straight-fronted dogs usually extends below the elbow, as shown in Figure 5-16. With a short upper arm, the Fox Terrier should be able to crawl through a burrow without elbows restricting the passageway. Although most Fox Terriers appear to have absolutely straight bone alignment, most do (and should) have the upper arm sloping toward the rear as shown. The short upper arm developed because of the desire to have legs that move "like the pendulum of a clock." A short upper arm is also advantageous in burrows.

We speak of the straight front on a Terrier, which is referred to as the Terrier front. The forelegs run parallel to each other from the chest to the ground when viewed from the front; the distance between the elbows, pasterns and feet is identical. When viewed from the side, the shoulder blade is well laid-back and the short upper arm slopes *slightly* to the rear; the foreleg is straight and the pasterns are short and straight with round, compact feet. The shoulder blade and the upper arm appear to be straight as the forechest, skin and hair form the straight line down to the foreleg. The bones are usually formed as shown in the dog silhouette of Figure 5-16.

Straight and Semi-Straight Fronts

In England packs of Beagles, Harriers or English Foxhounds were followed by huntsmen on horseback. A few Fox Terriers were carried by the horsemen to go after foxes in drains, burrows and hiding places.

The front structure of the above breeds is similar and somewhat like the legs of the hunter (horse). The Standards were all written by the same people.

In England, where there is plenty of soft grass footing, the effect of concussion (pounding) on feet and legs is minimized. Horses and dogs can hit the ground harder with their front feet since the ground is springy and takes up part of the shock. Horsemen commenting on the difference between English and American horses usually note that English horses have less bend in the pastern. The English Foxhound Standard was written by English horsemen and reads in part:

> **ENGLISH FOXHOUND** (1935)—*Every Master of Foxhounds insists on legs as straight as a post, and as strong; size of bone at the ankle being especially regarded as important. The desire for straightness had a tendency to produce knuckling-over, which at one time was countenanced, but in recent years this defect has been eradicated by careful breeding and intelligent adjudication, and one sees very little of this trouble in the best modern Foxhounds. The bone cannot be too large, and feet in all cases should be round and catlike, with well-developed knuckles and strong horn, which last is of the greatest importance.*

The current Smooth Fox Terrier Standard (1991) still maintains the portions of the old Standard, which was written by the same type of people who wrote the Foxhound Standard. The Smooth Fox Terrier Standard (1991) calls for "*symmetry of the Foxhound*" and "*should stand like a cleverly made hunter*" (horse).

> **SMOOTH FOX TERRIER** (1991)—*Speed and endurance must be looked to as well as power, and symmetry of the Foxhound taken as a model. The Terrier, like the Hound, must on no account be leggy, nor must he be too short in the leg. He should stand like a cleverly made hunter, covering a lot of ground, yet with a short back . . . Forequarters— . . . the forelegs viewed from any direction must be straight with bone strong right down to the feet, showing little or no appearance of ankle in front, and being short and straight in pastern. Both fore and hind legs should be carried straight forward in traveling . . .*
> *Gait— . . . The Terrier's legs should be carried straight forward while traveling, the forelegs hanging perpendicular and swinging parallel with the sides, like the pendulum of a clock.*

If the front legs move like a clock pendulum, little or no flexing of the pasterns or elbows occurs. A good Fox Terrier judge would have no trouble judging an English Foxhound or Beagle front since they are similar although not identical. Although the Beagle Standard is quite brief in describing the Beagle front (Figure 5-17), no doubt exists but that it is to be similar to the Foxhound, as stated below.

> **BEAGLE** (1957)—*A miniature Foxhound, solid and big for his inches, with the wear-and-tear look of the hound that can last in the chase and follow his quarry to the death.*

> **HARRIER** (1988)—*The Harrier should, in fact, be a smaller version of the English Foxhound.*

5-17. Beagle; note forequarters. *Photo by E. Shafer.*

The front shown in Figure 5-17 is typical of Beagles, Foxhounds, Harriers and Fox Terriers. Beagles are big for their inches, straight in front, and with moderate angulation in the rear. To satisfy type, the Beagle tail should be comparatively short and the ears houndy (soft and pendulous).

Pectoral Muscles

Pectoral muscles (superficial pectoral and deep pectoral), shown in Figure 3-4, run from the upper arm (humerus) to the breastbone (sternum) and tend to keep the legs from wobbling or paddling. In some dogs exercising (trotting behind a bicycle) will develop these muscles and eliminate movement faults.

Other Front Leg Bones

Shown in Figure 5-1 are the upper arm (humerus), forearm (radius and ulna) and the pastern (metacarpus). The upward extension of the forearm is known as the elbow or the tip of the ulna. Tendons attached to it, when pulled by muscles, move the forearm. At the elbow joint, the humerus is grooved and the top of the radius is formed to fit neatly into that groove. This construction limits the elbow joint to a forward and backward motion, like a hinge. Any malformation of the groove will give faulty leg motion.

The pisiform bone of the pastern joint acts like the upward extension of the ulna; a tendon pulling on it moves the pastern.

Bone in the Forearm

Bone in the forearm is either oval or round. In some cases different terms are used for "oval," such as "slightly flattened," "flat bone," "broad and flat," etc. When a Standard does not define the shape of the bone in the forearm, the following criterion can be used: Dogs with forward speed without great sidewise stress should have oval foreleg bones; those dogs that need to resist side forces should have round bone. This criterion is discussed below.

The horse's cannon bone is distinctly oval shaped to better absorb stresses. When viewed from the front, it is narrow; when viewed from the side, it is wide. The spires of the dog's vertebrae grow in a direction best calculated to resist stress. The spires at the withers slant toward the rear of the dog; those at the loin slant toward the front of the dog. The spires' slant is in opposition to the direction of the stress. Each of the above is an adaptation to overcome the stress in a given area.

Dogs used for speed, such as the Greyhound and the Whippet, illustrate that the lighter the leg bone, the faster the leg can move forward and back. Economy of leg bone weight is important to attain speed. In straightaway running the greatest stresses on the leg bones are on the front and rear edges, not on the sides. By making the leg bone oval with the long axis towards the front of the dog, the front and rear edges are reinforced without adding extra weight of bone on the sides.

Not all dogs' purposes demand maximum efficiency in running. The Bulldog, Bull Terrier and other wide-fronted dogs are designed for lateral stability (ability to resist side forces) as well as forward and backward stresses. For an American Staffordshire Terrier it is just as important to have leg bones equally strong sideways as forward; the Standard (1936) quite correctly says, *"round bones"* to take care of sideways forces.

Beagles, Harriers and English Foxhounds were originally used in packs and were scored on their ability to work as a group. Fast ones outrunning the pack and slow ones not keeping up were eliminated. In general these breeds call for heavy leg bones. Since forward speed with minimum weight bone is not demanded, oval bone is not necessary. Most of the breeds desiring flat or oval bones are in the Sighthounds and Sporting breeds.

Some of the Standards which define the bone shape are:

BORZOI (1972)—*Bones straight and somewhat flattened like blades, with the narrower edge forward.*

SCOTTISH DEERHOUND (1935)—*Legs should be broad and flat, and good broad forearms.*

BELGIAN MALINOIS (1990)—*The bone is oval rather than round.*

BELGIAN SHEEPDOG (1991)—*Bone oval rather than round.*

BELGIAN TERVUREN (1990)—*Bone oval rather than round.*

GERMAN SHEPHERD DOG (1994)—*The forelegs . . . bone oval rather than round.*

POINTER (1975)—*Forelegs straight and with oval bone.*

GERMAN WIREHAIRED POINTER (1989)—*Forequarters— . . . Leg bones are flat rather than round.*

ENGLISH SETTER (1986)—*Arm flat.*

ENGLISH SPRINGER SPANIEL (1994)—*foreleg . . . Bone is strong, slightly flattened, not too round or too heavy.*

FIELD SPANIEL (1990)—*Bone is flat.*

BASSET HOUND (1964)—*forelegs . . . heavy in bone.*

AUSTRALIAN TERRIER (1988)—*Forelegs— . . . the bone is round.*

BULLDOG (1990)—*forelegs . . . very stout.*

CHINESE SHAR-PEI (1992)—*The bone is substantial but never heavy.*

Pastern

The pastern joint can bend either forward or backwards; it is double jointed. The muscles that move the pastern are on the fore and rear parts of the leg. The muscles on the rear part move the leg while it is on the ground; they are much stronger than the muscles on the forepart of the leg. The pastern joint should readily fold to allow the leg to lengthen or shorten as the dog moves. A short pastern functions at a better mechanical advantage and imparts better endurance.

Hackney Action

Hackney horses are often seen in parades and exhibitions, never where serious work is being done. The hackney gait is beautiful to watch; it has artistic appeal but energy efficiency is nil.

In the hackney gait, the forefoot is raised too high for work efficiency and the toe (hoof) is kept pointed down and inward, as shown in Figure 5-18. This is not to be confused with flapping (Figure 5-19), where the toe of a dog flaps up. Technically a dog can never exactly imitate the horse; the leg bones are not the same. In the dog's hackney gait, the paw is not bent under like the horse's hoof in Figure 5-18. The name is the same but the action is not identical. Dogs tend to hold their paw in a more horizontal position.

There is no reason why a dog should not have a hackney action *provided* (1) the purpose of the gait is for aesthetic effect and (2) the breed is not intended to perform work other than as a companion. The Pekingese has a perfectly delightful roll and an inefficient gait. No one claims that the Pekingese is efficient at digging, sprinting or

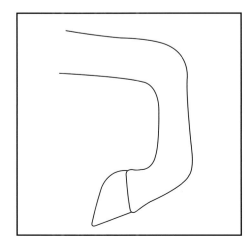

5-18. Position of the horse's leg in the hackney gait.

hunting, yet Pekingese are popular pets. Hackney-gaited dogs should serve a similar purpose. The Miniature Pinscher's (1990) *"hackney action is a high-stepping, reaching, free and easy gait in which the front leg moves straight forward and in front of the body and the foot bends at the wrist."* This hackney-like gait is a pleasure to watch.

Whenever legs are lifted too high, excess energy is used; efficiency is nil. A person jumping up and down tires quickly without much beneficial effect other than exercise.

> **BEDLINGTON TERRIER** (1967)—*Gait*— . . . *Springy in the slower paces, not stilted or hackneyed.*

> **STANDARD SCHNAUZER** (1991)—*Faults*— . . . *hackney gait, crossing over, or striking in front or rear.*

> **SHETLAND SHEEPDOG** (1990)—*Faults*— . . . *Lifting of front feet in hackney like action, resulting in loss of speed and energy.*

> **IRISH SETTER** (1990)—*Gait*— . . . *The forelegs reach well ahead as if to pull in the ground without giving the appearance of a hackney gait.*

In the showring, the higher the head is held, the higher the front paw will be lifted. A muscle extends from the upper arm along the neck to the head (brachicephalicus muscle). By holding the head high, the muscle is stretched. On the forward motion of the leg, the leg is lifted higher than normal. Show horses at a hackney gait always have a check rein designed to hold the head high. The dog show handler "strings a dog up" to attain a "high stepper," as is sometimes done in the Poodle ring.

Flapping

Figure 5-19 illustrates the fault of flapping. Some texts refer to this as padding, from the word "pad." The term "padding" as used by Dachshund breeders is spelled so similarly to "paddling" that the two are often confused. Herein flapping is equivalent to padding. If a Dachshund swings a front leg forward, and if the motion of the shoulder blade and upper arm stops, *and* if the lower arm continues moving so the foot flaps up, flapping occurs.

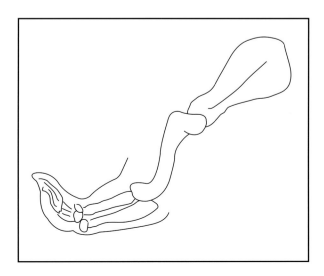

5-19. Dachshund front leg flapping—the foot flaps upward as shown.

Too steep a shoulder may cause this fault. As the dog moves, the forward swing of the shoulder blade and upper arm stops short of a full arc. The momentum built up in the lower arm and foot causes the lower arm to swing forward and the foot flaps up. In the hackney gait, the horse's tendons keep the hoof pointed downward. Hackney gait and flapping are entirely different motions.

No Standard approves flapping. Hackney action is artistically correct; flapping looks uncoordinated.

Paddling

Those who have paddled a canoe know that while the paddle swings backward in an arc, the blade must turn to prevent the canoe from going in a circle. Paddling in dogs is a circular motion of the front feet, best seen as the dog moves toward you. The two most common causes are: (1) muscles too loose, (2) shoulder blades too far forward on the chest.

No matter what causes paddling, it is a serious fault. Not even artists will claim this motion is appealing to the eye.

Paddling can occur at faster gaits and not at slower gaits or vice versa. Handlers usually know the best speed for their dogs. Handlers moving too slowly or too fast should be suspect. The judge should ask for a change of pace on a loose lead.

Padding

The term "padding" (not "paddling" and not "padding" as used by Dachshund breed-ers) is used to describe a dog whose pads hit the ground just prior to the completion of the forward leg swing. Theoretically a dog's front leg should swing forward and then backward before touching the ground. If the pad hits the ground prior to a full forward swing, the pad acts as a brake and slows the dog. "Pounding" and "padding" are similar terms. The dog *"pounds"* when the pad comes down with a "thud"; the dog is padding when the pad hits the ground before it should.

6-1. Three basic head types: (A) brachycephalic; (B) mesaticephalic; (C) dolichocephalic.

(A) Boston Terrier. Example of the brachycephalic head. *Photo by Rich Bergman.*

(B) Beagles. Examples of the mesaticephalic head. *Almstedt Photo.*

(C) Borzoi. Example of the dolichocephalic head. *Photo by Missy Yuhl.*

CHAPTER 6

The Head

Introduction

The head is the hallmark of every breed. Heads are divided into three types, as shown in Figure 6-1. The short-faced, wide-headed type, such as the Bulldog, Boston Terrier, Pekingese and Pug, is called *brachycephalic*. The long, narrow-headed type, such as the Collie, Afghan Hound, Borzoi and others, is called *dolichocephalic*. The intermediate type, such as the German Shepherd Dog, Beagle and all Setters, is called *mesaticephalic*. The short-jawed Bulldog type head probably started from a mutation; no comparable type is found in wild dogs. Each type of head will vary considerably between breeds.

The braincase remains approximately the same size in similar size dogs. This is true even though there is great size and shape variation of the head due to the three basic head types. The brain capacity of the three head types for similar size dogs is basically the same. Figure 6-2 illustrates how hair can create an illusion of an entirely different head shape than the dog possesses. The hair on the head of the Bichon Frise is trimmed to create an overall round impression.

The major causes of variations in the shape of the head are due to:

1. Occiput

2. Stop

3. Zygomatic arch

4. Sagittal crest

5. Muscles that activate the jaw

Refer to Figures 6-3, 6-4 and 6-5.

The occiput and the stop vary considerably depending upon the fancy. A deep stop allows good frontal vision. Lack of a stop restricts vision of each eye to the side. The depression of the skull between the eyes, or stop, is at the dividing point between the

6-2. Bichon Frise. Hair creates an illusion of entirely different head shape than the dog actually possesses. *Photo by Missy Yuhl.*

frontal bones of the braincase and the top plane of the muzzle. The stop is most developed in the short-faced breeds and is least developed in the long type of heads.

The zygomatic arch is well developed in the Bulldog and others with a *brachycephalic* head. The zygomatic arch (Figures 6-3 and 6-4) determines the width of the face. It is prominent on Bulldogs, Pugs and Pekingese; it is flat on Collies, Borzois, Greyhounds and Fox Terriers. Along with the well developed zygomatic arch there occur well developed cheek muscles that aid the dog in holding, as in the Bulldog, or in biting, as in the Staffordshire Terrier. Dogs that kill game by a quick snap (Terriers or Greyhounds) do not need well developed cheek muscles and usually have flat zygomatic arches and flat cheeks.

The sagittal crest is well developed in long-headed dogs (Borzoi) and almost absent in the Bulldog head (short-faced). Depending upon the development of the temporal muscles, the head can be narrow (Borzoi) or wide (Labrador Retriever).

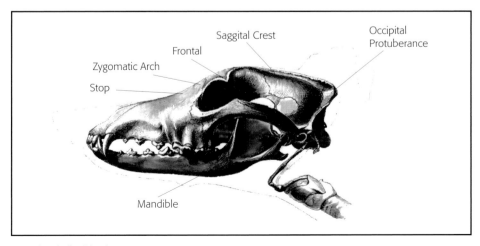

6-3. The skull—side view.

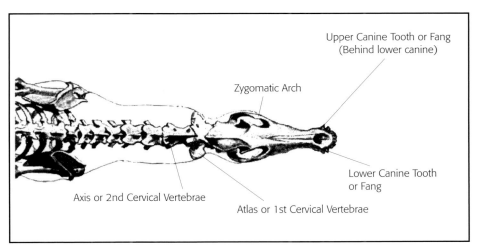

6-4. The skull—top view.

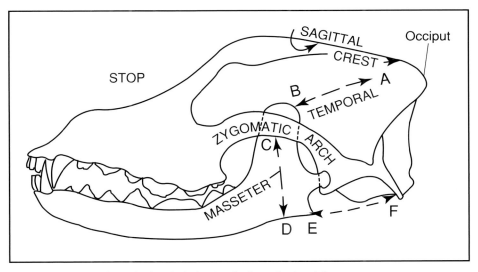

6-5. Bones and muscles of the head which primarily determine head shape.

Dogs that kill their prey by snapping (Terriers, Greyhounds, etc.) and dogs that retrieve game with a soft mouth (Brittanys, Cocker Spaniels, etc.) have poorly developed (not cheeky) masseter muscles (muscle C-D in Figure 6-5). The masseter is used to raise the mandible, closing the jaw. Staffordshire Terriers and others that hold on and bite prey have well developed (cheeky) masseter muscles. Refer to Figures 3-2 and 3-4 for the actual location of the masseter muscles.

The development of the temporal muscles, A-B in Figure 6-5 (used to close the jaw and located next to the sagittal crest), helps shape the head. The digastricus muscle, E-F in Figure 6-5, opens the mouth and is less developed than those closing the mouth. The location of the temporal muscle is shown in Figure 3-3, while the digastricus is shown in Figures 3-2 and 3-4.

6-6. Lhasa Apso. *Booth Photography.*

Nose

The nostrils of the scent breeds and some running dogs are large and open, as in the Bloodhound.

> **BLOODHOUND** (Undated)—*Nostrils—The nostrils are large and open.*

> **BASSET HOUND** (1964)—*The nose is darkly pigmented, preferably black, with large wide open nostrils.*

> **GERMAN SHORTHAIRED POINTER** (1992)—*The nose is brown, the larger the better, and with nostrils well opened and broad.*

> **BRITTANY** (1990)—*Nose—Nostrils well open to permit deep breathing of air and adequate scenting. Tight nostrils should be penalized.*

Most Standards are silent on the size of nostrils, but many specify skin color. The nose color, being quite obvious, does a great deal to set type. Of more importance, light colored noses easily sunburn. Dogs of northern regions, where sun rays are slanting, do not have sunburn problems. Nose pigment lightens during cold weather on some breeds.

> **GOLDEN RETRIEVER** (1990)—*Nose black or brownish black, though fading to a lighter shade in cold weather not serious. Pink nose or one seriously lacking in pigmentation to be faulted.*

Chocolate, liver or brown coated dogs usually have brown noses; the more dilute the brown coat, the lighter the brown is apt to be. Many dog Standards discriminate against light colored or parti-colored noses, such as the Lhasa Apso (Figure 6-6) Standard.

BRITTANY (1990)—*Color: fawn, tan, shades of brown or deep pink. A black nose is a disqualification. A two-tone or butterfly nose should be penalized.*

POINTER (1975)—*In the darker colors, the nose should be black or brown; in the lighter shades it may be lighter or flesh-colored.*

BORZOI (1972)—*Nose large and black.*

LHASA APSO (1978)—*Nose black . . .*

OLD ENGLISH SHEEPDOG (1990)—*Nose—Always black, large and capacious.*

ENGLISH SPRINGER SPANIEL (1994)—*The nostrils are well-opened and broad.*

AKITA (1972)—*Nose—Broad and black. Liver permitted on white Akitas, but black always preferred. Disqualification—Butterfly nose or total lack of pigmentation on nose.*

Eye Color

In theory a dark-colored iris protects the eye from the rays of bright sunlight. People native to the tropics have dark skin; those in the Arctic have light skin. Likewise, lighter eyes occur more commonly in the Arctic.

Eyes are black, brown, dilute brown, yellow, blue, ruby, albino, walleye, china (clear blue) and various intermixtures of pigments. By far the majority of Standards call for a dark eye.

FINNISH SPITZ (1987)—*Preferably dark in color with a keen and alert expression . . . light . . . eyes are to be penalized.*

BULL TERRIER (1974)—*Eyes . . . dark as possible . . . Blue eyes are a disqualification.*

AIREDALE TERRIER (1959)—*Eyes should be dark . . . Yellow eyes . . . are faults which should be severely penalized.*

SALUKI (1927)—*Eyes dark to hazel . . .*

SAMOYED (1993)—*Should be dark for preference . . .*

BRUSSELS GRIFFON (1990)—*black.*

CHIHUAHUA (1990)—*luminous dark or luminous ruby. (Light eyes in blond or white-colored dogs permissible.)*

POINTER (1975)—*The eye color should be dark in contrast with the color of the markings, the darker the better.*

BASSET HOUND (1964)—*colors are brown, dark brown preferred . . .*

BEAGLE (1957)—*brown or hazel color.*

COLLIE (1977)—*Except for blue merles, they are required to be matched in color . . . The color is dark . . . In blue merles, dark brown eyes are preferable, but either or both eyes may be merle or china in color without specific penalty.*

WEIMARANER (1971)—*In shades of light amber, gray or blue-gray* . . .

CHESAPEAKE BAY RETRIEVER (1993)—*Eyes* . . . *very clear, of yellowish or amber color* . . .

In theory, a blue-eyed or yellow-eyed dog in bright sunlight must squint more and is therefore at a disadvantage. The Chesapeake Bay Retriever was developed for retrieving in cold northern waters; yellow eyes are not a particular disadvantage.

Yellow or blue eyes are particularly noticeable because they stand out by contrast. As with a well-dressed person, brown eyes complement the coat; neither the eyes nor the coat are flashy or gaudy. Wolves and many cats have yellowish eyes. When they fix a gaze on a person, they look fierce and ready to attack. Is it this wild look of a yellow eye that causes dog people to be prejudiced? Possibly so. The fact that many wild animals do have yellowish eyes indicates that yellow is not as great a disadvantage as it seems.

Brown, the most common eye color, may be in shades from black-brown (many eyes that appear to be black are actually a very dark brown) to yellowish, dilute brown. Dilute brown (called hazel or amber), although yellowish in appearance, should *not* be confused with true yellow, which is a distinctly different pigment.

Ruby eyes give a ruby reflection of light as found in the raccoon. The color is not the color of the iris; it is the color of the *reflection*, as the reflection from a flashlight.

Ordinarily, eye color is not linked with coat color, i.e., a black dog can have light or dark brown eyes. But there are a few exceptions. The merle eye (also known as walleye, watch eye and pearly eye) or china eye (clear blue eye) occurs with the merle coat. One genetic liver coat (not all coats that are called liver are genetically the same) always is accompanied by yellow eyes. The liver and tan coat pattern is usually accompanied by yellow eyes. In the event of a merle spot around one eye and the remainder of the coat being a different pattern, the eye may be china or merle while the color is normal. Breed Standards that permit liver-colored coats usually permit yellow eyes. Disqualifying one eliminates the other.

COLLIE (1977)—*The four recognized colors are "Sable and White," "Tri-color," "Blue Merle" and "White."* . . . *Except for blue merles, they are required to be matched in color.* . . . *The color is dark* . . . *In blue merles, dark brown eyes are preferable, but either or both eyes may be merle or china in color without specific penalty.*

GREAT DANE (1990)—*Color—Brindle* . . . *Fawn* . . . *Blue* . . . *Black* . . . *Harlequin* . . . *Eyes* . . . *dark* . . . *In harlequins, the eyes should be dark; light colored eyes, eyes of different colors and walleyes are permitted but not desirable.*

SHETLAND SHEEPDOG (1990)—*Color—Black, blue merle, and sable (ranging from golden through mahogany); marked with varying amounts of white and/or tan. Eyes* . . . *Color must be dark, with blue or merle eyes permissible in blue merles only.*

CARDIGAN WELSH CORGI (1991)—*Color—All shades of red, sable and brindle. Black with or without tan or brindle points. Blue merle (black and gray, marbled) with or without tan or brindle points* . . . *Eyes* . . . *Clear and dark in harmony with coat color. Blue eyes (including partially blue eyes), or one dark and one blue eye permissible in blue merles, and in any other coat color than blue merle are a disqualification.*

LABRADOR RETRIEVER (1994)—*Eye color should be brown in black and yellow Labradors, and brown and hazel in chocolates. Black or yellow eyes give a harsh expression and are undesirable. (Author's note: Due to non-conformity of coat color names, chocolate is often called liver. When changing from one breed to another, color naming may vary.)*

In early times it was believed that light-eyed dogs could see better at night and dark-eyed dogs could see better at day. For this reason, it is claimed that shepherds preferred dogs with one light-colored eye to see at night and one dark colored eye to see better in daylight. While this may explain the frequency in occurrence of mismatched eyes in Collies and Shelties, it is difficult to assign the same reason to Siberian Huskies, which commonly have one brown eye and one blue eye. Northeastern Siberia is a long way from Europe.

Some drugs dilate eyes. Dilated eyes appear darker. If a dog's pupils look as though they are excessively dilated, a shadow should be cast over the dog's eyes. If the pupils fail to change in diameter, the dog is suspect. If the dog is in the show ring and the pupils will not dilate, the owner may be charged with faking. Clever handlers with light-eyed dogs in bright outdoor rings will keep their shadow over the dog's eyes, thus allowing as much natural dilation as possible. Such procedure is not faking; use of drugs is.

Eye Rim Color

The eye rim color and the nose color are usually the same. Since dark rims absorb sunlight and do not reflect rays into the eyes, dark colors are preferred for most breeds. Eyes with flesh-colored rims tend to water more. A similar effect can be found in Fox Terriers with a black spot around one eye and a white spot around the other eye; a noticeable increase in wetness occurs on the white spot.

Eye Placement and Size

Eyes do not increase or decrease in size in proportion to body size. Eyes on big dogs are relatively small compared to the size of the dog. An elephant's eyes are microscopically small for the size of the animal. Eyes on little dogs do not get proportionately smaller with diminishing size. In proportion to size, Toys and small dogs tend to have large eyes. Although most Toy Standards fault pop eyes, some do call for large and prominent eyes.

BRITTANY (1990)—*Eyes—Well set in head. Well protected from briars by a heavy expressive eyebrow. A prominent, full or popeye should be heavily penalized. It is a serious fault in a dog that must face briars. Skull well chiseled under the eyes, so that the lower lid is not pulled back to form a pocket or haw that would catch seeds, dirt and weed dust. Preference should be for the darker colored eyes . . .*

BEDLINGTON TERRIER (1967)—*Eyes—Almond shaped, small, bright and well sunk with no tendency to tear or water. Set is oblique and fairly high on the head . . .*

SMOOTH FOX TERRIER (1991)—*Eyes and rims should be dark in color, moderately small and rather deep set, full of fire, life and intelligence and as nearly possible circular in shape.*

BEAGLE (1957)—*Eyes large, set well apart—soft and houndlike—expression gentle and pleading . . .*

COCKER SPANIEL (1992)—*Eyeballs are round and full and look directly forward. The shape of the eye rims gives a slightly almond shaped appearance; the eye is not weak or goggled . . .*

BRUSSELS GRIFFON (1990)—*Eyes set well apart, very large, black, prominent and well open . . .*

CHIHUAHUA (1990)—*Eyes—Full, but not protruding, balanced, set well apart . . .*

ITALIAN GREYHOUND (1976)—*Eyes . . . medium in size.*

PEKINGESE (1995)—*Eyes—They are large, very dark, round, lustrous and set wide apart.*

Figure 6-7 illustrates variations in eye shape and placement. The Chow Chow (Figure 6-7 A) shows the Standard (1990) requirement for eyes that are "*deep set and placed wide apart and obliquely, of moderate size, almond in shape. The correct placement and shape should create an Oriental appearance.*" The Cairn Terrier (Figure 6-7 B) shows the Standard (1938) requirement for eyes that are "*set wide apart, rather sunken, with shaggy eyebrows, medium in size . . . with a keen terrier expression,*" while the Pug (Figure 6-7 C) shows the Standard (1991) requirement for eyes that are "*very large, bold and prominent, globular in shape . . . .*"

Eyes and Their Purpose

The Bulldog head is wider, and the eyes normally are set forward on the frontal plane of the face. The narrow head, such as found on the Borzoi and Collie, is more apt to have side placement of the eyes. For fighting dogs and those going after game, especially in burrows, the Standard often calls for deep set eyes as a protection from claws or dirt.

Behind the eyeballs are pads of fat. As in humans, if the body is sickly, the pad decreases in size and the eyes become sunken.

Many of the hooved animals that depend upon speed for escape have their eyes set nearly on the sides of their heads. Since one eye can see about 180 degrees, side placement enables these animals to see nearly 360 degrees. Horses have a long face with eyes high up on the side of the forehead to enable them to see 360 degrees and graze simultaneously. Because horses can see ahead as well as behind, lions have difficulty in making a surprise attack; wide angle vision is a defense mechanism.

When human eyes focus on a doorknob, each eye sees the knob from a different angle. The difference in angle is a rough measure of the distance to the doorknob. The closer the doorknob is to the eye, the more accurate the measure of distance (called stereoscopic vision). Dogs can't talk, so it is difficult to test them for stereoscopic vision. In 1956, Smythe reported that Pekingese and some of the Toy Spaniels with frontally placed eyes might have such vision.

For the purpose of deciding what type of eyes are needed for a given dog breed, the following scientific principles can be stated:

1. Wide-angle vision is attained by eyes placed on the sides of the face.

2. Deep-set eyes and eyes close together decrease the field of vision.

6-7. Variations in eye shape and placement.

(A) The deepset, widely placed eyes of the Chow Chow.

(B) A Cairn Terrier with eyes set wide apart, rather sunken, medium in size, with a keen terrier expression.

(C) The very large, bold and prominent, globular shaped eye of the Pug. *Photographer Joan Ludwig.*

3. Deep-set eyes are protected from dirt, briars and claws.

4. Frontally placed eyes can have stereoscopic vision.

Bird dogs and other hunting dogs that are looking for game need a large field of vision, and their eyes tend to be flush with the plane of the face and set towards the sides. Fighting dogs need protection more than wide-angle vision. Most Terriers have small, deep-set eyes. Attacking animals (eagles and cats) seem to have eyes closer together than do animals depending upon speed for escape. Sled dogs have problems with the sun's reflection off snow. To avoid snow blindness dogs "squint down," that is, they look through the narrowest eye slit formed by almost shut lids.

Tendency towards cataracts occurs more frequently in a few breeds. Cataracts are not mentioned as a fault in any Standard, but they do contribute to blindness. Blind dogs must be disqualified at a show and obviously should be eliminated from any breeding program.

A dog with wetness around the eye usually has a defect. The lower eyelid may be inverted (turned in) so the hairs scratch the eyeball. In dogs with prominent eyes the tear duct may close the passage to the nose.

Lower Eyelid and Haws

The lower eyelid protects the eye from dirt, seeds and foreign objects. A loose lower lid allows the accumulation of dirt and objects in direct contact with the eyeball. Furthermore, red blood vessels on the lower lid's inner surface are not pretty to look at. Most Standards prohibit loose lids; exceptions are found in the Standards of extremely loose-skinned dogs such as the Bloodhound. Prohibiting the loose lid and exposure of the haw would eliminate the loose skin; genetically they go together.

> **BLOODHOUND** (Not dated)—*Eyes—The eyes are deeply sunk in the orbits, the lids assuming a lozenge or diamond shape, in consequence of the lower lids being dragged down and everted by the heavy flews.*

> **BASSET HOUND** (1964)—*The eyes are soft, sad, and slightly sunken, showing a prominent haw . . .*

> **BULLDOG** (1990)—*Eyes and eyelids— . . . The lids should cover the white of the eyeball, when the dog is looking directly forward, and the lid should show no "haw."*

Skull or Braincase

Technically the skull consists of the bony components of the head and is divided into two sections, the braincase and the foreface. Standards have misused the term "skull" to mean "braincase"; some Standards use the term "skull" and "head" interchangeably. Other terms used for "braincase" are "topskull" and "backskull." The braincase section of the skull houses the brain and inner ear, and partially encloses and protects the eye. The three major bones of the braincase, starting from the back of the head, are the occipital, parietal and frontal. The ossification (hardening) of the parietal and frontal bones may not be complete in a young puppy, thus this area (top of the braincase) may be soft. Many adult Chihuahuas have incomplete hardening in this area. The Standard refers to this as a molera.

CHIHUAHUA (1990)—*Head*—*A well rounded "apple dome" skull, with or without molera.*

Jaw and Muzzle

Those breeds that need strong and powerful jaws need strong muscles to activate the jaw. The muscles that close the jaw (temporal muscles) are located in the rear of the mouth. The muscles that allow side-to-side movement (masseter) are located in the cheeks. Dogs that chew and hold their prey require strong cheek muscles, as in the Staffordshire Terrier. Most Sporting dogs must be soft-mouthed (that is, they are supposed to retrieve without marring the object retrieved); strong jaw muscles are undesirable. For this reason Sporting breed Standards often call for "no cheekiness." If puppies and dogs are often given bones to chew on, they develop the cheek muscles. Chew objects are withheld from Sporting dogs, but supplied for "cheeky" dogs.

A long muzzle on a digging dog projects teeth out far enough to protect the front feet from rodent bites. Many Fox Terrier breeders look upon long slim heads with considerable favor.

The fill under the eyes and square muzzle indicate good bone to back up the molars. Snipy muzzles have poor support for teeth.

COCKER SPANIEL (1992)—*The bony structure beneath the eyes is well chiseled with no prominence in the cheeks.*

CHOW CHOW (1990)—*The muzzle is broad and well filled out under the eyes . . .*

LAKELAND TERRIER (1991)—*The muzzle is strong with straight nose bridge and good fill-in beneath the eyes.*

STAFFORDSHIRE BULL TERRIER (1989)—*very pronounced cheek muscles . . .*

Bite

Types of bites found in breed Standards are overshot, undershot, level and scissors. In defining overshot and undershot the *lower* jaw is considered as fixed. A dog is overshot if the upper jaw extends beyond the lower. A dog is undershot (Bulldog) if the upper jaw does not reach as far forward as the underjaw. A bite is level if the incisors meet tip to tip (upper and lower). A bite is scissors if the inside edge of the upper incisors just meets the outside edge of the lower incisors.

Fixed Bite

A normal level bite is shown in Figure 6-8. If a dog is overshot or undershot, the teeth can be fixed. Any time teeth slant in the wrong direction it is possible that the position of the teeth may have been altered by the use of a brace. Even though the judge may be unable to prove that the teeth have been fixed, the dog can be penalized for having abnormal position of teeth.

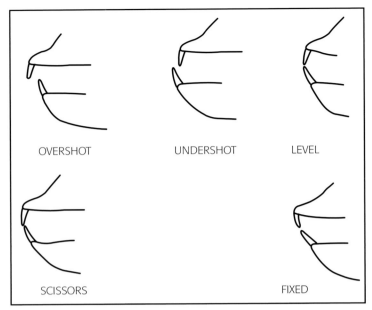

OVERSHOT   UNDERSHOT   LEVEL

SCISSORS   FIXED

6-8. Types of bites.

Some dogs have a temporary brace placed on their teeth to bind the teeth together. This is done to prevent the natural development of the bite. If this is done, the dog is ineligible to compete under the provisions of Chapter 14, Section 8, of the *Rules Applying to Registration and Dog Shows*. When a judge detects any type of brace, band, string, etc., used to restrain the teeth in any fashion, the dog must be disqualified, and a note placed in the judge's book explaining what was found. Not only is the show eligibility of the dog affected by this disqualification, but the owner and/or handler will be subject to further disciplinary action.

Teeth

Some exhibitors and breeders may concentrate on external characteristics rather than internal. Some breeds have serious teeth problems. A normal mouth has forty-two properly placed teeth, twenty in the upper jaw and twenty-two in the lower jaw.

Refer to Figure 6-9. In counting teeth it is much easier to remember the number of teeth in the upper half of the jaw: *three* incisors, *one* canine, *four* premolars and *two* molars. The lower jaw has an additional molar (three instead of two). With practice, it should not be necessary to count teeth; the eye should instantly recognize the pattern of correctly placed teeth. In most large dog breeds there is spacing between the teeth; do not confuse the spacing with missing teeth. *Teeth* must be counted, not gaps.

Narrow-headed breeds (Poodles, Borzois, etc.) have problems with missing incisors and/or premolars, whereas Bulldogs and other breeds with similar heads sometimes have extra teeth (a fault). Many times missing incisors leave no discernible gaps. A dog may have extra teeth and may have forty-two teeth yet still have a tooth missing. Remember, an extra tooth does not make up for a missing tooth—in this case the dog has *two* bite faults.

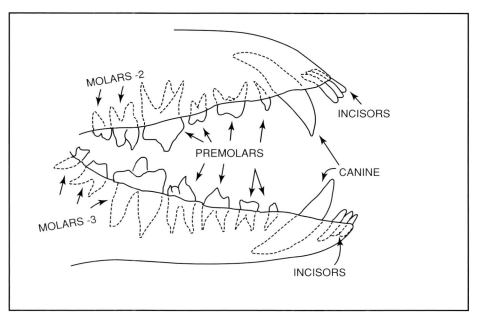

6-9. Half set of teeth.

Ears

Ears are quite variable. For dogs going after game, the ear set and size are designed to be out of reach of the prey. Some breeds have an ear style calculated to set type. Large prick ears, in the evolutionary process, evolved for hearing sounds. The ability to turn ears and focus on noises is of special benefit to animals hunting in dense cover or hunting at night. (Refer to Figure 6-10.)

> **BASENJI** (1990)—*Ears—Small, erect and slightly hooded, of fine texture and set well forward on top of head.*

If an animal relies upon odor to detect game or enemies, the need for acute hearing is not as important. Most of the tracking dogs, such as Bloodhounds, Beagles and Fox-hounds, have soft, drooping ears that interfere with good hearing, but do help to gather scent.

Scott and Fuller, in their experiments at Bar Harbor, Maine, reported in *Genetics and Social Behavior of Dogs/Dog Behavior, The Genetic Basis* that deaf dogs were usually superior in other traits. In tracking, they were not distracted by noises and performed above average. It is possible that in the selection of superior tracking dogs, those with long, pendulous ears had poorer hearing and better trailing efficiency.

The rough-coated Otterhound was one of the primary early crosses used to pro-duce the Airedale Terrier. The Otterhound had a rough wire coat, long ears and loose skin. The tendency for hound ears on the Airedale has not been entirely eliminated to this day.

Swimming dogs may have special designs to keep water out of the inner ear. The Newfoundland has ear flaps designed to fit over the ear canal in such a way that water does not readily enter the canal. The Poodle has an overabundance of hair at the ear

6-10. Basenji ears are of benefit for hunting. *Photo by Missy Yuhl.*

canal opening on the theory that the hair will keep out the water. Excess hair seems to be more trouble than it is worth; dead hair gets into the ear and causes infections.

The projecting parts of dogs, such as ears, tend to be smaller in cold countries and bigger in the desert. Small ears with a small area prevent excessive heat loss. An accumulation of snow on the top of large ears causes the ear to fall over from weight. Soon they freeze, and when thawed out, bloodblisters form. Short ears are desirable in cold countries.

In theory people reduced the size of some dogs without reducing the skin. With surplus skin the ears drooped, as in hounds. Dogs with large pendulous ears have very loose skin (Bloodhounds, Coonhounds, etc.). Rose ears (Greyhounds) are formed by the cartilage in tight-skinned dogs. Bulldogs (with loose skin) are supposed to have rose ears, but breeders find them difficult to keep.

The ear is held erect by muscles and the skin on the neck. Loose skin causes droopy ears. An overly fat dog, upon reducing, may even change from a prick ear to a drop ear because the skin becomes loose upon losing fat. A dog with one drop ear and one erect ear has a fault; both sides are not balanced. A puppy with one drop ear and one erect ear usually has ear defects as an adult.

CHAPTER 7

Posed Examination

Why a Posed Examination

Dogs in motion cannot be observed in detail. The shape of the eyes, the number of teeth, dewclaws, texture of the coat, height of the dog and many other points are best observed as the dog is posed. Some qualities, such as firmness of muscles, slope of the shoulder, monorchidism, crytorchidism, hair type and rib spring are judged by feel. All good judges see with their hands as well as with eyes.

Posed Examination

An individual examination of each dog, both visually and manually, is performed while the dog is posed (stacked). Breed custom indicates how this is done. For breeds not examined on a table, it is often customary to examine and move each contestant individually. This relates structure with movement; that is, if a shoulder feels too steep when the dog is posed, an immediate check on reach is made.

Table Examination

Toy breeds, also Beagles, Dachshunds, Cockers, most Terriers and some of the other small breeds are examined on a table. Tabling calls for a slightly different procedure since one extra step is added. To save time as well as correlate movement with observed structural traits, it is expedient to move each dog immediately after the table examination.

If you are judging in the show ring, establish a convenient location for the table where you can get a good front, side and rear view of the dog. This location should be chosen to provide efficiency of judging and require a minimum of motion on the judge's part. Check that the table is solid and relatively level. Make sure that the table surface does not get too hot for the dog's comfort. Ideally on a hot day the table should be set in the shade.

Wait for the handler to set the dog up before examining the exhibit. Each exhibit is gently examined on the table and then individually gaited. This individual examination on the table needs to be followed up with an evaluation of the dog standing on the ground. Some exhibits will tense up when on the table and generally distort their overall outline. This is evidenced by one or more of the following: going up on the toes, bracing, roaching the topline and trembling. When the exhibit is on the ground it will be relaxed and will then present its true outline. If outdoors, hopefully the grass has been properly mowed so that the outline can truly be evaluated.

Type

Type is the characteristic qualities that distinguish a breed, i.e., the embodiment of a Standard's essentials (*The Complete Dog Book*).

Breed type as based upon physical characteristics is best studied by looking at superior dogs of a given breed. Regardless of how perfectly an author describes a breed, it is almost impossible for the reader to form a picture of what is being described. Photographs help. Observing good specimens along with a commentary from an expert telling what is being seen is ideal. No attempt will be made here to describe the type of all breeds.

Type in a dog can be classified as naturally occurring or artificially produced. Smooth-coated dogs, being exhibited naturally, have a type that is not altered by trimming. Some breeds, Terriers in particular, depend on trim plus naturally occurring features to show type. An untrimmed Kerry Blue Terrier may look like a mutt. Indeed, the skill and imagination of the dog's groomer profoundly influence how a dog looks.

Disqualifications in a breed Standard tell what a breed is *not*. The Miniature Schnauzer Standard (1991) states: *Disqualifications—Dogs or bitches under 12 inches or over 16 inches. Color solid white or white striping, patching, or spotting on the colored areas of the dog, except for the small white spot permitted on the chest of the black.*

The height limitation is a definite measurable quantity and the white color is observable. But if a superbly moving Schnauzer of the correct height and color, but not quite looking like a good Schnauzer, is shown against a poorly moving dog that looks like a typical Schnauzer should look, who would win? *How important is type as compared to soundness?* Judging type, after a dog meets the minimum requirements for the breed, is more of an art than a science. The set of the eyes, head expression, silhouette, shape of body and many features difficult to describe are compared and judged.

The type of Cocker Spaniel now exhibited is quite different from what was formerly considered correct. Type is the current opinion of experts; it changes with time. As proof of this, look up the early champions of almost any breed. Refer to Figure 1-6 for the change in the Wire Fox Terrier type. Early head studies of Collies are vastly different from those today.

Standards are changed. The Basset Hound Standard *prior* to January 14, 1964, read:

> *Forelegs—The forelegs should be short, very powerful, very heavy in bone, close fitting to the chest with a crook'd knee and wrinkled ankle ending in a massive paw.*

> *Feet—He must stand perfectly sound and true on his feet, which should be thick and massive, and the weight of the forepart of the body should be borne equally by each toe of the forefeet so far as is compatible with the crook of the legs.*

The Basset Hound is a very massive, short-legged hound. The crook placed the paws well under the dog and decreased lateral stability. After January 14, 1964, the Standard became:

> *The forelegs are short, powerful, heavy in bone, with wrinkled skin . . . The paw is massive, very heavy with tough heavy pads, well rounded with both feet inclined equally a trifle outward, balancing the width of the shoulders . . . The toes are neither pinched together nor splayed, with the weight of the forepart of the body borne evenly on each.*

The words "crook'd knee" and "crook of the legs" were omitted. In fact, the new Standard very carefully avoids mention of the knee's shape.

Type can change without a change in the written Standard for the following reasons: (1) Many English words are variable in meaning and interpretation, especially over time. (2) Type is judged by people. (3) Selection toward a goal can change the composition of a breed to accent that goal.

Dogs in Breed "A" have a medium-length coat and the Standard is not specific on coat length. A new, consistently winning dog of Breed "A" arrives with a longer coat. Now everyone breeds for a longer coat and the longer coat becomes a fixed part of the breed. Later a better angulated dog with a longer coat is exhibited and he consistently wins. Now the accent is on breeding for better angulation. Finally, after several such changes, type is drastically different. This is the rule of graduality: Many small changes gradually make a larger change. It takes more than a few years to realize what has taken place.

In most breeds the tendency is toward larger dogs (Toys excepted). In Beagles those at the upper limits of height tend to have an advantage over those at the lower limits; they usually have better developed bone and appear more mature. A good big dog in some breeds often wins over a good little dog.

The Cocker Spaniel Standard did not mention height prior to October 12, 1943, but stated weight as follows: *Not under 18 nor exceeding 24 pounds.* No one enforced the weight limitation. Soon the Standard was changed to conform to the larger dogs. In 1943 this was changed to: *Not under 22, nor over 28 pounds . . . severely penalize . . . Puppies exempt from minimum.* Then the December 10, 1957, change eliminated any reference to weight and put in the present height and added the height disqualification: *Males over 15 1/2 inches; females over 14 1/2 inches.* The type of Cocker Spaniel now being shown is bigger than it used to be.

Frequently, an argument arises over what is proper type for a given breed. The reason for argument is a failure to define terms. When we speak of type, do we mean (1) the average type as determined by what is being shown, (2) the type that someone believes most nearly conforms to the written Standard, or (3) the type that is winning? The type that is winning reflects the type that a breed is headed *toward*; the average type being shown is what the breed *is*; the type an individual believes to be correct is a *personal opinion*.

Type cannot be measured in the same sense as structure. Type is the opinion of the observer. The average judge's opinion on type is certainly better than that expressed by the average exhibitor. The judges, by their composite decisions, determine what type is.

Symmetry or Balance

Symmetry has several meanings. *Webster's New World Dictionary (Third College Edition)* includes the following among its definitions: *"balance or beauty of form or proportion resulting from such correspondence."* In the dog game, symmetry is a word commonly used to mean beauty of form, as well as proportion of parts. In judging symmetry, first impressions are often best. Are the legs, body and head matched proportionately? Is there beauty of form?

Symmetry is judged when the dog is in motion and when posed. A dog that is eye-catching at first glance, moves gracefully, has parts that appear to fit one another, and is artistically correct, has symmetry. Symmetry of the dog is not a measurable quality; it is what *appears* right to the observer. Correct symmetry is what knowledgeable judges (more than one) declare to be right.

A dog can have good symmetry when posed and not when moving or vice versa. A dog with poor layback of shoulder may pose with a beautifully sloping backline, yet move with short, choppy strides and rough gait. Judging symmetry is an acquired knowledge derived from constant observation. Some people are experts at knowing correct symmetry; others always seem to be wrong. Perhaps this is one reason why some judges are superior.

Attitude–Facing Off or Sparring

Terrier judges generally have two dogs spar, or face off, to show their attitude. Sparring is *not fighting*; it is checking the dog for alertness, self-control and sensible courage. Good Terriers do not start a fight; they only finish the fight someone else starts.

The judge indicates which dogs are to face off. The handlers then bring the dogs out of the line to stand facing each other naturally. They should not enter each others' "safety zone" when they face off. Baiting at this time would only ruin the natural arch of the neck. The dogs should be up on their toes, alert, and looking at each other. The dogs should hold their own and exude the attitude of a winner without having fought. Sparring is used to see the dog *naturally*. It should only be done two dogs at a time. The judge is checking to find dogs that pull themselves together, holding head and tail high and showing like winners. This is spelled out in some of the Standards.

> **WIRE FOX TERRIER** (1991)—*The Terrier should be alert, quick of movement, keen of expression, on the tip-toe of expectation at the slightest provocation. Character is imparted by the expression of the eyes and by carriage of ears and tail.*

> **IRISH TERRIER** (1968)—*The temperament of the Irish Terrier reflects his early background: he is family pet, guard dog, and hunter. He is good tempered, spirited and game. It is of utmost importance that the Irish Terrier show fire and animation. There is a heedless, reckless pluck about the Irish Terrier which is characteristic, and which, coupled with the headlong dash, blind to all consequences, with which he rushes at his adversary, has earned the breed the proud epithet of "Daredevil."*

Sparring is done with most Terrier breeds. Terrier breeds *not* sparred are the Border, the Bull breeds, Dandie Dinmont, Bedlingtons, and the Skye Terriers. Rarely, some judges will have Chihuahuas face off. The rest of the Toys and all of the Sporting, Hound, Working, Non-Sporting and Herding breeds are never sparred.

Head

The head is the most obvious part of a dog, usually the most important part as it establishes type. The shape of the eyes, ears and muzzle; the color of the eyes; wrinkles and many other details produce the picture of the dog. A Bloodhound with prick ears is no Bloodhound at all. Regardless of the perfection of the body or legs, a Corgi with hanging ears is not a Corgi. Without question, a dog that fails to look like its breed, regardless of structural perfection, should not win.

Breeder judges (those judges who have specialized in one breed) that have not spread their knowledge beyond their immediate sphere of interest are apt to be very critical of minute type characteristics and pass over important structural features. The multi-breed judge is more apt to be critical of structural defects and overlook minor type defects. Having both kinds of judges probably improves the breed. One feature is less apt to be exaggerated at the expense of another.

Body Structure

The vertebral or spinal column and ribs, from the neck through the tail, are shown in Figures 7-1 and 7-2. From the nose to the end of the tail, including the ribs, is what is referred to as the axial skeleton. The fore and hind limbs comprise the appendicular skeleton. The spinal column is composed of the seven **cervical** or neck vertebrae; thirteen **thoracic** vertebrae; seven **lumbar** vertebrae; three fused **sacral** vertebrae; and twenty **caudal** (coccygeal or tail) vertebrae. The tail vertebrae number varies by breed, but is generally twenty.

The thirteen thoracic vertebrae are divided into the nine withers and four (mid or true) back vertebrae. The thirteen ribs articulate with the thoracic vertebrae. The first nine ribs are called **true ribs** and the next three are called **false ribs**, while the last rib is referred to as the **floating rib**. The bottom of the rib cage has eight bones, or sternebrae, which are joined together by cartilage. (Refer to Figure 7-3.) This is called the "breastbone," "sternum" or "brisket."

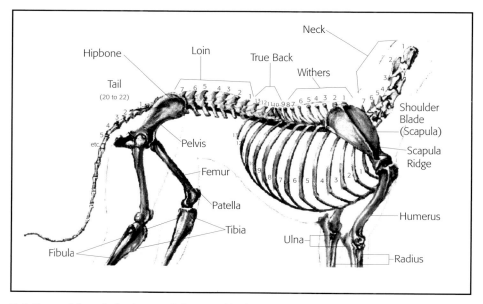

7-1. Bones of the spinal column and rib cage—side view.

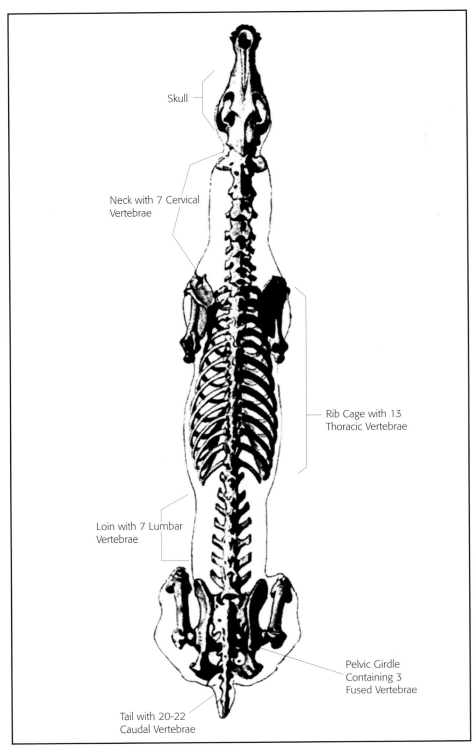

Skull

Neck with 7 Cervical
Vertebrae

Rib Cage with 13
Thoracic Vertebrae

Loin with 7 Lumbar
Vertebrae

Pelvic Girdle
Containing 3
Fused Vertebrae

Tail with 20-22
Caudal Vertebrae

7-2. Bones of the spinal column and rib cage—top view.

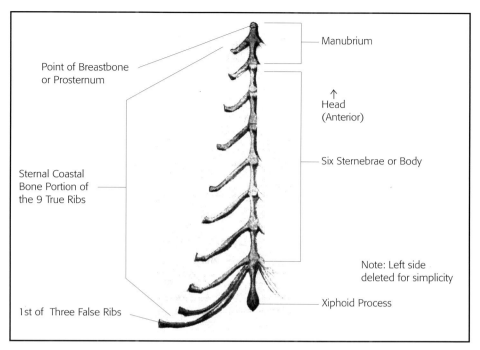

7-3. Breastbone or sternum as seen from below.

Neck

The neck provides both support and movement to the head. Figure 7-4 shows the seven cervical vertebrae. The first vertebra is known as the "atlas" and provides up-and-down motion to the head. The joint between the atlas vertebra and the skull is known as the "yes joint" due to this up-and-down motion. The axis or second vertebra provides rotary movement to the head, and the joint between the atlas and the axis vertebrae is known as the "no joint."

The neck and head are held up by a cervical (nuchal) ligament extending from the withers to the axis vertebra of the neck. The cervical ligament is one of the few body ligaments that is capable of contracting or expanding. By contraction it can pull the neck up, or by relaxing, the head can be lowered.

The most powerful muscles of the neck activate the shoulder blades. One of these muscles, the brachicephalicus (Figure 3-4), extends from an attachment on the head to an attachment on the shoulder blade. Others extend from the shoulder blades to the neck's vertebrae. (Refer to Figure 7-5.) An arch (as in an arched doorway) is structurally stronger than other forms. Since the shoulder blade muscles are attached to the neck, an arched neck is structurally superior at withstanding the "pull" from the shoulder blade muscles. Therefore an arched neck is superior to a ewe neck (named after sheep necks).

There is a correlation between the length of the neck and the steepness of the shoulder. Dogs with long necks usually have well laid-back shoulder blades; dogs with short necks usually have steep shoulders. Steep-shouldered dogs appear to have short necks because the distance between the head and shoulders appears shorter than normal.

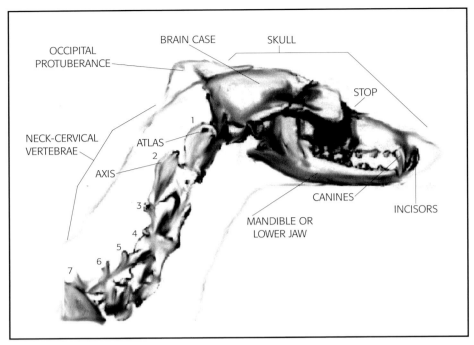

7-4. Neck or cervical vertebrae.

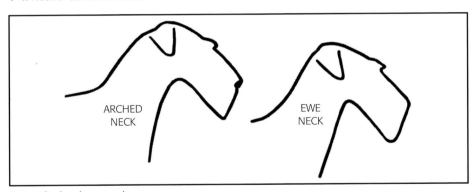

7-5. Arched and ewe neck.

The length of the neck does not correlate with speed; the world's fastest animal has a very short neck. Those animals that use the double suspension gallop (cheetah, many cats, Sighthounds, etc.) have either a small head or a short neck or both. The Greyhound has a thin neck, long enough to reach down to catch a rabbit, and a small head. It is frequently stated that a long neck has long muscles that aid speed (especially in shoulder rotation). This is simply not true. A long neck helps a grazing animal's mouth reach the ground, but has little correlation with speed.

POINTER (1975)—*Neck—Long, dry, muscular and slightly arched, springing cleanly from the shoulder.*

AFGHAN HOUND (1948)—*The neck is of good length, strong and arched, running in a curve to the shoulders . . .*

DACHSHUND (1992)—*Neck—Long, muscular, clean-cut, without dewlap, slightly arched in the nape, flowing gracefully into the shoulders.*

ALASKAN MALAMUTE (1994)—*Neck—The neck is strong and moderately arched.*

DANDIE DINMONT TERRIER (1991)—*The neck is very muscular, well developed and strong, showing great power of resistance. It is well set into the shoulders and moderate in length.*

ITALIAN GREYHOUND (1976)—*Neck—Long, slender and gracefully arched.*

BULLDOG (1990)—*Neck—The neck should be short, very thick, deep and strong and well arched at the back.*

COLLIE (1977)—*Neck—The neck is firm, clean, muscular, sinewy and heavily frilled. It is fairly long, carried upright with a slight arch at the nape and imparts a proud, upstanding appearance showing off the frill.*

Shoulder (Blade) Angle

The approximate angle of the shoulder blade can be determined with the hand. But the accuracy of the observation depends upon the position of the neck, the front pads and the rear. If the pads are well forward, extra stress is placed upon the front of the shoulder and causes the blade to rock back at the withers. Pulling the rear feet way back straightens out the shoulder blade. To judge the angle of the blade properly, all feet must be in a normal position.

If a dog is well muscled or overweight, the shoulder is difficult to feel. The action of the front legs at a trot is then the best indicator. A good reach without bounce at the withers indicates a well laid-back shoulder blade. Some Standards refer to the tops of shoulder blades as the points.

Loaded Shoulders

Muscles that rotate the shoulder blade are located above and below the blade. If the muscle under the blade becomes too well developed (loaded shoulders), the enlarged muscle pushes the shoulder blade out from the body, especially at the blade's top (withers area). This pulls in the shoulder blade and pushes the elbow out. "Out at the elbows" may be caused by what is described by the term "loaded in the shoulders."

The amount of separation of the shoulder blades at the withers is an indicator of being "loaded in the shoulders." The separation varies from the width of one finger to more than the width of four fingers, depending upon the dog's size and breed. If the tops are separated by more than the *usual* amount *for the breed*, the dog's elbows should be checked to see if they are out when posed or moving.

BELGIAN TERVUREN (1990)—*Top of the shoulder blades roughly two thumbs width apart.*

KERRY BLUE TERRIER (1992)—*Shoulders fine, long and sloping, well laid back and well knit.*

GORDON SETTER (1990)—*Shoulders fine at the points, and laying well back. The tops of the shoulder blades are close together.*

SCOTTISH DEERHOUND (1935)—*Shoulders should be well sloped; blades well back and not too much width between them. Loaded and straight shoulders are very bad faults.*

A dog with good muscles under the blade should not be penalized because it has exercised more than another exhibit. A wide separation at the shoulder blade tops is an indicator of a possible defect; out at the elbows is proof of a defect. A dog may have a wide separation and *not* be out at the elbows.

As a dog's head lowers, muscles of the neck pull the shoulder blade points forward and together. If the blade tops touch one another before the dog's head reaches the ground, the dog will be unable to lower its head to the ground without bending the front legs or spreading the front legs. A tracking dog trailing with nose close to the ground must always have sufficient separation at the withers to allow lowering of the head to the ground. Stated conversely, the rule is:

Dogs with shoulder blade tops (points) touching have a serious fault. Surprisingly few Standards say so.

Withers

Muscles work in pairs. Shoulder blade muscles are attached to the neck. Another set of muscles and tendons must keep the neck from being pulled down when the blade is activated. The cervical ligament attached from the withers to the neck is the main stabilizer. To form a good base of attachment for the cervical ligament, the withers must be well developed; that is, the bones that cause the withers to rise should be noticeable by feel. The *heavier the head* of the dog, the *higher the withers* should be. A bison has high withers and a very large head.

Elbows

In dogs designed for speed or trotting, out at the elbows is a serious fault. Clever handlers hide this fault in smaller dogs. When dogs are posed, they can place a hand under the chest of the dog, and with the thumb and little finger manipulate the upper arm to place the elbows in line. Handlers cannot hide this fault as successfully when dogs are moving. Common causes of out at the elbows are: (1) loaded shoulders (muscles under the shoulder blade too heavy); (2) shoulder blade too far forward on the chest. Item (2) more commonly occurs in the reduced leg bone length breeds such as Scotties, Corgis, Sealyhams, Dachshunds, etc., but can also occur in larger breeds.

Pasterns

Pasterns can be straight, knuckled over or bent. (Refer to Figure 7-6.) When dogs are standing still, the most comfortable (and also statically correct) position is to have the paws directly under the center of the shoulder blades. In some average build dogs, correct pasterns are vertical since this puts the pads directly under the center of the shoulder blade. Dogs with long upper arms have their forearms (radius and ulna) extending behind the center of their shoulder blades. Their *pasterns* in a posed position are *bent forward* to allow the pads to be directly under the center of the shoulder blades.

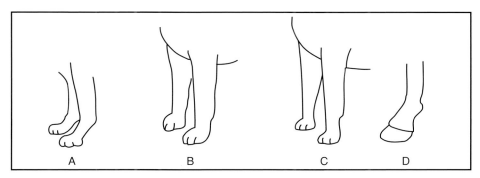

7-6. Pasterns.

Figure 7-6A illustrates pasterns bent at approximately 25 degrees as called for in the German Shepherd Dog Standard. On a Beagle these pasterns would be totally unacceptable and would be called "down in the pasterns." The pasterns in Figure 7-6B are correct for a Beagle. Pasterns knuckling over, as shown in Figure 7-6C, are unacceptable in all dogs except the Harrier. As stated in the Harrier Standard (1989): *"inclined to knuckle over very slightly but not exaggerated in the slightest degree."* Breeds with straight fronts (Beagles, Foxhounds, Fox Terriers and others) are more likely to have knuckling over. Most Sporting dogs have pasterns "slightly" bent but not as extreme as in Figure 7-6A. A good pastern for a hunter horse is shown in Figure 7-6D; horses have bent pasterns.

Terriers with short upper arms have forearms too far forward to allow the pads to be under the center of the shoulder blade. A straight pastern is a necessity.

The calf muscles of a human leg are much larger than those on the shin. Muscles behind the leg do the work; muscles in front carry the leg forward. The Fox Terrier, Beagle, Foxhound and Harrier, with front legs far forward, have excess strain on the muscles in the front of the leg. If these muscles are in the least bit weak, knuckling over or quivering pasterns results. Dogs with bent pasterns do not quiver.

Dogs with weak leg muscles and bent pasterns may become "down in the pasterns" (the muscle unable to hold the pastern up). In such dogs the pastern always rests on the ground. The term "down at the pasterns" is relative. The meaning of the term as applied to a German Shepherd Dog is distinctly different from the meaning as applied to a Fox Terrier. "Down in the pasterns" means "as compared with the normal position of the pasterns for a given breed of dog."

Many Standards call for the front legs to be perfectly straight, presumably when looking head on, *not* viewed from the side. "Perfectly straight" depends on the structural requirements of a breed. It can *not* always be interpreted to mean perfectly straight from *both* the front and side views. How can legs be perfectly straight at the elbow? Most Standards mean "perfectly straight" when viewed head on. Legs can be perfectly straight and yet slant inward while single tracking. "Perfectly straight" does not always imply 90 degrees to the ground or square with the ground. Beagles, Foxhounds, Fox Terriers, Harriers and many other breeds have legs 90 degrees to the ground when posed.

AFGHAN HOUND (1948)—*He has a straight front . . . Forelegs are straight and strong with great length between elbow and pastern; elbows well held in.*

AMERICAN FOXHOUND (Undated)—*Forelegs—Straight, with fair amount of bone. Pasterns short and straight.*

SMOOTH FOX TERRIER (1991)—*The forelegs viewed from any direction must be straight with bone strong right down to the feet, showing little or no appearance of ankle in front, and being short and straight in pastern.*

BRITTANY (1990)—*Front Legs—Viewed from the front, perpendicular, but not set too wide . . . Pasterns slightly sloped.*

AKITA (1972)—*Forelegs heavy boned and straight as viewed from the front. Angle of pastern 15 degrees forward from the vertical.*

POMERANIAN (1991)—*Forelegs are straight and parallel . . . Pasterns—The Pomeranian stands well up on his toes. Down in pasterns is a major fault.*

FINNISH SPITZ (1987)—*Legs—Viewed from the front, moderately spaced, parallel and straight with elbows close to the body and turned neither out nor in . . . Pasterns—Viewed from the side, slope slightly. Weak pasterns are to be penalized.*

GERMAN SHEPHERD DOG (1994)—*The forelegs, viewed from all sides, are straight and the bone oval rather than round. The pasterns are strong and springy and angulated at approximately a 25 degree angle from the vertical.*

Structurally, a pastern that knuckles over is a fault; a bent pastern is not. *A strong and flexible pastern produces a smooth gait.* Some of the Standards that call for a "vertical pastern" do so for aesthetic reasons, not structural reasons.

Feet

When a dog is posed, the feet can be examined in detail for quality or faults as described in Chapter 4, under **Feet in Motion.**

Back, Backline and Topline

The terminology associated with the back, backline and topline is often misapplied in Standards, dog books and articles, and in conversations. The proper uses of the terms are shown in Figure 7-7. Unfortunately, the Chihuahua Standard (1990) states: "*Topline—Level.*" "Backline level" was probably intended.

Most Standards call for a level back; a few call for an arch and a few for a dip. When a Standard says a "level back," does it include the withers, the loin and the area above the pelvis? The upward projection of the vertebrae at the withers, to be correctly developed in most dogs, arches above the backline. In horses the withers are particularly noticeable. Figure 7-8 shows a race horse backline with a level back, an arch over its pelvis and an arch at the withers. Dogs with this type of backline are said to have a "dip in the back." The muscles of dogs are not as well developed and do not produce pronounced arches. A number of dog Standards call for a slight arch over the loin. If a dog is properly developed at the withers, and if the withers *are* included in the words "level back," the back can never be absolutely level. Some breeds call for a level back and an arched loin. If the loin is part of the "level back," there can't be a level back *and* an arched loin.

The better concept is to treat the term "level back" in such Standards as excluding the withers and loin, as shown in Figure 7-7. A well developed dog would have a topline as follows: (1) arched neck, (2) neck to withers to back forming a curve, (3) back level,

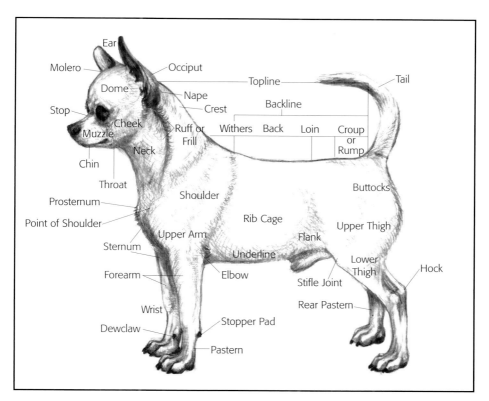

7-7. Back, backline and topline. *Chihuahua artwork by Nancy Shonbeck.*

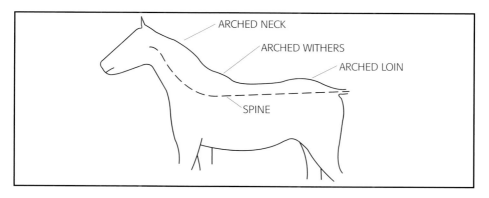

7-8. Race horse backline.

(4) loins arched or level as called for and (5) croup and tail coming off level, rounded or low set as called for in the breed Standard.

A few Standards call for a small dip in the back. If the rear is higher than the front end (Bulldog), there must be a transition from the neck to the back to the rear that becomes a dip. The following Standards state:

FRENCH BULLDOG (1991)—*The back is a roach back with a slight fall close behind the shoulders . . .*

CHINESE SHAR-PEI (1991)—*The topline dips slightly behind the withers, slightly rising over the short, broad loin.*

BULLDOG (1990)—*There should be a slight fall in the back, close behind the shoulders (its lowest part), whence the spine should rise to the loin (the top of which should be higher than the top of the shoulders), thence curving again more suddenly to the tail, forming an arch (a very distinctive feature of the breed), termed "roach back" or, more correctly, "wheel back."*

POODLE (1990)—*The topline is level, neither sloping nor roached, from the highest point of the shoulder blade to the base of the tail, with the exception of a slight hollow just behind the shoulder.*

For most dogs, a dip in the back is undesirable, but the withers and loin must not be mistaken for the back. In Figure 7-8 the horse has an arch over the pelvis, level back, rise at the withers and an arched neck. A level back of this type on most dogs would be considered a fault. In horses, the well developed rearing muscles produce an illusion of a dip, especially in heavy work horses. The spine of the horse in Figure 7-8 is level; the muscle outline is not. If a dip in the backline of a dog is caused by a sagging spine, the dog should be severely penalized; however, if the dip is an illusion caused by excellently developed rearing muscles of a sled or running dog, the dog should be praised.

The Chesapeake Bay Retriever (Figure 7-9) has a topline that is unique to that breed. The Standard (1993) states:

Topline should show the hindquarters to be as high as or a trifle higher than the shoulders. Back should be short, well coupled and powerful. Chest should be strong, deep and wide. Rib cage barrel round and deep. Body is of medium length, neither cobby nor roached, but rather approaching hollowness from underneath as the flanks should be well tucked up.

7-9. Chesapeake Bay Retriever. *John Ashbey Photography.*

Figure 7-10 illustrates various breed toplines as copied from photographs. The Dandie usually has a small dip at the base of the tail and the Bedlington has a low tail set. It is interesting that in the history of these two breeds, according to some writers, they have common ancestors.

In most cases, when the term "backline" is used in a Standard it is used correctly. Several examples follow:

> **GERMAN WIREHAIRED POINTER** (1989)—*The entire backline showing a perceptible slope down from withers to croup.*

> **GOLDEN RETRIEVER** (1990)—*Backline strong and level from withers to slightly sloping croup, whether standing or moving.*

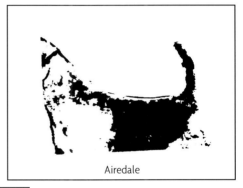

Airedale

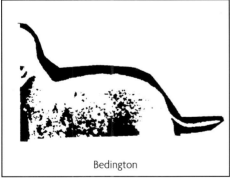

Bedington

Dandie Dinmont

7-10. Dog toplines.

We speak of a level back and think that the spine is also level. This is not true. The vertebrae of the spine have bony projections above them. These projections are longest at the withers and vary in height along the remainder of the back, as shown in Figure 7-1. For the skin of a dog's back, loin and pelvis to be level, the bony projections would have to be level. If the bony projections were not of uniform length, the spine could not be parallel with the skin. All level-back (including loin) dogs have a slightly S-curved spine. The level back is due to the muscle formation above and along the spine.

One of the few Standards that uses the term "topline" correctly is the Ibizan Hound (1989); it states: *"The topline, from ears to tail, is smooth and flowing. The back is level and straight."* But some Standards misuse the term "topline." Refer to Figure 7-7 for the proper definition. The following are examples of misuse:

BRITTANY (1990)—*Topline—Slight slope from the highest point of the shoulders to the root of the tail.*

FLAT-COATED RETRIEVER (1990)—*Topline strong and level.*

COCKER SPANIEL (1992)—*Topline—sloping slightly toward muscular quarters.*

HARRIER (1989)—*The topline is level.*

WEST HIGHLAND WHITE TERRIER (1989)—*Topline—Flat and level, both standing and moving.*

BICHON FRISE (1988)—*The topline is level except for a slight, muscular arch over the loin.*

GERMAN SHEPHERD DOG (1994)—*Topline—The withers are higher than and sloping into the level back.*

SCOTTISH TERRIER (1993)—*The topline of the back should be firm and level.*

BRIARD (1992)—*Topline—the Briard is constructed with a very slight incline, downward from the prominent withers to the back which is straight, to the broad loin and the croup which is slightly inclined.*

CHOW CHOW (1990)—*Topline straight, strong and level from the withers to the root of the tail.*

Much of the misuse of these terms is not confusing when reading a particular Standard—but can be confusing when using that definition in relation to other breeds.

Loin

The loin is part of the back *above* the flank (there are no ribs below the loin). Galloping dogs freely flex this part of the back. The muscle in the loin area is shown in Figure 7-11. Some of the Standards call for a slightly arched loin; a few call for a well arched loin. The Saluki Standard (1927) is probably worded better than other Standards. It calls for *"muscles slightly arched over the loin,"* thus stating what is the cause of the arch.

DALMATIAN (1989)—*The loin is short, muscular and slightly arched. The flanks narrow through the loin.*

SCOTTISH DEERHOUND (1935)—*The loin well arched and drooping to the tail.*

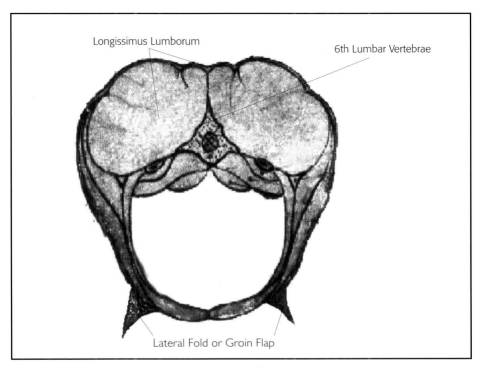

Longissimus Lumborum

6th Lumbar Vertebrae

Lateral Fold or Groin Flap

7-11. Cross section of the loin, just before hip bone at sixth lumbar vertebrae.

GREYHOUND (Undated)—*Loins—Good depth of muscle, well arched, well cut up in flanks.*

POINTER (1975)—*Loin of moderate length, powerful and slightly arched.*

SAMOYED (1993)—*Loins strong and slightly arched.*

BEDLINGTON TERRIER (1967)—*Back has a good natural arch over the loin, creating a definite tuck-up of the underline.*

MANCHESTER TERRIER (1991)—*The topline shows a slight arch over the robust loins falling slightly to the tail set.*

CHINESE SHAR-PEI (1991)—*The topline dips slightly behind the withers, slightly rising over the short, broad loin.*

In the portion of the Scottish Deerhound Standard quoted above, the inference is that the loin extends to the tail. The croup was omitted. However, the words clearly indicate that the backline should "droop" from the loin, across the croup to the tail.

No Standard calls for a dip in the loin; several call for an arch. Ordinarily the arch is not a roach; it is a *downward curve* from a level back. The Greyhound Standard calls for a well arched loin, i.e., the back is level and the loin slopes downward to form a "fall-off" arch over the loin (not up then down so as to form a roach). The Bedlington Terrier has the roach type of arch, as shown in Figure 7-10.

In writing about the Greyhound, Stonehenge (1872) made it clear that the Greyhound was used for coursing, not track racing. Present day track Greyhounds are usually much flatter in the loin and have higher hocks to attain greater short distance speed. Many of the Sporting dogs were developed from a cross with the Greyhound, and several call for a small arch over the loin. The arch is advantageous for agility and running uphill.

Bottom Line

In horse show judging, the lower line of the chest and belly is known as the bottom line. The term is perfectly applicable to dogs.

In many dogs the important ribs judged are the last two. If these are large so as to increase the chest cavity, lung room is increased. Large lungs are found in "stayers," especially in fast races. A herring-gutted dog has the upward slope of the keel starting at the front of the chest (between the front legs) and sloping upward steeply to the rear. The last two ribs are small and there is little tuck-up. Structurally, herring gut is a serious fault. In those Standards that call for a tuck-up, the bottom line should slope upwards slightly to the end of the ribs and then have a quick tuck-up.

> **POINTER** (1975)—*Tuck-up should be apparent, but not exaggerated.*

> **VIZSLA** (1983)—*underline exhibiting a slight tuck-up beneath the loin.*

> **AFGHAN HOUND** (1948)—*well ribbed and tucked up in flanks.*

> **BORZOI** (1972)—*Loins—Extremely muscular, but rather tucked up, owing to great depth of chest and comparative shortness of back and ribs.*

> **DOBERMAN PINSCHER** (1990)—*Belly well tucked up, extending in a curved line from the brisket.*

> **MANCHESTER TERRIER** (1991)—*The abdomen should be tucked up extending in an arched line from the deep brisket.*

> **ITALIAN GREYHOUND** (1976)—*back curved and drooping at hindquarters, the highest point of curve at start of loin, creating a definite tuck-up at flanks.*

> **KEESHOND** (1990)—*belly moderately tucked up.*

> **BELGIAN MALINOIS (1990)**—*The underline forms a smooth ascendant curve from the lowest point of the chest to the abdomen. The abdomen is moderately developed, neither tucked up nor paunchy.*

Ribs

Figure 7-12 shows a cross section of the ribcage at the deepest part of the chest (the fifth thoracic vertebra). Most Standards use the expression "well sprung ribs" and some use the expression "well ribbed up" or "last rib well developed." In most of the following Standards the terms "ribs well sprung" are used.

> **WHIPPET** (1993)—*Ribs well sprung but with no suggestion of barrel shape.*

> **BULLMASTIFF** (1992)—*Chest wide and deep, with ribs well sprung and well set down between the forelegs.*

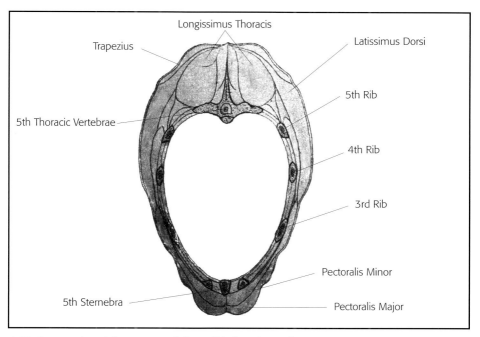

7-12. Cross section of deepest part of chest—fifth thoracic vertebrae.

WEST HIGHLAND WHITE TERRIER (1989)—*Ribs deep and well arched in the upper half of rib, extending at least to the elbows, and presenting a flattish side appearance. Back ribs of considerable depth, and distance from last rib to upper thigh as short as compatible with free movement of the body.*

SUSSEX SPANIEL (1992)—*The chest is round, especially behind the shoulders, and is deep and wide which gives a good girth. The back and loin are long and very muscular both in width and depth. For this development, the back ribs must be deep.*

PUG (1991)—*The body is short and cobby, wide in chest and well ribbed up.*

POODLE (1990)—*Chest deep and moderately wide with well sprung ribs.*

GERMAN SHEPHERD DOG (1994)—*Ribs well sprung and long, neither barrel-shaped nor too flat, and carried down to a sternum which reaches to the elbows. Correct ribbing allows the elbows to move back freely when the dog is at a trot. Too round causes interference and throws the elbows out, too flat or short causes pinched elbows. Ribbing is carried well back so that the loin is relatively short.*

The Whippet is narrow in the chest and the Bullmastiff is wide. How can both have well sprung ribs? In common usage "well sprung ribs" indicates a dog with a barrel chest. However, if the ribs spring out well from the backbone and also have an oval shape, the dog is also said to have well sprung ribs. The Whippet has a deep chest and well sprung ribs, whereas the Bullmastiff has a wide chest and well sprung ribs.

Ribs are attached to the backbone by a ball and socket joint so ribs will rotate. If humans take a deep breath and throw out their chests, muscles rotate the ribs upward and cause the chest to expand. As the chest expands, the lung capacity increases.

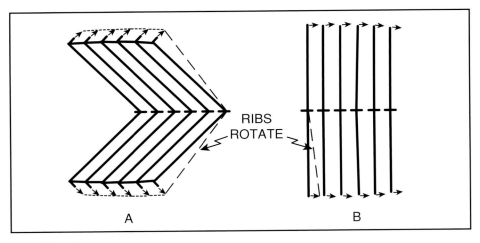

7-13. Rib rotation.

Figure 7-2 illustrates the dog's ribcage as viewed from above, while Figure 7-13 illustrates rib rotation. The ribs, as illustrated, have a 45 degree layback (the ribs slant 45 degrees toward the rear). Arrows show the direction ribs rotate and the dotted lines show the *expanded* chest. After rotation occurs, the lungs expand to fill the expanded chest cavity and air enters the lungs through the nasal passage. Ribs are rotated by muscles. If ribs are laid back at an angle (as in Figure 7-13A) and are rotated, the chest expands as shown to increase lung capacity. If ribs are at 90 degrees to the spine (as shown in Figure 7-13B), rotation does not increase lung capacity. Dogs with rib structures indicated in Figure 7-13B have breathing problems when they exert themselves.

Breathing is caused by two forces: (1) ribs rotating and (2) diaphragm moving up and down.

In an effort to attain a barrel chest, as required in the Bulldog, dogs have been developed with ribs at 90 degrees to the spine. The chest capacity of dogs lacking rib layback (ribs 90 degrees to the spine) cannot be increased by rotating the ribs; air intake is impaired. The Bulldog's breathing problems can be attributed to two factors: restricted nasal passages from the pushed-in face, and 90 degree ribs.

In evaluating dogs the fingers should be run down the back to check rib layback. When a Standard says "well ribbed up," the meaning includes "ribs well laid back."

As shown in Figures 7-1 and 7-2, there are thirteen paired ribs, the first nine called true ribs, the next three called false ribs, and the last rib called the floating rib. The true ribs are attached to the breastbone and are more rigid than the false ribs. The false ribs are usually attached one to the other by cartilage, while the last rib is unattached and is a true floating rib. When the ribs swing outward and forward, the space within the chest cavity is increased. Lungs are an elastic tissue; they will expand and air will be drawn in. When the chest muscles relax, the ribs return to their original position and the lung contracts and forces air out. True ribs have a lesser effect on increasing the chest cavity. To increase the dog's breathing power, the rearward ribs are more important.

Lung capacity can be increased by: (1) well sprung ribs, (2) long ribcage, (3) ribs oblique to the spine (turned toward the rear), (4) deep ribcage. The diaphragm that causes the lungs to inhale and exhale air is attached across the last ribs on a diagonal. The longer the rear ribs, the better the attachment. A long floating rib with good layback indicates a "well ribbed up" dog. Standards calling for the last rib well developed or well ribbed up are describing a dog with plenty of lung room.

Judging ribs is difficult when a dog is in "show condition." Usually "show condition" means that the dog is fat enough to hide poor rib conditions; the hand cannot feel the floating rib and the fat conceals a herring gut. In the leaner breeds, such as Salukis and Greyhounds, the ribs are exposed to view. The judge must feel the ribs on long-haired dogs.

Exhibitors of some of the short-legged breeds have found that by adding weight, a pad of fat will develop under the chest and make the chest look much deeper. Your hand must be run along the keel line to determine absence or existence of fat. Rarely, a projection of cartilage will be found on the chest keel. This cartilage gives the illusion of a full chest, yet in reality, lung capacity is not enlarged one iota. *Such structure is without merit.*

Croup

The croup is the part of the topline above the hind legs. A low tail set indicates a steep pelvis; a steep pelvis probabaly indicates poor backward reach. To best check the pelvis, watch the dog in motion.

A steep pelvis is not always a disadvantage; for agility and quick turning it is desirable. For more discussion on the croup refer to Chapter 4 under **The Pelvis and its Slope.**

Hocks

Long hocks, high initial speed; short hocks, endurance. Posed, the relative length of hock to arm can be critically observed. In the Smooth Fox Terrier, hocks are apparently higher than those of the Wire Fox Terrier. Genetically linked factors are hard to eliminate, and it appears that longer hocks are linked to the smooth coat. This variation is apt to be around for a long time.

Stifles

Many Standards call for a well bent stifle. This does help reach, provided the joint can be straightened when in motion. A check is always desirable since some dogs cannot completely straighten their well bent stifles.

Coat Colors

Most coat colors of wild animals evolved for camouflage, not protection from the elements. Samoyeds are white to match snow, not dark-colored to absorb the sun's rays. With the wide variation in existing environments it is not surprising that animals have developed numerous coat patterns. In hunting, flashily marked animals are at a disadvantage. For some animals, such as the skunk, bright colors are a warning to stay away.

Coat colors as specified in dog Standards have been developed by people for camouflage and artistic appeal.

Dr. Clarence C. Little states, in *The Inheritance of Coat Color in Dogs*, "dogs appear to have two major types of pigment in their coats. One of these is yellow, the other dark (brown or black). The color varieties of dogs have to be formed by various genes controlling the amount, extent, and distribution of these pigments, both individually, in combination, or in competition with one another." Dilute black can become blue. Dilute brown becomes tan. Yellow and brown can produce orange. Absence of hair pigments produces white (albinos have absence of pigments in the eyes and skin as well as hairs).

The pattern of coat pigments is controlled by genes different from those genes that control coat pigment colors. A pattern usually occurs in any of the pigment colors as ticking (blue belton, orange belton, Dalmatian spots, tan ticking and black ticking). Merle can be true merle, dappled in Dachshunds (brown, red-yellow or black pigment), harlequin in Danes (black pigments). One gene controls the merle pattern; another controls the pigment colors.

When judging coat colors, a person looks for traces of unwanted colors and traces of undesirable patterns. A merle coat is a case in point. The merle is dominant; a dog with one merle gene (Mm) is always merle in pattern. Also occurring on the same chromosome with the merle gene are recessive genes for deafness and blindness. The two are linked; one comes with the other. When two merle genes occur in a dog (MM), there usually occurs a deaf, blind or deaf and blind dog. For this reason most Standards that permit merle also fault excessive white. The Collie Standard (1977) permits white dogs and permits blue merle markings on a predominantly white dog. This color could indicate an undesirable double merle gene (MM). For the dappled Dachshund the Standard (1992) states: *"Neither the light nor the dark color should predominate."* The predominance of a dark color is probably not genetically harmful, whereas the excess white definitely is.

Another link with dog coat color is the liver or tan coat's link with light eyes. Standards that allow liver or tan coats also allow light-colored eyes; Standards that call for a solid black or white coat usually call for dark-colored eyes. The hazel eye color, usually associated with tan coats, is a dilute brown that looks almost yellow. The yellow eyes associated with true liver coats have yellow pigments, not dilute brown.

Genes that control coat patterns are imperfect. Black and white patterns (Irish spotting) can occur as mostly black with a little white on the chest, feet and body, or it can occur as white with a little black on the head and body. When an imperfect pattern of white is narrowly limited as in the Boston Terrier Standard (1990), breeding acceptable show specimens within the precise pattern cannot be consistently done. Puppies are frequently neutered because they have imperfect color patterns. In such breeds, structural perfection tends to become subordinate to patterns and pigments.

Dogs with the solid (self) color gene and black pigment gene often have a few white hairs. Many of the Standards that call for a dark self-colored dog (black or brown) also allow a small amount of white on the chest.

LABRADOR RETRIEVER (1994)—*A small white spot on the chest is permissible, but not desirable.*

SCHIPPERKE (1990)—*The outer coat must be black . . . occasional white hairs should not be penalized.*

A few breed Standards allow any color: Afghan Hound, Beagle, Borzoi, Greyhound, Whippet and others. The Afghan Hound Standard (1948) allows all coat colors provided the dog has dark eyes and a black nose. The eye and nose color limit the coat color. Merle coats are associated with walleyes, and walleyes are not permitted.

In many breeds coat color variation is allowed within limits. Allowing a coat variation for hunting dogs allows the hunter to select the best color for a given hunting environment.

BORZOI (1972)—*Any color, or combination of colors, is acceptable.*

BEAGLE (1957)—*Any true hound color. (Note: Hound people consider this to mean any solid color or combination of colors as stated in the English Foxhound Standard (1935) as listed below. This excludes merle, Dalmatian spotting, Norwegian Elkhound color, and harlequin.)*

ENGLISH FOXHOUND (1935)—*Color and Coat—Not regarded as very important, so long as the former is a good "hound color" . . . Hound colors are black, tan, and white, or any combination of these three, also the various "pies" compounded of white and the color of the hare and badger, or yellow, or tan.*

GREYHOUND (Undated)—*Color—Immaterial.*

WHIPPET (1989)—*Color immaterial.*

Coat Texture

Coats protect the dog from cold, heat, moisture, briars and rough hunting conditions. A naturally oily coat, as oily as duck feathers, prevents the skin from getting wet. Air, if not in motion, is a poor conductor of heat. Air entrapped between hairs in a dense fine coat is not in motion; it is the major factor in preserving body heat. For protection from briars coarse, heavy hairs are needed. Dogs designed for the cold regions have two coats: (1) a fine-textured undercoat that prevents the escape of body heat by entrapping air; (2) a strong outer guard coat called a wire coat or guard coat.

CHESAPEAKE BAY RETRIEVER (1993)—*Coat should be thick and short, nowhere over 1 1/2 inches long, with a dense fine woolly undercoat. Hair on face and legs should be very short and straight with tendency to wave on the shoulders, neck, back and loins only. Moderate feathering on rear of hindquarters and tail is permissible. The texture of the Chesapeake's coat is very important, as the Chesapeake is used for hunting under all sorts of adverse weather conditions, often working in ice and snow. The oil in the harsh outer coat and woolly undercoat is of extreme value in preventing the cold water from reaching the Chesapeake's skin and aids in quick drying. A Chesapeake's coat should resist the water in the same way that a duck's feathers do. When the Chesapeake leaves the water and shakes, the coat should not hold water at all, being merely moist.*

In extremely cold countries long guard hairs accumulate snow (especially wet snow). Most Arctic dogs do not have guard hairs extending out from the thick undercoat. They have a heavy "stand off" coat that does not readily part, especially on top of the back where snow can accumulate.

Arctic dogs in cold weather sleep with nose in the hair of the tail plume. The filtered air is a little warmer than the outside temperature. For this reason, dock-tailed Arctic dogs have a greater incidence of pneumonia.

SAMOYED (1993)—*The Samoyed is a double coated dog. The body should be well covered with an undercoat of soft, thick, close wool with longer and harsh hair growing through it to form the outer coat, which stands straight out from the body and should be free from curl. The coat should form a ruff around the neck and shoulders, framing the head (more on males than on females). Quality of coat should be weather* *resistant and considered more than quantity. A droopy coat is undesirable. The coat should glisten with a silver sheen. The female does not usually carry as long a coat as most males and it is softer in texture.*

ALASKAN MALAMUTE (1994)—*Coat—The Malamute has a thick, coarse guard coat, never long and soft. The undercoat is dense, from one to two inches in depth, oily and woolly. The coarse guard coat varies in length as does the undercoat. The coat is relatively short to medium along the sides of the body, with the length of the coat increasing around the shoulders and neck, down the back, over the rump, and in the breeching and plume. Malamutes usually have a shorter and less dense coat during the summer months. The Malamute is shown naturally. Trimming is not acceptable except to provide a clean cut appearance of feet.*

Dogs designed for use in hotter climates need a thin, hard coat that will allow heat to escape. In the dryer areas, an oily coat is not needed or desirable.

SALUKI (Undated)—*Coat—Smooth and of a soft silky texture . . .*

In some environments, the show ring among them, coats are to please the eye, not necessarily to serve a hunting or working purpose. In the city a dog's survival depends more upon pleasing the owner than on a dingy coat ideally suited for sneaking up on a nonexistent badger.

CHINESE SHAR-PEI (1991)—*Coat—The extremely harsh coat is one of the distinguishing features of the breed. The coat is absolutely straight and off standing on the main trunk of the body but generally lies somewhat flatter on the limbs. The coat appears healthy without being shiny or lustrous. Acceptable coat lengths may range from extremely short "horse coat" up to the "brush coat," not to exceed one inch length at the withers . . . The Shar-Pei is shown in its natural state.*

Dark coat colors absorb heat rays; light coat colors reflect heat rays. If heat absorption were the only consideration, dogs in snow country should be black and dogs in the tropics white. Usually camouflage is more important; white dogs are found in snow country. It is easier to grow a slightly thicker coat than it is to hide a black dog in the snow.

The importance of a coat is illustrated in the origin of the Borzoi. According to *The Complete Dog Book* (1968), a Russian Duke imported a number of Arabian Greyhounds, but they were unable to withstand the cold winters and soon died out. A second importation was crossed with a Collie-like dog that had a very heavy, wavy or curly coat with a tendency to be woolly. Selection produced the Borzoi.

The wire coat of Terriers becomes dormant and dull approximately twice a year. If dormant hairs are hand plucked, hair regrowth will commence immediately; clipping does no good. The trick in hand stripping is to remove the hair from the slower growing areas first and leave the faster growing areas until later.

MINIATURE SCHNAUZER (1991)—*Coat—Double, with hard, wiry, outer coat and close undercoat. The head, neck, ears, chest, tail, and body coat must be plucked. When in show condition, the body coat should be of sufficient length to determine texture. Close covering on neck, ears and skull. Furnishings are fairly thick but not silky.*

WELSH TERRIER (1993)—*The coat is hard, wiry and dense with a close-fitting, thick jacket. There is a short, soft undercoat. Furnishings on muzzle, legs, and quarters are dense and wiry.*

A curly coat helps to increase the density of the coat. A hair of round cross section grows straight; an oval-shaped hair grows curly (thin, flat wood carvings curl).

> **CURLY-COATED RETRIEVER** (1993)—*Coat*— . . . *distinguishing characteristic and quite different from that of any other breed. The body coat is a thick mass of small, tight, crisp curls, lying close to the skin, resilient, water resistant, and of sufficient density to provide protection against weather, water and punishing cover. Curls also extend up the entire neck to the occiput, down the thigh and back leg to at least the hock, and over the entire tail. Elsewhere, the coat is short, smooth and straight, including on the forehead, face, front of forelegs, and feet . . .*

The Flat-Coated Retriever Standard (1990) covers trimming: *"The Flat-Coat is shown with as natural a coat as possible and must not be penalized for lack of trimming, as long as the coat is clean and well brushed. Tidying of ears, feet, underline and tip of tail is acceptable. Whiskers serve a specific function and it is preferred that they not be trimmed. Shaving or barbering of the head, neck or body coat must be severely penalized."*

Winter and Summer Coats

Dogs, like many wild animals, have a heavy winter and a light summer coat. The length of daylight, not temperature, causes the change in coat. People who have raised chickens know that by turning on lights in the hen house during the winter night, hens will lay earlier than normal. Since winter eggs sell at a higher price than summer eggs, a profit is realized.

If dog show exhibitors want to have their dog's winter coat develop early, locking the dog in a dark room for part of the day will be effective. Fox breeders control light to regulate winter coat; it is desirable to have a prime pelt early to meet the early winter demand. Most dogs kept as pets are exposed to excessive artificial light; they tend to shed hair continuously.

Tying Back of Hair

There are only four breeds whose Standards permit the breed to be shown with the hair tied back: Maltese, Shih Tzu (Figure 7-14), Yorkshire Terrier and Poodle. No other breed is permitted in the ring if anything is used to hold back the hair, whether elastic, ribbon or barrette. Judges shall excuse from their ring any dog that uses any device to tie back the hair, except for the following breeds:

> **MALTESE** (1964)—*The long head-hair may be tied up in a topknot or it may be left hanging.*

> **SHIH TZU** (1989)—*Hair on top of head is tied up.*

> **YORKSHIRE TERRIER** (1966)—*The fall on the head is long, tied with one bow in center of head or parted in the middle and tied with two bows.*

> **POODLE** (1990)—*In all clips the hair of the topknot may be left free or held in place by elastic bands. The hair is only of sufficient length to present a smooth outline. "Topknot" refers only to hair on the skull, from stop to occiput. This is the only area where elastic bands may be used.*

7-14. Shih Tzu.
Photo by Missy Yuhl.

Inheritance

In some Standards, points that indicate that a dog is a genetic carrier of an undesirable trait are severely penalized. As an American Kennel Club rule, all dogs that are blind, deaf, changed in appearance by artificial means, or males that do not have two normal testicles normally located in the scrotum are disqualified from competing at dog shows.

The genetic makeup of dogs cannot be evaluated by observing individual dogs. However, certain points can be observed that sometimes prove that a dog is a carrier of a given undesirable trait. Yellow eyes are recessive, and a dog with yellow eyes must be genetically pure for yellow eyes. Eyes are obvious. Disqualifying faults may be genetic. Some disqualifications are due to undesirable non-functional traits that entered the gene pool at some time during its development, such as color, coat texture or length.

> **BRITTANY** (1990)—*A black nose. Black in the coat.*
>
> **AMERICAN WATER SPANIEL** (1990)—*Yellow eyes.*
>
> **WEIMARANER** (1971)—*A distinctly long coat. A distinctly blue or black coat.*
>
> **WHIPPET** (1993)—*Blue or wall eyes. Any coat other than short, close, smooth and firm in texture.*

Testicles

The American Kennel Club *Rules Applying to Registration and Dog Shows (1991)*, in Chapter 14, Section 8, states: "A dog which is . . . castrated . . . or a male which does not have two normal testicles normally located in the scrotum, may not compete at any show and will be disqualified."

The Basenji, a dog native to Africa, is of ancient origin and is not closely related to other American Kennel Club breeds. Adult males have a unique ability to retract their testicles. Two male Basenjis sparring or growling at each other may not have testicles in the scrotum. The AKC rule was carefully written to say "normally located in the scrotum," not "always" located in the scrotum. When judging Basenjis and testicles are not down, the best procedure is to separate the dogs, walk them (walking the dogs in tight circles gets the dogs dizzy and they relax), then reexamine.

Faking and Artificial Means

During the posed examination faking is looked for. Dogs lacking prick ears sometimes have wires inserted to hold the ears erect. Coats are dyed. Small amounts of arsenic in the dog's diet cause the dog to gain weight and grow hair. However, the hair has a characteristic dead look. Handlers have been known to straighten a crooked tail. Black polish can hide a butterfly nose—while a tattoo can change it permanently. Looking for faking is one of those disagreeable jobs that one must be constantly aware of when evaluating a dog either for breeding or in the show ring.

The American Kennel Club *Rules Applying to Registration and Dog Shows (1991)*, in Chapter 14, Section 8, states: "A dog . . . which is changed in appearance by artificial means except as specified in the standard for its breed . . . will be disqualified . . . A dog will not be considered to have been changed by artificial means because of removal of dewclaws or docking of tail if it is of a breed in which such removal or docking is a regularly approved practice which is not contrary to the standard."

Dogs that have been changed in appearance by artificial means are barred from show competition because the judge is required to evaluate each dog on the basis of natural appearance. This cannot be done if the dog's natural appearance has been altered. Any surgery or other procedure, any drug or other substance that may have the effect, whether deliberate or not, of changing a dog's appearance, makes the dog disqualifiable or ineligible to compete.

Trimming coats in the manner that is customary for the breed, or as stated in the breed Standard, *is acceptable*. Trimming that has the effect of concealing or removing a condition that would be a fault under the breed Standard is changing a dog's appearance by artificial means. Trimming a distinctly long coat in a Weimaraner or a Basset Hound, where a distinctly long coat is a disqualification, would be considered as changing appearance by artificial means.

Any substance left in a coat, even if used for cleaning purposes, that alters the coat's texture or body falsifies coat quality. If, in the judge's opinion, there is any substance present that prevents the proper evaluation of the natural texture or body of the coat, the judge shall excuse the dog from the ring. The judge's book shall be marked "Excused—foreign substance—unable to judge coat's texture." A judge shall not permit any spray or other substance except plain water to be used on a dog in the ring. If such a substance is being applied, the judge should excuse both the dog and the exhibitor from the ring.

Drugs or other substances that affect the nervous system by stimulation, sedation, tranquilization or otherwise are clearly prohibited. Drugs that can alleviate pain or discomfort of a dog with an arthritic condition will change the appearance of the gait, and are also prohibited. Steroids, which can stimulate muscle development, would deceive a judge as to the dog's natural appearance and are also prohibited.

Surgical procedures for cosmetic reasons must not be performed on dogs that are to be shown. This surgery has the purpose of concealing the natural condition of the dog, thereby deceiving judges as well as breeders. Straightening misaligned teeth or the use of tattooing to conceal a lack of pigment is *not* permitted and is in direct violation of the rules as mentioned above.

Some procedures are performed on a dog for health and well being. Even so, these disqualify the dog from competition. As necessary as the procedure may have been, if it resulted in a change in appearance by artificial means, it makes it impossible for the judge to evaluate the dog based on the natural condition.

The purpose of the AKC regulations is to promote the breeding of dogs that can lead normal, comfortable lives without surgery or drugs. We all need to enforce these regulations in order to promote the best interests of purebred dogs.

Vicious Dogs

No one should be exposed to a dog that habitually bites. The AKC rule printed in *Rules Applying to Registration and Dog Shows*, Chapter 14, Section 8-A, is as follows:

> A dog that in the opinion of the judge menaces or threatens or exhibits any sign that it may not be safely approached by the judge or examined by the judge in the normal manner shall be excused from the ring. When the judge excuses the dog, he shall mark the dog 'Excused,' stating the reason in the judge's book. A dog so excused shall not be counted as having competed.

> A dog that in the opinion of the judge attacks any person in the ring shall be disqualified. When the judge disqualifies the dog, he shall mark the dog 'Disqualified,' stating the reason in the judge's book. When a dog has been disqualified under this section, any awards at that show shall be canceled by The American Kennel Club, and the dog may not again compete unless and until following application by the owner to The American Kennel Club, the owner has received official notification that the dog's show eligibility has been reinstated.

The Guidelines for Conformation Dog Show Judges states as follows:

Shy and Vicious Dogs

Excuse any dog that in your opinion:

- menaces
- threatens
- exhibits any sign that it may not be examined in the normal manner

When you excuse the dog mark your judge's book 'excused.' State the reason in the book.

Disqualify any dog that in your opinion attacks any person in the ring. Mark your book, 'disqualified attacked . . . ' *Clearly communicate your decision to the exhibitor of the dog.*

Be certain to tell the exhibitor exactly what action you have taken . . .

Breeders and judges must understand the traits of dogs and know how to approach them.

CHAPTER 8

Front and Rear Acting Together

Dog's Origin

Up to this point the parts of a dog have been considered as separate pieces. Now we will consider parts acting together. Prior to studying the action in detail, the origin of the dog and the characteristics of wild dogs should be understood.

Most authorities agree that the domestic dog evolved from similar ancestors of wolves, with minor contributions from jackals. It is doubtful that the short-legged bush dog (Figure 1-4), the African hunting dog (Figure 8-1) and the maned wolf had any part in producing domestic dogs. While the African hunting dog is not closely related to the domestic dog, in early history it did have a common ancestor with the domestic dog. Note the long legs, the bat ears and the bend of the hock and stifle. It is fairly swift and hunts in packs.

True wolves are basically carnivores but are capable of scavenging, eating berries, fruit or vegetables. In traveling they run with great endurance and fair speed. On first thought it would seem that wolves should be able to run faster than their prey, but if this were true, wolves would soon multiply and eliminate their prey. Wolves rely more upon cunning, teamwork and endurance; the prey relies upon speed to get away. Jackals are more often scavengers, extremely cunning, cursorial with fair speed, and above all have endurance.

Wolves are specialists in stamina and endurance; they surpass most mammals in this respect. Natural dogs (undistorted for a special purpose) should excel in the trot and be built for endurance. The trotting style used by wild dogs (wolves and coyotes) is assumed to be ideal for the endurance trot. The domestic dog rarely trots to the perfection displayed by the wolf.

In the dry plains area, by selective breeding, people developed a flexible-back domestic dog fast enough to catch most prey. Speed was not a natural development in wolves; man, by selecting faster animals for breeding, was responsible. This was done at

125

8-1. African hunting dog. *Photo by Ron Garrison, courtesy San Diego Zoo.*

the expense of endurance. At a trot, day in and day out, wolves leave Greyhounds far behind. It cannot be expected that Greyhounds will perform a trot to the perfection of wolves; they are not built that way.

Running animals (cursorial), in the process of evolving speed and endurance, developed these specialized characteristics:

1. Legs that move in a single plane (they cannot rotate like the human arm)

2. Muscles that tend to concentrate in the upper portion of the legs

3. Legs that are longer

4. Paws and leg extremities that are as small as possible

5. An increase in the effective number of joints that are used in running. Refer to Figure 8-2 for a comparison between the feet of the dog and the horse

6. The back is used by Sighthounds in running (Refer to Figures 2-8 and 2-9)

A most frequent statement in the biological world is: Form follows function. The function of dogs to meet our needs (herding, speed, catch game, bull baiting, going to ground, retrieving, swimming, fighting, etc.) changed dogs' form. With a change in form came a change in efficiency and style of trotting. Today there are many breeds of dogs whose form precludes the possibility of the endurance trot displayed by the wolf.

Gaiting

In the showring each entry is gaited individually. This should afford ample opportunity to observe the rear, side and front action. Different judges utilize different ring patterns

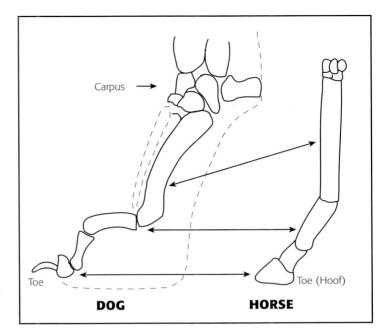

Carpus

Toe

Toe (Hoof)

DOG　　　　**HORSE**

8-2. Comparison of the foot of the dog and the horse.

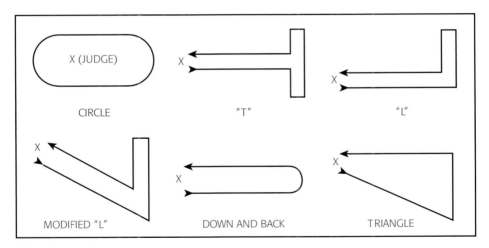

X (JUDGE)

CIRCLE

"T"

"L"

MODIFIED "L"

DOWN AND BACK

TRIANGLE

8-3. Gait patterns.

that they wish the handler to take. Straight across the ring, circling at the end and returning in a straight line to the judge, then circling to the the end of the line is the simplest. Other patterns are shown in Figure 8-3.

An efficient pattern is the path of a triangle. The judge sees the dog going, in side view, and coming without steps being retraced. In large breeds shown in a small ring, the triangular path allows the handler continuous motion without breaking stride, and one extra triangle can be completed in the time consumed by the stop in the up-and-back pattern. German Shepherd Dogs require greater speed to demonstrate the flying trot; the judge, in addition to the up-and-back pattern, usually requires the full circle.

Dogs that have a tendency toward hip dysplasia or locomotion problems may limp or slip down when turning square corners; square corner patterns help detect faults.

The Legs in Action at a Trot

When breeding dogs for a particular purpose, one or more of several objectives should be kept in mind.

1. To develop dogs with maximum galloping speed

2. To develop dogs with both endurance and good galloping speed

3. To develop superior endurance trotters

4. To develop superior speed trotters (German Shepherd Dog)

5. To develop superior ability to perform a specific function (catching game, bull baiting, swimming, etc.) and allow dogs to trot as best they can

6. Since the advent of dog shows a sixth item is added: To develop dogs that travel in the most graceful manner with animation (alert expression of eyes and ears, high head carriage, etc.)

Each of these objectives demands a different style of trotting.

When judging the quality of leg and body motions for endurance at the trot, any motion that wastes energy is undesirable. *Without considering body shape or size*, the following principles are important for evaluating efficiency for endurance:

1. The legs on each side should have single plane motion; that is, legs should move back and forth in a straight column and in the direction of travel (no paddling, weaving, cow hocks, out at the elbows, bow legs, etc.).

2. At faster speeds the legs on each side should converge in a straight column towards the dog's centerline (almost single tracking or single tracking).

3. The spine should point in the direction of travel (no crabbing).

4. Up-and-down motion of the topline should be minimal.

5. Paw lift should not be excessive. Generally, paw elevation during the endurance trot should not be higher than the height of the pastern joint in the posed position.

6. Each side's motion should be symmetrical to the other side (no lameness).

Remember that the principles listed above are for the endurance trot. A German Shepherd Dog (Figure 8-4), when viewed from the side, moves neither up nor down at the withers; it glides. But not all dogs' purpose in life is to produce a perfect flying trot or have an endurance trot. The coyote and wolf at a trot have a little up-and-down motion at the withers. The Bulldog and all dogs with wide spread legs must roll to be correct. Steep-shouldered dogs (designed for draft or to have straight hocks) cannot move without some up-and-down motion at the withers.

8-4. German Shepherd Dog in flying trot. *COOK phoDOGraphy.*

Defects Found When Front and Rear Are Out of Balance

When a dog's legs fail to move in a single plane, most Standards call the movement a fault (paddling, weaving, out at the elbows, cow hocked, pin toed, east and west feet, and bowlegged). Some dogs' legs in uniquely shaped breeds (Bulldog especially) do not move in a single plane.

Movement is a cooperation between front and rear legs. When a rear moves with power behind a front that can't move as well, compensation must take place. One solution is to have the rear quit pushing as hard and thus ease the burden on the defective front.

Dog "A" has an excellent rear assembly capable of full stride and full push, but also has defective shoulder layback with a front incapable of a full stride. At a trot the rear can take it easy and shorten stride to fit the front. Due to steep shoulders, the withers will bob up and down as the dog moves. However, at a fast trot the front cannot reach far enough forward to keep up with the rear. To compensate, the rearing muscles of the hindquarters lift the front off the ground so that during part of the stride the front travels suspended in the air. This lengthens the front stride, but it also bobs the front up and down (rocking-horse effect—all calves run this way), and it is exceedingly tiring. The energy used for lifting (suspending the front in the air) sacrifices endurance. Except for dogs designed for special purposes, this action is faulty. A perfectly good rear assembly that is not using its potential casts suspicion upon the front. When rearing muscles lift the front to lengthen the stride, the front feet must come down with a thud. It is like jumping; you come down hard. The feet are said to be pounding.

Dog "B" has an excellent front and too steep a croup. The rear legs reach too far forward and not far enough back. In the trot, if the rear legs of this dog reach as far forward as they can, the front and rear feet will hit. To compensate the dog can shorten the stride, or it can crab (move with its back out of line with its direction of travel). The more common compensation is to shorten the stride. At dog shows a dog persistently moved at a slow trot is suspected of having a defective reach.

Speed of Leg Movement

To a certain degree, the speed of leg movement, especially the front ones, is determined by the same rules that determine the speed of pendulums. Those people fortunate enough to have a grandfather clock know that by shortening the pendulum's length, they can cause the clock to run faster. Short pendulums (also short legs as found on Toy breeds) are capable of moving back and forth at a faster rate than are long pendulums (as on the Weimaraner). Little dogs and small rodents with short legs can move their legs with surprising speed; however, their short strides do not allow them to cover as much ground as longer-legged dogs do. Long legs are not the only determinant for speed. Whippets in short dashes are faster than Greyhounds. The cheetah or lion can outsprint the longer-legged gazelle. The longest-legged mammal of all (giraffe) is not as fast as the cheetah. Long thin legs tend to give greater speed *provided* muscles are also capable of producing speed.

Toy dogs have short, light legs that move rapidly. For this reason Toy dogs at a trot do not move like larger dogs; they have quick strides that are difficult to follow with the eye. Because of the speed of travel of the legs, many observers are unable to see defects that are readily seen in longer-legged, slower moving dogs.

We know that the heavier the object, the greater force needed to accelerate it. Pushing a ten-pound object is easy; pushing a fifty-pound object is more difficult. Fast sprinting animals (deer, gazelle, Greyhound and others) have thin legs; less force is needed to accelerate lightweight legs. Furthermore, the more the leg is lightened at its extremity, the less force is needed. The Standard for the Pointer illustrates this principle.

> **POINTER** (1975)—*Pasterns of moderate length, perceptibly finer in bone than the leg . . .*

Animals traveling with speed tend to have their muscles concentrated in the shoulder and have their legs operated by tendons. The maximum rate of speed for fast animals is determined by the length of stride and the frequency of stride.

A paw must be on the ground before it can deliver force to the body. As a dog trots, part of the time a forefoot is in front of the shoulder blade. At the same time a hind foot is in front of the hip joint. Both the front and rear paw have a force that tends to slow (decelerate) speed. Dogs do not have the ability to pull on the ground when the front paw is ahead of the shoulder blade. In the trot, only after the paw passes behind the shoulder blade or hip joint does the paw develop forward thrust.

Both the front and the rear provide forward thrust. Forward reach is primarily to maintain balance, while rearward extension provides thrust. For a full discussion on locomotion and its dynamics refer to Curtis M. Brown's *Dog Locomotion and Gait Analysis*, Chapter 5.

Not all animals' legs are designed for speed on firm footing. Traveling in snow (reindeer or Samoyed) or on sand requires big paws capable of distributing weight over large surfaces. On soft footing, large feet increase running speed. On firm footing, large feet decrease speed.

> **CHESAPEAKE BAY RETRIEVER** (1993)—*Well webbed hare feet should be of good size with toes well-rounded and close. (Note: For swimming).*

> **SAMOYED** (1993)—*Feet—Large, long, flattish—a hare-foot, slightly spread but not splayed; toes arched; pads thick and tough, with protective growth of hair between the toes. (Note: For snow).*

8-5. Cheetah—Reputed to be the world's fastest land mammal. *Photo by Ron Garrison, courtesy San Diego Zoo.*

AFGHAN HOUND (1948)— . . . *pads of feet unusually large and well down on ground. (Note: For hilly desert country).*

By studying fast running animals, certain conclusions regarding correct build of legs to produce running speed can be reached. Most authorities agree that there are several combinations of parts capable of yielding equal speed. A visual comparison of the legs of a horse, a rabbit and a fox (all capable of approximately the same speed) is proof. Though *the combinations of parts to produce speed may vary,* certain scientific principles can be used to select dogs that will probably run faster.

The approximate maximum speeds of some mammals are: cheetah, 70 miles per hour (see Figure 8-5); pronged antelope, 70 miles per hour; horse and rider, 48 miles per hour; rabbit (hare) and red fox, 45 miles per hour; Greyhound, 40 miles per hour. Both the cheetah and racing Greyhound are propelled by a lever system designed for speed, yet the cheetah is much faster in the sprint. It is quite apparent that Greyhounds on the racetrack have plenty of room for speed improvement. The most obvious advantage of the cheetah is its superior muscles (especially in the shoulder), short neck and vertical shoulder blades.

Figure 8-5 shows the cheetah, which is reputed to be the world's fastest land mammal. As is characteristic of animals that have quick speed without much endurance, the head is small, the neck is short, the shoulder blades are vertical, the hindquarters are powerful, the back is very flexible, the body is lean and the legs are long and slender. Unlike other cats, the pads of the cheetah's feet are dog-like and the claws are not retractable. The tail is long and fairly heavy; it is used for balance in fast turns. Angulation in the rear is not as much as seen on some dogs. The pasterns are bent.

When designing a lever system (as legs are) to obtain an end purpose, the result is dependent upon the product of numbers. How many ways can you multiply two numbers together and get twelve?

$$1 \times 12 = 12 \qquad 4 \times 3 = 12$$

$$2 \times 6 = 12 \qquad 6 \times 2 = 12$$

$$3 \times 4 = 12 \qquad 12 \times 1 = 12$$

Applying the same principle to leg assemblies, there are various arrangements of bones and muscles that will produce a speed of 70 miles per hour. The only mammals that may be faster than the cheetah are the pronged antelope and lion. The pronged antelope has hoofs, thin legs, high hocks and long neck (muscles of the shoulder blade are attached to the neck). The cheetah has dog-like feet (not cat-like), medium hocks, shorter and heavier legs, shorter neck and smaller head. Both have powerful muscles. The leg structures of each and the necks are miles apart in type, but both have nearly the same speed!

As illustrated above for speed, it can be shown that for any end purpose (digging, trotting, jumping, high initial speed, endurance or draft), there are several possible arrangements of bones and muscles that will accomplish similar end results.

Single Tracking

Running dogs are said to *single track* when their pawprints are in a straight line. The legs of most dogs converge as they increase in speed.

At an early age, Sir Isaac Newton discovered and stated one of his fundamental laws of motion: bodies in motion continue in motion in a straight line until deflected by another force. When you are on a bicycle, it is no trick to stay in balance while moving, but try to do it when motionless! Dogs, when standing, spread their feet for balance. When moving, they have no reason to keep their feet far apart; the faster the dog runs, the closer the feet converge. But remember, not all dogs are designed exclusively for running. The Bulldog's feet are kept far apart to prevent overturning. Draft animals pulling a heavy load at a slow gait must keep their feet apart to effectively put weight on the collar.

To illustrate the effect of a wide front, slowly walk toward a full length mirror with your feet spread apart and watch your shoulders. They weave to the right, then to the left (lateral instability). Why would anyone, including a dog, ever try to trot while weaving the shoulders from one side to the other? Trotting dogs that have endurance keep their feet under the center of gravity; that is, as nearly directly under the keel as possible. Any other position wastes energy.

Short-legged dogs, such as the Dachshund, Scottish Terrier and Basset Hound, cannot get their legs completely under their keel; the legs are not long enough. However, these dogs do get their legs under their chests as far as is practical. The old Basset Hound Standard, until the revision of 1964, stated: "*The forelegs should be short, very powerful, very heavy in bone, close fitting to the chest with a crook'd knee and wrinkled ankle, ending in a massive paw.*" A crook in the legs was required to get the legs under the heavy dog. Not a bad idea!

Some of the Standards are excellent at stating how the running dog's legs should converge; others ignore the subject. A few of the Standards clearly imply that the dog is not to single track.

SHETLAND SHEEPDOG (1990)—*Viewed from the front, both forelegs and hind legs should move forward almost perpendicular to ground at the walk, slanting a little inward at a slow trot, until at a swift trot the feet are brought so far inward toward center line of body that the tracks left show two parallel lines of footprints actually touching a center line at their inner edges.*

GERMAN SHEPHERD DOG (1994)—*The dog does not track on widely separated parallel lines, but brings the feet inward towards the middle line of the body when trotting, in order to maintain balance.*

BOXER (1989)—*The legs are parallel until gaiting narrows the track in proportion to increasing speed, then the legs come in under the body but should never cross.*

GOLDEN RETRIEVER (1990)—*As speed increases, feet tend to converge toward center line of balance.*

BELGIAN TERVUREN (1990)—*He single tracks at a fast gait, the legs both front and rear converging toward the center line of gravity of the dog.*

SCOTTISH TERRIER (1993)—*The forelegs do not move in exact parallel planes; rather, in reaching out, the forelegs incline slightly inward because of the deep broad forechest . . . The action of the rear legs should be square and true . . .*

WELSH CORGI, CARDIGAN (1991)—*The forearm (ulna and radius) should be curved to fit spring of ribs. The curve in the forearm makes the wrists (carpal joints) somewhat closer together than the elbows.*

BULLDOG (1990)—*The forelegs should be short, very stout, straight and muscular, set wide apart, with well developed calves, presenting a bowed outline, but the bones of the leg should not be curved or bandy, nor the feet brought too close together.* (Author's Note: For the Bulldog, preventing overturning is far more important than the efficiency gained by single tracking.)

BULLMASTIFF (1992)—*Forelegs straight, well boned, and set well apart; elbows turned neither in nor out.*

Daisy Clipping/Skimming

If a dog's feet in motion skim the ground without enough ground clearance, it is called "daisy clipping" or "skimming." In rough terrain, dogs that do not lift their feet high enough will develop sores on the tops of their toes and will tend to stumble. While high action (hackney gait) is wasted motion and wasted energy, the opposite extreme (daisy clipping) can also cause problems for dogs in rough country. In smooth terrain and at a slow trot, daisy clipping uses less energy.

GERMAN SHEPHERD DOG (1994)—*The feet travel close to the ground on both forward reach and backward push.*

SHETLAND SHEEPDOG (1990)—*The foot should be lifted only enough to clear the ground as the legs swing forward.*

At a fast trot or at a gallop dogs that daisy clip use excess energy. This sounds like a paradox since it takes energy to lift a paw. Earlier, the action of a pendulum was discussed. The time it takes a free-swinging pendulum to swing back and forth is solely dependent upon its length. The shorter the pendulum, the faster the swing. If the walk or trot is slow, the natural swing of the leg corresponds to the time for a pendulum to swing. A person with a stiff leg can walk by allowing the leg to swing forward like a pendulum. Whenever a dog wants to move faster, muscles must pull the leg forward. Shortening the pendulum (lifting the feet higher by folding the leg upward) allows the leg to naturally swing forward faster and conserve energy. The faster an animal moves, the larger and heavier the leg, the more important it is to lift the legs high. Most fast animals do this at a gallop, especially the long-legged hooved varieties such as the horse.

At different speeds there is a given height to which paws should be lifted for *minimum* energy expenditure. The hackney action of a horse at slow speeds looks good but requires excessive energy.

Number of Joints

If an animal uses leg segments properly, the speed of each segment can be additive. This is like riding down an escalator and walking down the steps at the same time. The speed of travel is the sum of the escalator speed plus the walking speed. A baseball pitcher can attain high velocity in throwing a baseball provided he can synchronize the velocity of each segment of his arm so that the speed of the upper arm, lower arm, wrist and fingers are all cumulative. As shown in Figure 8-2, the hoof of a horse corresponds to the toenail of the dog; the horse has more joints that can be effectively used to attain speed. In spite of its heavier weight, a horse can move as fast as a Greyhound.

When evaluating dogs, it is important to watch how dogs use their joints. If the joints are not straightened and folded during motion, the dog has a serious fault (sickle hock).

Animals that move in the double suspension gallop have greater speed because the back is used as an extra joint. The speed of bending and straightening the back is additive to the leg speed.

Flank and the Flex of the Back

The "back" of a dog is an ill-defined term. Probably the most common definition of the back is any part of the spinal column from the neck to the pelvis; however, many dog people think of the back as extending from the neck to the tail. The anatomical division of the spinal column is neck, withers, back, loin and croup. By this definition the "back" is only four vertebrae long. Since very few dog people use "back" in this context, we will use the term "back" to include the area from the withers to the croup. In dog Standards the word "back" has several meanings.

The flank is the space where the dog's intestines are thinly covered with skin and muscles. This is the distance between the last rib and the hindquarters; the area on the side of the dog that is free of ribs.

Ribs do not compress appreciably; the spine in the area of the ribs bends some but not much. The spine above the flanks, being free of ribs, bends more readily than any other part of the back.

Greyhounds or any of the faster dogs, when at a gallop, bend their backs most noticeably just above the flank. At times the bend is almost a sharp angle. The least flexible portion of the back is where the pelvis is attached; the joints are fused. Near the forepart of the chest (withers), where the shoulder blades are attached by muscle, the backbone is not as flexible as it is further astern. When Sighthounds fold their legs under themselves, and the legs overreach one another, the back is relatively flat at the withers, arched over the ribcage, bent downward in the flank, and extended downward on a rigid line along the pelvis. The back does not form a symmetrical curve even though the eye may think it sees a symmetrical arch.

Back Movement to the Side

The back, in addition to being able to arch vertically, can arch laterally. Those who have watched lizards move (Figure 8-6) know that bending the back sideways increases reach. Puppies (especially with short legs, such as Dachshunds) and dogs moving with legs far apart (Bulldog) show this type of back bending. To a limited extent this sideways movement also occurs in trotting dogs, especially those that move with feet wide apart, but it is not readily visible in adult dogs.

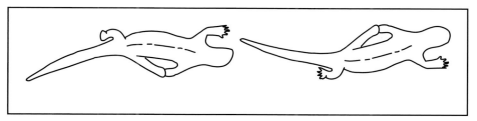

8-6. Sideways back movement. As lizards and amphibians move with legs in the same sequence as in the trot, bending the back sideways gives extra reach.

Effect of Head and Neck in Motion

The head and neck of a dog (or any other animal) is used to maintain balance. For dogs to run faster, the neck extends forward, puts more weight on the forequarters, and increases the forward falling force (also speed). In order to pull on a harness, a draft animal extends neck and body forward to put more weight into the collar. If the footing is slippery, as on ice, the head is raised to improve balance on the feet. When turning a corner, a dog moves the head and neck towards the center of the turning curve to overcome centrifugal force. In the trot or pace the head can be moved to one side, then to the other to counterbalance side sway forces.

A common fallacy among dog people is that a long neck improves speed. Many of the fast-moving predators (cheetah and other members of the cat family) have short necks, small heads and speed. The speed of movement depends more upon the length of fibers within a muscle than upon the length of the muscle. Grazing animals developed long necks to enable their mouths to reach the grass on the ground; the evolutionary adaptation was unrelated to speed. The most extreme neck adaptation is the giraffe; its long neck and exceptionally long legs allow feeding on high trees.

Greyhounds are coursing dogs; the long neck was developed to enable the dog to (1) reach down and grab rabbits and (2) see in the distance. Most speedy animals using the double suspension gallop have either a small head or a short neck or both; Greyhounds and Borzois have the smallest head per pound of body weight for dogs.

Dogs have a muscle that runs from the shoulder blade to the head. They also have a muscle that runs from the upper arm to the head (brachicephalicus muscle). In pulling the leg forward the brachicephalicus muscle contracts. If the head is held high to put tension on the muscle, the front legs will be pulled up extra high; a prancing gait results. Poodles carry themselves *"proudly"* and Afghan Hounds have a *"proudly carried head."* Both hold their heads high and tend to lift their feet higher than many other breeds. At a horse show the horse's head is held high by harness; at a dog show the dog's head is held high by the handler who "strings the dog up" with a tight lead.

Tail

The tail of a dog, in addition to showing happiness, acting as a rudder or pointing birds, helps maintain balance for the head and neck.

Tails are docked for aesthetic or historical reasons, not moving efficiency. In the eighteenth century drovers' dogs (for driving cattle and sheep) were exempt from taxes. Docked tails proved their occupation. The Old English Sheepdog, to this day, must either be born bobtailed or have a docked tail.

Arctic dogs sleep with their noses in the plumes of their tails. Freezing air is partially warmed before entering the lungs.

An adult Fox Terrier should have at least four inches of tail to act as a handle when pulling the dog out of a foxhole.

Wolves, foxes and jackals keep their tails down to mask odors, especially when hunting. At times of sexual excitement the tail is raised. The position of the tail on domestic dogs is to please humans.

Endurance

Endurance is staying power; the word can be applied in relation to speed or strength. A lightweight dog may show more running endurance than a heavyweight dog. In snow, a heavyweight dog may show greater endurance for pulling a sledge than a lightweight dog.

Short and Long Bodies

Some Standards use the term "cobby" when referring to the build. This term comes from the Cob horse, which is a thickset, stocky, short-legged horse; a cobby dog is compact, strong, thickset and relatively short, both in body height and length.

Many Standards call for a square dog; usually that means the height at the withers equals the length from forechest to stern. Race horses use the single suspension gallop, run with a relatively stiff back and have short (square) bodies.

Figure 8-7 illustrates the term "daylight." Horsemen often use the term "standing with a lot of daylight." The outline of the Basenji is of a lightly built, short-backed dog with plenty of daylight. The Boxer, with a larger body, has less daylight underneath.

8-7. Daylight under a dog.

When considering leverage, the short body has an advantage in the single suspension gallop, in the canter and in running uphill (jumping), but not in the regular trot or the double suspension gallop. The rearing muscle of the dog (the muscle that extends from the point of the pelvis to the lower thigh) assists in lifting the front of the dog; if the body is short, less energy is needed to lift the forequarters. Try this experiment: Place a fairly heavy object on a table. Next, stand close to the table and lift the object. Next, stand away from the table, reach out (arms extended) and lift the same object. With the arms extended, considerably more force will be needed to lift the object. Dachshunds with their long bodies and short legs are inefficient at the single suspension gallop. Dogs running uphill or jumping or both (Afghan Hound and Puli) should be square-bodied.

In the ordinary trot, one forepaw is on the ground at all times; it is unnecessary for the rearing muscle to lift the front from the ground. Longer-bodied dogs do not use excess energy in the trot. Shorter-bodied dogs, trotting with a long stride, tend to have paws interfering with one another. At the slow trot used in the showring, square dogs are apt to display more faulty movement than longer-backed dogs.

The unique feature of the double suspension gallop is that the dog is short-bodied when it folds its back and long-bodied when it stretches out. At the moment the Greyhound is ready to take a forward leap, the rear legs are well under the forechest and the body is as short as possible (see Figure 2-8); after the leap is made the body is stretched out to give maximum distance. It is the flexible back that gives the Greyhound its extra speed.

The lengths of backs mentioned in a few breed Standards are as follows:

BASENJI (1990)—*Body—Balanced with a short back, short coupled and ending in a definite waist.*

NORWEGIAN ELKHOUND (1989)—*The body is short and close-coupled with the ribcage accounting for most of its length.*

COCKER SPANIEL (1992)—*Proportion—The measurement from the breast-bone to back of thigh is slightly longer than the measurement from the highest point of the withers to the ground. The body must be of sufficient length to permit a straight and free stride; the dog never appears long and low.*

CARDIGAN WELSH CORGI (1991)—*Body long and strong.*

POMERANIAN (1991)—*The body is cobby, being well ribbed and rounded.*

PUG (1991)—*The body is short and cobby, wide in chest and well ribbed up.*

GERMAN WIREHAIRED POINTER (1989)—*The body is a little longer than it is high, as ten is to nine.*

GERMAN SHEPHERD DOG (1994)—*The German Shepherd Dog is longer than tall, with the most desirable proportion as 10 to 8$^1/_2$.*

Optical Illusions

Spots and uneven markings on dogs often cause optical illusions, such as the appearance of a dip in the back where none exists. Different colors on separately moving legs make the eye seem to see what is not there.

On particolored dogs the hair in differently colored spots usually grows at different rates. The brown hair may grow at a slower rate than the white background. If the brown spot occurs at the withers, the shorter brown hair produces what appears to be a dip in the back. If the brown hair is on the outside of one rear leg and the other rear leg is white, the longer white hair makes one leg appear crooked compared to the other.

By using colors, artists can produce the illusion of depth on a flat canvas, even though no objects are pictured. The trick is to duplicate the brightness or dullness of colors in the sequence the eye sees them in nature. The eye records the brightest brights and the darkest darks in the foreground; that is: white, brilliant yellow, black, dark brown, etc. In depth the eye loses its ability to distinguish bright colors; colors fade into greyed or dull colors. By merely painting bright or dark colors on the exterior edges of a canvas and dull or greyed colors in the center, the illusion of depth is obtained. Multiple colors on dogs can cause distortion of depth perception, especially if duller-colored spots adjoin a brighter area. When bright and dull colors occur on opposite legs, critical observation must be made to avoid doing an injustice to a moving dog. Color illusions are deceptive.

Where longer hair adjoining shorter hair causes the illusion of a dip or hole, trimming hairs to equal length can relieve some of the distortion. It is difficult to overcome color depth perception effect; the brighter-colored hair must be slightly shorter than the dull hair.

When a dog with one black and one white paw moves, a judge must be aware of the limitations in interpreting what the eyes see. All that the brain records is an eggbeater coming forward. Perhaps the best way to judge such dogs is to look for other symptoms of poor movement and correlate these with what is observed. Bouncing hair on long-coated dogs indicates a rough gait. Do the withers glide, or bounce up and down? Does the dog roll? If all these indicate a smooth gait, maybe the fault is with the eye. Straightness of leg can be checked when the dog is posed; rapid movement of variable colors often causes the illusion of bending.

Long-coated dogs with color variations and in motion are extremely difficult to evaluate correctly. Fine silky coats flow in the breeze created by the dog's own motion. Flying leg feathering with multiple colors camouflages what the legs are doing. In particular, black and tan pattern on the hocks can cause optical illusions of poor movement when the dog is in fact moving correctly.

Stringing Up the Dog

People showing dogs with poor front movement have learned that holding up the head with a tight lead sometimes conceals faulty leg movement. Most pendulums move fairly straight.

In the German Shepherd Dog ring the process of "stringing up the dog" by a tight lead is not obvious. The forward momentum of a fast moving, *heavy* dog requires the handler to pull straight back on the lead to take weight off the front. Thus, the process of "stringing up" the German Shepherd Dog merely consists of the handler slowing down a bit so that the dog is pulling the handler around the ring. To all appearances, it looks like the handler cannot keep up with the dog. Stringing up a small dog is obvious; the lead is pulled up (vertically) and the tight lead is apparent.

To evaluate true movement dogs must move freely on a loose lead. Many wise older judges refuse to put a dog up that is shown on a tight lead; the handler either loosens the lead or the dog is not considered.

Some breed Standards require the dog to be shown on a loose lead.

> **FLAT-COATED RETRIEVER** (1990)—*Judging the Flat-Coat moving freely on a loose lead . . .*

> **GOLDEN RETRIEVER** (1990)—*It is recommended that dogs be shown on a loose lead to reflect true gait.*

> **AFGHAN HOUND** (1948)—*When on a loose lead, the Afghan can trot at a fast pace; stepping along, he has the appearance of placing the hind feet directly in the foot prints of the front feet, both thrown straight ahead.*

> **SIBERIAN HUSKY** (1990)— *. . . when in the show ring should be gaited on a loose lead at a moderately fast trot.*

Crabbing

Figure 8-8 shows a posed dog. Assuming that in the trot the front paw will be lifted off the ground in the middle of the dog's body (point O) and that the rear paw will be set down at that point, one stride will be from P to O or about equal to the height of the dog at the point of the shoulder blade. For the slow trot as usually performed in the ring, the dog's reach is about as shown (O to P). Whenever short body breeds go at a faster trotting rate, the feet must overreach one another. The correct sequence is to have the front paw lift off the ground just prior to the arrival of the rear paw. At the fastest trotting speeds, because of longer strides, many dogs have the rear paw move either inside or outside of the front paw. This is permitted in the German Shepherd Dog Standard: (1994)—*"The overreach of the hindquarters usually necessitates one hind foot passing outside and the other hind foot passing inside the track of the forefeet, and such*

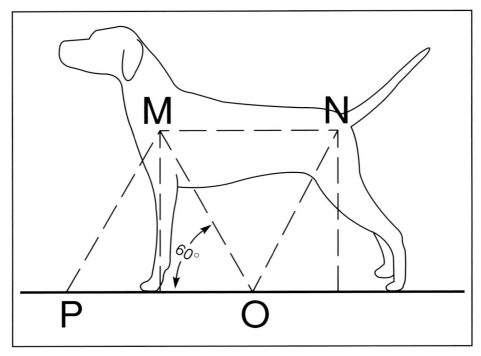

8-8. The posed dog.

action is not faulty unless the locomotion is crabwise with the dog's body sideways out of the normal straight line." Regardless of the method used to overreach, the dog should never crab; that is, the spine should be straight and pointed in the direction of travel. A dog that moves its rear out of line with the front, in order to avoid nicking feet, is faulty.

Excessive Angulation

As will be frequently stressed, every point on a dog has two limits: too much and too little. Excessive angulation of the rear quarters always seems to be a judging merit. *Because a Standard states "well angulated," it does NOT mean the more angulation the better.* Some attitudes seem to be, "If a little is good, a lot is better." A little bit of arsenic can be a medicine; a lot can be poison.

We must admit that because of time constraints at a show, dogs are judged on what *looks* correct, not on what *is* correct. So be it. Dog showing is a fancy, not a contest of speed, endurance, coursing of game, pointing or retrieving of game, herding, guarding or function. Excess angulation does not necessarily improve speed, endurance or function, but to some it looks nice.

Some breeds with greater than normal angulation have hip dysplasia problems. Wild dogs have medium angulation and shorter strides; the rotation of the hip socket is not excessive. Longer strides cause greater rotation in a ball and socket joint designed for lesser rotation. Some believe that some hip dysplasia is the result of excess rotation. Others think that the cause is poor breeding practices on the part of dog fanciers. Probably both contribute to the problem.

Rhythm Defects in Short-Legged Dogs

Short-legged dogs such as the Dachshund never have trouble in the trot with the rear feet hitting the front feet; the rear legs cannot reach as far forward as the front pawprints. Because of this reason, rear legs can travel out of rhythm with front legs.

Suppose that the rear legs have less reach than the front legs. Therefore, for both ends to cover the same distance in the same time, the rear legs must take more steps than the front legs. The legs, as the dog travels, will change rhythm. An unbalanced short-legged dog may start at a trot and change to an irregular gait rhythm. You can check your dog's pawprints in snow or sand. Short-legged dogs with legs out of rhythm often hop to get legs in cadence. This is similar to a soldier out of cadence who makes a quick double step to get into step. Hopping is an indication of a fault.

Experienced judges learn that some dogs are trained to trot at a given rate. Suppose that a short-legged dog with a good front and a poor rear was trained to trot in cadence at a slow speed. The front stride is adjusted to the rear stride; at faster speeds the rear cannot keep up. By asking the handler to move the dog faster, the judge discloses the problem; the dog will either occasionally hop with the rear legs or break into a gallop.

Balanced legs (front and rear legs capable of equal performance) on short-legged dogs are best observed by having the dogs move at different speeds.

The Roll (Old English Sheepdog)

Unlike other dogs, the Old English Sheepdog (Figure 8-9) is supposed to roll while at a slow trot. The Standard (1990) states: *"May amble or pace at slower speeds."* In effect this means that the dog, when trotting, rolls like a pacing (ambling) animal. This Standard means "amble" as used by horsemen. It is probably best described as a fast walk wherein the footfall is nearly, but *not exactly*, as that in the pace. The roll is not attained by moving with the feet far apart as in the Bulldog, but by flexible joints. It is best seen at a walk or a slow trot, and disappears at a gallop.

Handling Tricks

Usually the judge determines how and where dogs move in the ring. Clever handlers watch the judge prior to going into the ring to take full advantage of the time their dog will be evaluated by the judge.

If a judge allows the dogs to move in the order that they appear at the entrance to the ring, a handler with a dog whose profile looks best at a fast gait will try to be first in line. A handler with a dog whose profile looks best at a slow gait will aim for the end of the line (never the middle). Chances are there will be a slow-moving dog towards the middle of the line; the dog at the end of the line will appear to be moving slowly because of the slow-moving dogs ahead. The judge will not know whether the dog looks unfavorable at a faster rate or not.

The judge usually individually moves the dogs to carefully examine each (1) going away, (2) coming toward, (3) in profile. A wise handler knows the rate of speed at which a dog looks best for each of the three views. Thus, a dog going away may move best at a fast trot. On the other hand, the same dog with a serious front fault should be moved toward the judge at a slower rate. If a dog is poor in profile, side exposure to the judge should be as little as possible; the handler merely takes a U-turn and moves towards the judge, unless a judge's pattern dictates otherwise.

Dogs often show their best when baited with bits of food. When baiting small dogs, the handler often holds the bait too high, especially so if the dog is moving. If the dog's head is held high, the result is a hackney-like gait. While this result might be desirable for a Miniature Pinscher, it is a disaster for a short-legged Terrier.

Interfering

When the moving foot strikes the support foot, the fault is called interfering.

8-9. Old English Sheepdog (OES) and OES Herding.

(A) *Ashbey Photography Inc.*

(B) Herding—note gait is the amble.

Rope Walking or Weaving

When the moving leg swings around and in front of the supporting leg, the fault is called "rope walking" or "weaving." This fault is distinguished from paddling by the fact that in paddling the leg swings wider in an arc.

Lame Dogs

The AKC *Rules Applying to Registration and Dog Shows*, dated July 1, 1991, in Chapter 14, Section 8-B, states:

> *A dog that is lame at any show may not compete and shall not receive any award at that show. It shall be the judge's responsibility to determine whether a dog is lame. He shall not obtain the opinion of the show veterinarian. If in the judge's opinion a dog in the ring is lame, he shall withhold all awards from such dog and shall excuse it from the ring . . .*

Hip dysplasia, a degenerative disease of the ball and socket joint, which connects the pelvis and upper thigh, is prevalent among larger dogs and is often the cause of lameness. Most authorities believe that the disease can be controlled by selective breeding. Since hip dysplasia often results in lameness, this is just one justification for the AKC rule.

When a dog tends toward lameness, the fault is most readily observed on sharp turns. Wise judges insist upon handler and dog making right-angle turns during the individual examination.

9-1. Alaskan Malamute. *Booth Photography.*

CHAPTER 9

Application of Scientific Principles

Studying Standards by Similarities

The question frequently asked multi-breed judges is, "How can you possibly remember all of the points in breed Standards?" It is difficult. Most judges review frequently, especially the night before a show. The task is simplified by studying dogs of similar type, structure or movement as, for example, short-legged dogs (Dachshund, Basset, Corgi, Scottie, Skye, etc.). If the leg movement of one of these breeds is studied thoroughly, the knowledge gained can be applied to others. The AKC divisions of breeds by Group may or may not be a satisfactory study classification. The Sighthounds (similar in speed structure) are all in the Hound Group whereas the short-legged dogs are in the Terrier, Herding, Hound and Sporting groups. The Arctic dogs are in the Hound, Working, Non-Sporting and Toy Groups.

A person well acquainted with dogs should be able to picture what the structural design of a dog must be to efficiently perform a given task. Dogs used for like purposes tend to have similar builds.

A number of breeds or groups of breeds that have similarities are discussed below. There are other combinations besides those discussed, such as Retrievers, European gun dogs, Spaniels, Setters, sheep dogs, Poodles, Hounds, drovers and herding dogs. Those looking at Arctic breeds soon realize that they come from a common source.

Arctic Breeds

Arctic breeds (Alaskan Malamute, Akita, American Eskimo, Chow Chow, Keeshond, Norwegian Elkhound, Eskimo Dog, Samoyed, Finnish Spitz, Siberian Husky, Schipperke, Shiba Inu, Pomeranian) have heavy coats, straight to moderately angulated stifles and similar heads with small erect ears. These breeds are part of the Spitz group of dogs.

A summary of the desirable points of those Arctic dogs that do *heavy* draft work is as follows:

1. *Heavy muscles and heavy weight*

2. *Relatively steep shoulder blades*

3. *Tendency to straight stifles and hocks*

4. *Shorter legs than racing dogs (or longer bodies)*

5. *Short, heavily muscled neck and heavy head*

6. *Wide in the front and rear*

7. *Good footing (large feet)*

8. *Dense coat that readily sheds snow*

9. *Well furred (plume) tail*

In motion, heavy draft horses can use lateral instability to aid in pushing (pulling of the harness) by shifting weight in the collar, first to the right and then to the left. At heavy work, wide rears that enable the legs to be well apart are advantages. However, when moving at a brisk trot, even heavy animals tend to converge their feet.

The Alaskan Malamute (Figures 9-1, 11-1 and 11-2) is the heavy freighting dog of the Arctic breeds. Following are selected passages from its Standard (1994):

> The Alaskan Malamute, one of the oldest Arctic sled dogs, is a powerful and substantially built dog with a deep chest and strong, well-muscled body . . . The tail is well furred, carried over the back, and has the appearance of a waving plume. The Malamute must be a heavy boned dog with sound legs, good feet, deep chest and powerful shoulders, and have all of the other physical attributes necessary for the efficient performance of his job . . . He is not intended as a racing sled dog designed to compete in speed trials. The Malamute is structured for strength and endurance, and any characteristic of the individual specimen, including temperament, which interferes with the accomplishment of this purpose, is to be considered the most serious of faults . . . The feet are large, toes tight fitting and well arched. There is a protective growth of hair between the toes. The pads are thick and tough; toenails short and strong . . . IMPORTANT—In judging Malamutes, their function as a sledge dog for heavy freighting in the Arctic must be given consideration above all else . . .

The Akita (Figure 9-2) is a powerful Arctic dog. Its legs are particularly massive. In Japan, the lighter, more racy types are often seen, but in this country the Standard quite clearly describes the heavier dog with the Arctic coat and Arctic features.

For medium draft work, speed becomes more important, and lighter dogs intermediate between the racing dog and the heavy dog are wanted. Most intermediate and lightweight draft dogs are used for additional work purposes: herding and draft or hunting and draft, or all of these. The Samoyed (Figure 9-3) is a dog developed for herding reindeer and pulling sledges. The dog is neither racy nor slow; it is an intermediate type. Modification of structure, as compared to the Alaskan Malamute, requires flatter shoulder blades, more angulated legs, shorter body (but *not* square), rear not as wide, and nearly single tracking at faster gaits. Those who wrote the Samoyed Standard (1963 and 1993) knew their structural principles. Selected passages are as follows:

> The Samoyed should never be so heavy as to appear clumsy nor so light as to appear racy.

9-2. Akita. *Kohler Photo.*

Coat (*Texture and Condition*)—*The Samoyed is a double-coated dog. The body should be well covered with an undercoat of soft, short, thick, close wool with longer and harsh hair growing through it to form the outer coat, which stands straight out from the body and should be free from curl . . .*

Gait— *. . . Moving at a slow walk or trot, they will not single track, but as speed increases the legs gradually angle inward until the pads are finally falling on a line directly under the longitudinal center of the body. As the pad marks converge the forelegs and hind legs are carried straight forward in traveling, the stifles not turned in nor out. The back should remain strong, firm and level. A choppy or stilted gait should be penalized . . .*

Rear End—*Upper thighs should be well developed. Stifles well bent . . . Hocks should be well developed, sharply defined and set at approximately 30 per cent of hip height . . .*

Front End—*Legs should be parallel and straight to the pasterns. The pasterns should be strong, sturdy and straight, but flexible with some spring for proper let-down of feet. Because of depth of chest, legs should be moderately long. Length of leg from the ground to the elbow should be approximately 55 per cent of the total height at the withers—a very short-legged dog is to be depreciated. Shoulders should be long and sloping . . . and be firmly set. Out at the shoulders or out at the elbows should be penalized. The withers separation should be approximately 1–1$^{1}/_{2}$ inches.*

Feet—Large, long, flattish—*a hare-foot, slightly spread but not splayed; toes arched, pads thick and tough, with protective growth of hair between the toes.*

9-3. Samoyed. *Photo by Rich Bergman.*

Feet should turn neither in nor out in a natural stance but may turn in slightly in the act of pulling . . .

Neck *should blend into shoulders with a graceful arch.*

The withers forms the highest part of the back. Loins strong and slightly arched. The back should be straight to the loin, medium in length, very muscular and neither long nor short-coupled. The dog should be "just off square"—the length being approximately 5 per cent more than the height. Females allowed to be slightly longer than males.

The tail should be moderately long with the tail bone terminating approximately at the hock when down. It should be profusely covered with long hair . . .

The Norwegian Elkhound (Figure 3-8) is one of the better hunting dogs, primarily for moose or big game. Because of its ability to detect odors (trail), it has been placed in the Hound group at dog shows. However, it is not genetically related to the hounds. While the Elkhound did develop independently as a breed over thousands of years in Norway, its origin must have been from a common ancestor with other Arctic breeds.

NORWEGIAN ELKHOUND *(1988) — Hindquarters — Moderate angulation at stifle and hock. Thighs are broad and well muscled. Seen from behind, legs are straight, strong and without dewclaws.*

When a bull moose attacks the Elkhound, the short back and hind legs well under allow the dog to jump nimbly in and out, thus avoiding horns and forefeet. The ability to bounce like a rubber ball as well as trail are the essence of its structural perfection.

The Chow Chow was a Chinese hunting dog of Arctic origin. It has the straightest hock joint of the group, as shown in Figure 9-4. The Standard (1990) states:

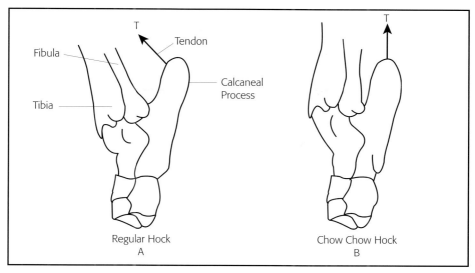

9-4. Regular hock vs. Chow Chow hock.

> *Hock joint well let down and appears almost straight. The hock joint must be strong, well knit and firm, never bowing or breaking forward or to either side. The hock joint and metatarsals lie in a straight line below the hip joint.*

The Keeshond was a Dutch dog used as a watchdog to sound an alarm. Early breeders preferred dogs that did not hunt; they wanted their dogs to stay home and protect the house. Breed structure is similar to ancestors of the north. The Pomeranian was bred down from the Spitz group of Arctic dogs used to pull sleds in Iceland and Lapland. Another of the Spitz group is the Finnish Spitz, noted as a companion and natural bark pointer.

The Siberian Husky was imported into Alaska as a sled dog of moderate speed, yet fairly strong. As a result the structure is more toward speed, as stated in the Standard (1990):

> *The Siberian Husky is a medium-size working dog, quick and light on his feet and free and graceful in action . . . He performs his original function in harness most capably, carrying a light load at a moderate speed over great distances. His body proportions and form reflect this basic balance of power, speed and endurance.*

Sighthounds

The Sighthounds (Gazehounds) are of desert origin and later adapted to other areas, as the Greyhound did in England. The Scenthounds are quite different in that they lack the "racy" build. Originally the purpose of Sighthounds was to have a dog fast enough to catch and strong enough to kill the game. Straightaway speed was not the only consideration; strength, courage, endurance and sagacity ranked high. Thus, the Deerhound had to be bigger and stronger than the "rabbit hound," but both needed speed, agility and cleverness to catch the game.

The pelvis and loin formations account for obvious variations between Sighthound breeds. To understand the differences a definition of the terms "roached" and "arched" is needed. If the backline rises from the withers to the loin in a curve and if the topline then falls away to the tail, it is a roach. A roached back has an outline similar to an arched doorway or the Bedlington Terrier. Many breeds require an arch over the loin; the arch is due to loin muscle development. Strong loin muscle is a requirement in all Sighthounds.

In England until 1831 only the upper class were permitted to keep Greyhounds. After that date, with repeal of the law, public coursing became popular. At the time the Sighthound Standard was written, a coursing dog was described, not a sprinter (Figure 1-2). Dogs seen on the racetrack do not conform to the AKC Standard, nor should they. Their purpose is different.

The Greyhound was described by Dame Juliana Berners, in her "Boke of St. Albans" of 1486, the first sporting book published in English.

The Properties of a Good Greyhound

A Greyhound should be headed like a snake,
And necked like a drake,
Footed like a cat,
Tailed like a rat,
Sided like a teme,
Backbone like a beam.

The small head ("headed like a snake") was to give added speed. The neck of the drake (long) was long enough to allow the dog to reach down and readily grasp a running hare. The cat foot was insisted upon by many of the early breeders (to give agility and endurance). It should be noted that the cheetah has doglike pads and non-retractable claws on catlike paws. Speed can be attained without the hare foot. The present Greyhound Standard calls for a foot rather more hare- than cat-feet. The word "teme" has been written as "bream" (a sunfish) by many writers.

Although the Greyhound Standard is short (refer to Chapter 1 for the full Standard), those who understand structure for speed, endurance and agility can quickly grasp the intent of the words. In coursing hare, the fastest dog is not always the best. Those with sufficient speed to overtake the hare and the ability to maneuver quickly usually catch the rabbit.

The structure required for straightaway speed for short distances (Whippet racing and short Greyhound races in particular) is different from that advantageous for long runs with agility. High hocks, straight front assembly (including shoulder blade) and long bodies can produce high initial speed.

A fall away of the croup on a coursing Greyhound is not a disadvantage **provided** that the loin is flexible enough to allow the rear legs to fully extend in a gallop. A good galloping Greyhound, when airborne, has the front and rear legs *as well as* the body extended in an almost straight line. (Refer to Figure 2-8.) In the exploding portion of the gallop (legs over-reaching one another) the back is doubled under so that the pelvis is at a steep angle. A very essential feature of the Greyhound is a **flexible back**; the most serious fault is an arched back without the ability to straighten, or a flat back that cannot flex. Most coursing Greyhounds have a flat back with the loin and pelvis falling away (not roached). If speed alone were the consideration, the Standard would not call for low hocks.

The Whippet (Figure 10-6) should suggest speed with its flowing lines, balance and elegance. A dog with the proper length of neck will *appear* to be much taller than a dog with a short neck. In proportion the Whippet is basically a square dog. The fact that the Whippet looks long and *should* look long comes from a long, sweeping, well angulated rear. The Whippet should cover ground; i.e., pasterns to rear hocks. A Whippet with a properly constructed rear will have a broad hock.

The Afghan Hound (Figure 4-11) originated in Afghanistan, a hilly and mountainous country. The Afghan Hound has much of the speed of the Greyhound, even though it is a specialist in negotiating crags, ravines and uneven ground. For this, a compact and well coupled dog is necessary rather than a long-loined racing dog whose first quality is speed. The Afghan Hound has agility, and as a hurdle racer it has no equal. The structural features of the Greyhound are altered in the Afghan Hound. The prominent hip bones, modified pelvis and large but springy feet are the most obvious features advantageous for leaping. A bounding gait is best attained by the rear legs well under, strong rearing muscles, a short body and springy feet. In the following Standard (1948) the words, *"Tail set not too high on the body,"* and *"faults, goose rump"* should be noted; the dog is intermediate between these two extremes. The head carried high aids jumping since the center of gravity is shifted toward the rear.

Neck—*The neck is of good length, strong and arched, running in a curve to the shoulders which are long and sloping and well laid back. Faults—Neck too short or too thick; a ewe neck; a goose neck; a neck lacking in substance.*

Body—*The back line appearing practically level from the shoulders to the loin. Strong and powerful loin and slightly arched, falling away toward the stern, with the hipbones very pronounced; well ribbed and tucked up in flanks. The height at the shoulders equals the distance from the chest to the buttocks; the brisket well let down, and of medium width. Faults—Roach back, sway back, goose rump, slack loin; lack of prominence of hipbones; too much width of brisket, causing interference with elbows.*

Tail—*Tail set not too high on body, having a ring, or a curve on the end; should never be curled over, or rest on the back, or be carried sideways; and should never be bushy.*

Legs—*Forelegs are straight and strong with great length between elbow and pasterns; elbows well held in; forefeet large in both length and width; toes well arched; feet covered with long thick hair, fine in texture; pasterns long and straight; pads of feet unusually large and well down on the ground. Shoulders have plenty of angulation so that the legs are well set underneath the dog. Too much straightness of shoulder causes the dog to break down in the pasterns, and this is a serious fault. All four feet of the Afghan Hound are in line with the body, turning neither in nor out. The hind feet are broad and of good length; the toes arched, and covered with long thick hair; hindquarters powerful and well muscled, with great length between hip and hock; hocks are well let down; good angulation of both stifle and hock; slightly bowed from hock to crotch. Faults—Front or back feet thrown outward or inward; pads of feet not thick enough; or feet too small; or any other evidence of weakness in feet; weak or broken down pasterns; too straight in stifle; too long in hock.*

Gait—*When running free, the Afghan Hound moves at a gallop, showing great elasticity and spring in his smooth, powerful stride. When on a loose lead, the Afghan can trot at a fast pace; stepping along, he has the appearance of placing the hind feet directly in the footprints of the front feet, both thrown straight ahead. Moving with*

9-5. Saluki. *Photo by E. M. Gilbert Jr.*

> *head and tail high, the whole appearance of the Afghan Hound is one of great style and beauty.*

The Standard for the Saluki (Figure 9-5) under *General Appearance* sums up the essence of the breed. One point that seems to bewilder the newcomer to the breed is the wide variation in height—"*Dogs should average in height from 23 to 28 inches and bitches may be considerably smaller, this being very typical of the breed.*" This variation in size is due to the wide environmental extremes in which the Saluki lived, and therefore the wide variation in game that it hunted. Salukis ranged from Egypt throughout the Middle East to the mountains of Iraq and Iran bordering on the Caspian Sea, down to the southern tip of the Arabian peninsula on the Indian Ocean. The environmental extremes in this area of the world vary from hot and dry (little to no rainfall) to moderate temperatures and normal rainfall. As a result, the size of the game varied from the small gazelle (19 inches at the shoulder) in Yemen, to the wild ass and normal size gazelle in the mountains of Iraq. The Saluki Standard (adopted by AKC in 1929) under *General Appearance* states: "*The whole appearance of this breed should give an impression of grace and symmetry and of great speed and endurance coupled with strength and activity to enable it to kill gazelle or other quarry over deep sand or rocky mountains. The expression should be dignified and gentle with deep, faithful, far-seeing eyes. Dogs should average in height from 23 to 28 inches and bitches may be considerably smaller, this being very typical of the breed.*"

There are two varieties of the Saluki: the feathered and the smooth. The coat of the feathered is *"smooth and of a soft silky texture, slight feather on the legs, feather at the back of the thighs and sometimes with slight woolly feather on thigh and shoulder."* In addition the feet are *"well feathered between the toes,"* and the tail is *"well feathered on the underside with long silky hair, not bushy."* The smooth has the same conformation as the feathered *"with the exception of the coat, which has no feathering."* It should be pointed out that the texture of coat of the smooth is a harsh, not a soft, silky texture.

When describing the neck and back, the Scottish Deerhound Standard (1935) clearly states the purpose of this dog as compared to the Greyhound.

> **Neck**—*The neck should be long—of a length befitting the Greyhound character of the dog. Extreme length is neither necessary nor desirable. Deerhounds do not stoop to their work like the Greyhounds . . . The neck, however, must be strong as is necessary to hold a stag.*

> *The loin well arched and drooping to the tail. A straight back is not desirable, this formation being unsuitable for uphill work, and very unsightly.*

Some hooved animals have structures designed to give them superior ability to run uphill and thus escape. Using an arched loin to get the legs well under would give the dog better performance going uphill. In the showring the reason given, *"very unsightly,"* is a command to the judge to approve the arched loin, irrespective of whether he thinks it is scientifically correct or not. If the Standard is clear, that is the rule; personal opinion is without merit.

The Ibizan Hound (Figure 9-6) is a Sighthound whose primary quarry is hares and rabbits. Above all, this is a hound of function, not fashion. It should be in lean, hard running condition. The last few ribs and the points of the hip are visible when the hound is in show or hunting condition. The Ibizan is a hound of moderation and, with the exception of the ears, brisket and prominent breastbone, should not be extreme or exaggerated. The distinguishing features of the breed are light pigment; large, erect, properly shaped ears; prominent, sharply angulated breastbone; and the lithe, racy, sinewy, angular-bodied, fine-boned appearance.

The chest *"is deep and long with the breastbone sharply angled and prominent. The ribs are slightly sprung. The brisket is approximately $2^1/_2$ inches above the elbow. The deepest part of the chest, behind the elbow, is nearly to or to the elbow."* The abdomen is well tucked up, but not as deeply tucked as the Greyhound.

The deepest part of the brisket is behind the elbow because of a rather upright upper arm. *"The shoulder blades are well laid back. At the point of shoulder they join to a rather upright upper arm. The elbow is positioned in front of the deepest part of the chest . . . "*

The gait of the Ibizan is quite different from the other Sighthounds. The gait from the side view should show joint flexion. It is not a hackney but rather an up-and-forward movement that is not desirable in the other Sighthounds. This movement is elegant, graceful and floating. As the Standard (1989) states: *"An efficient, light and graceful single tracking movement. A suspended trot with joint flexion when viewed from the side. The Ibizan exhibits smooth reach in front with balanced rear drive, giving the appearance of skimming over the ground."*

The Standard (1989) for the Pharaoh Hound (Figure 9-7) states: *"General appearance is one of grace, power and speed. The Pharaoh Hound is medium sized, of noble bearing with hard clean-cut lines—graceful, well balanced, very fast with free easy movement and*

9-6. Ibizan Hound. *Kohler Photo.*

9-7. Pharoah Hound. *Photo by Joan Ludwig.*

alert expression . . . Length of body from breast to haunch bone slightly longer than height of withers to ground . . . Deep brisket almost down to the point of elbow . . . Moderated sweep of stifle . . . Gait—Free and flowing; the head should be held fairly high and the dog should cover the ground well without any apparent effort. The legs and feet should move in line with the body; any tendency to throw the feet sideways, or a high stepping 'hackney' action is a definite fault."

Even though there are many similar conformation characteristics between the Ibizan and the Pharoah, they move quite differently. The suspended trot with joint flexion is peculiar to only the Ibizan. The Pharoah has a higher front action than the other Sighthounds, but definitely less front action than the Ibizan.

Terriers

Terrier breeds can be classified as long-legged or short-legged. Long-legged Terriers have straight legs with feet pointing straight forward. When they dig they throw the earth back under the body and through their spread rear legs. Short-legged Terriers, having their body close to the ground, throw the earth to the side. Therefore the short-legged, based on their function, should have feet that toe out slightly. If a short-legged Terrier does not toe out, most would overlook this functional fault—as some of the Standards do, e.g., Australian, Border and Sealyham Terriers.

The other short-legged Terrier Standards read as follows:

> **CAIRN TERRIER** (1938)— . . . *forefeet may be slightly turned out.* (Refer to Figure 4-18 for the Cairn.)

> **DANDIE DINMONT TERRIER** (1991)—*Feet point forward or very slightly outward.*

> **NORFOLK TERRIER** (1990)—*Short, powerful legs, as straight as is consistent with the digging terrier.*

> **NORWICH TERRIER** (1990)—*Short, powerful legs, as straight as is consistent with the digging terrier.*

> **SCOTTISH TERRIER** (1993)—*The forefeet should be larger than the hind feet, round, thick and compact with strong nails. The front feet should point straight ahead, but a slight "toeing out" is acceptable.*

> **SKYE TERRIER** (1990)—*Large hare-feet preferably pointing forward . . .*

> **WEST HIGHLAND WHITE TERRIER** (1989)—*Forefeet . . . they may properly be turned out slightly.*

The Scottish Terrier (Figure 9-8) is a digging breed, so its feet are important, as noted above. The General Appearance portion of the Standard (1993) provides a concise description of the breed. It states: "*General Appearance—The Scottish Terrier is a small, compact, short-legged, sturdily-built dog of good bone and substance. His head is long in proportion to his size. He has a hard, wiry, weather-resistant coat and a thick-set, cobby*

9-8. Scottish Terrier.
Photo by Ashbey.

body which is hung between short, heavy legs. These characteristics, joined with his very special keen, piercing, 'varminty' expression, and his erect ears and tail are salient features of the breed. The Scottish Terrier's bold, confident, dignified aspect exemplifies power in a small package."

The body is moderately short, comprising a long ribcage that is heart-shaped in cross section, with a short, strong loin that is deep in the flanks. The coat is a broken coat—*"hard, wiry outercoat with a soft, dense undercoat."*

The head of the Scottish Terrier has several unique features associated with the length of the head, its nose, eyes and ears. The head is quite long for a ten-inch dog, but it is also strong in that it is of medium width. In addition the nose projects somewhat over the lower jaw, giving the impression of a longer upper jaw, and also making the muzzle appear longer than the braincase. The eyes are dark brown, small, almond shaped and set wide apart and with the proper stop well in under the brow. The ears are natural, small, prick, set well up on the skull and pointed. Their use, size, shape and placement and their "erect carriage are major elements of the keen, alert, intelligent Scottish Terrier expression." This expression combines with the bold, confident carriage of head and tail and temperament to provide the Terrier character that all Scotties must possess in the showring.

The Sealyham Terrier (Figure 9-9) Standard (1974) defines the essence of the breed by stating: *"should be the embodiment of power and determination, ever keen and alert, of extraordinary substance, yet free from clumsiness."* The English Standard states, *"presenting a balanced picture of great substance in a small compass"*—meaning much in little.

The head is long, approximately three-quarters the height at the withers, broad and powerful, with keen Terrier expression. The ears are thin, folded level with the top of the head, and well rounded at the tip. The neck is relatively long, slightly less than two-thirds of the height at the withers. The entire dog is built for hunting on both land and water, and going to ground for such game as the Badger. He should not be so heavy that he lacks endurance, nor so light that he cannot fight his prey if the occasion demands it. He has a broken coat. In the show ring, he must display that Terrier spirit, along with movement that is *sound, strong, quick, free, true and level.*

9-9. Sealyham Terrier.

9-10. Welsh Terrier.

Those Terrier breeds that require an upright tail have the tail set well up on the back, such as the Airedale, Smooth and Wire Fox Terrier, Irish and others. In general the longer-backed Terriers carry their tails down.

The so-called Terrier front as exemplified by the Fox Terrier is common to some Terriers, certainly not all. In addition to Terriers, the Beagle, Harrier and American Foxhound Standards describe the same type of front.

The Terriers, as a group, are noted for courage. Their work is to force game out of its lair (not to kill the game underground) or to indicate the game's whereabouts by barking. Most Terriers are diggers. The Fox Terrier (Figure 10-1) worked with hounds (usually Foxhounds), and was usually carried on horses until a fox was holed. The dog was then set down to drive the fox into the open.

The "Fox Terrier front" (Figure 5-16) has a short upper arm that is about level with the keel; it has a pendulum-like motion rather than the flexing motion of the joints. This does not mean that the Fox Terrier does not bend its pasterns when in motion; it does, but not as much as some other breeds.

The short upper arm is due to the way the front is assessed. (Refer to Chapter 5, Figure 5-6.) The hand is used to span from the top of the shoulder (A) to the point of the shoulder (B); therefore the head of the upper arm or humerus is included in the "measurement" of the shoulder. The hand then spans from the point of the shoulder (B) to the elbow (C); the actual upper arm is not measured. The more upright the upper arm is, the longer the "measurement" of the shoulder becomes, and the shorter the "measurement" of the upper arm becomes.

Some authors believe that the short upper arm evolved because it was advantageous in going to ground; the dog could work on its keel with legs free to dig. While the short upper arm is advantageous for digging, it is difficult to explain by the same reason why some of the non-digging Terriers and the Beagle have similar fronts. Other reasons must exist.

9-11. Kerry Blue Terrier. *Photo by Joan Ludwig.*

The Welsh Terrier (Figure 9-10), a long-legged Terrier, was used on otter, fox and badger. As stated in the Standard (1993): "*The Welsh Terrier is a sturdy, compact, rugged dog of medium size with a coarse wire-textured coat. The legs, underbody, and head are tan; the jacket black (or occasionally grizzle). The tail is docked to a length meant to complete the image of a 'square dog' approximately as high as he is long. The movement is a terrier trot typical of the long-legged terrier. It is effortless, with good reach and drive. The 'Welsh Terrier expression' comes from the set, color, and position of the eyes combined with the use of the ears. The Welsh Terrier is friendly, outgoing to people and other dogs, showing spirit and courage.*"

The Kerry Blue Terrier (Figure 9-11), another long-legged Terrier, is an Irish dog used for trailing, retrieving (land or water), herding cattle or sheep, guarding and small-game hunting. The dog was not developed for a specialized purpose; the breed's structure and parts must be all-purpose. The joints are more angular than the Fox Terrier's and in the gait the joints flex more. It is only by watching the breed in the ring that this is observed; the following Standard does not point out these differences.

KERRY BLUE TERRIER (1992)— . . . *Head*—Long, but not exaggerated, and in good proportion to the rest of the body. Well balanced . . .

Neck, Topline, Body—Neck—Clean and moderately long, gradually widening to the shoulders upon which it should be well set and carried proudly. Back short, strong and straight (i.e., level), with no appearance of slackness. Chest deep and of but moderate breadth. Ribs fairly well sprung, deep rather than round. A slight tuck-up, loin short and powerful. Tail should be set on high, of moderate length and carried gaily erect, the straighter the tail the better.

Forequarters—Shoulders fine, long and sloping, well laid back and well knit. The elbows hanging perpendicularly to the body and working clear of the side in movement.

The forelegs should be straight from both front and side view. The pasterns short, straight and hardly noticeable. Feet should be strong, compact, fairly round and moderately small, with good depth of pad free from cracks, the toes arched, turned neither in nor out, with black toenails.

Hindquarters—*Strong and muscular with full freedom of action, free from droop or crouch, the thighs long and powerful, stifles well bent and turned neither in nor out, hocks near the ground and, when viewed from behind, upright and parallel with each other, the dog standing well up on them . . .*

Gait—*Full freedom of action. The elbows hanging perpendicularly to the body and working clear of the sides in movement; both forelegs and hind legs should move straight forward when traveling, the stifles turning neither in nor out.*

Short-Legged Dogs

Regardless of what short-legged dogs are used for, they have several similar structural limitations. Short legs are useful for digging, crawling through low passageways, and getting the mouth and nose close to the ground. But short legs decrease speed and jumping ability.

The most efficient way to lower a dog's body and yet retain a long stride is to have well angulated legs. The well built Dachshund (Figures 9-12 and 5-9) represents structural perfection for a short-legged digging dog. The leg parts are of equal length to fold under the dog; the dog rests on its keel when digging; the body is tapered in order to get through the narrow passages (either by going forward or backing out). The neck is powerful and the teeth sharp. When moving the head back and forth, the quick-acting neck muscles allow the eye to see only a blur, an ideal defense mechanism. The important words of the Standard describing structural conformation are:

DACHSHUND (1992): *General Appearance—Low to ground, long in body and short of leg with robust muscular development . . . the Dachshund is well-balanced with bold and confident head carriage . . . His hunting spirit, good nose, loud tongue and distinctive build make him well-suited for below-ground work and for beating the bush . . .*

Jaws *opening wide and hinged well back of the eyes, with strongly developed bones and teeth.*

9-12. Dachshund.
Photo by Kohler.

Teeth—Powerful canine teeth: teeth fit closely together in a scissors bite . . .

Neck—Long, muscular, clean-cut, without dewlap, slightly arched in the nape, flowing gracefully into the shoulders.

Trunk—The trunk is long and fully muscled. When viewed in profile, the back lies in the straightest possible line between the withers and the short very slightly arched loin.

Forequarters—For effective underground work, the front must be strong, deep, long and cleanly muscled. Forequarters in detail: **Chest—***The breastbone is strongly prominent in front so that on either side a depression or dimple appears. When viewed from the front, the thorax appears oval and extends downward to the mid-point of the forearm. The enclosing structure of well-sprung ribs appears full and oval to allow, by its ample capacity, complete development of heart and lungs. The keel merges gradually into the line of the abdomen and extends well beyond the front legs. Viewed in profile, the lowest point of the breast line is covered by the front leg.* **Shoulder Blades—***Long, broad, well laid-back and firmly placed upon the fully developed thorax, closely fitted at the withers, furnished with hard yet pliable muscles.* **Upper Arm—***Ideally the same length as the shoulder blade and at right angles to the latter, strong of bone and hard of muscle, lying close to the ribs, with elbows close to the body, yet capable of free movement.* **Forearm—***Short; supplied with hard yet pliable muscles on the front and outside, with tightly stretched tendons on the inside and at the back, slightly curved inwards. The joints between the forearms and the feet (wrists) are closer together than the shoulder joints, so that the front does not appear absolutely straight. Knuckling over is a disqualifying fault.* **Feet—***Front paws are full, tight, compact, with well-arched toes and tough, thick pads. They may be equally inclined a trifle outward. There are five toes, four in use, close together with a pronounced arch and strong, short nails. Front dewclaws may be removed.*

Hindquarters—Strong and cleanly muscled. The pelvis, the thigh, the second thigh, and the metatarsus are ideally the same length and form a series of right angles. From the rear, the thighs are strong and powerful. The legs turn neither in nor out.

Metatarsus—Short and strong, perpendicular to the second thigh bone. When viewed from behind, they are upright and parallel. **Hind Paws—***Smaller than the front paws with four compactly closed and arched toes with tough, thick pads. The entire foot points straight ahead and is balanced equally on the ball and not merely on the toes. Rear dewclaws should be removed.* **Croup—***Long, rounded and full, sinking slightly toward the tail.* **Tail—***Set in continuation of the spine, extending without kinks, twists, or pronounced curvature, and not carried too gaily.*

The Pembroke Welsh Corgi (Figure 9-13), from the point of view of origin, is probably related to the Arctic breeds and the Border Collie. It is said that the Pembroke is *not* of common ancestry with the Dachshund as is the Cardigan Welsh Corgi. In the nineteenth century the two were crossed to a limited extent.

At the time the king owned most of the land, Welsh tenant farmers were permitted to fence off a few acres around their houses. Cows could be pastured on common land. Corgis drove the cows as far out as possible to the better grass areas and brought them in the evening. They also chased other cows away by nipping at their heels.

9-13. Pembroke Welsh Corgi. *Photo by Rich Bergman.*

Their short legs enabled them to duck kicks from the cow and put the teeth down where they were most effective.

The Pembroke is shorter in body than the Cardigan, higher on leg, with a finer coat, straighter legs and lighter boned. The Cardigan (Figure 10-2) Standard reads in part:

> **WELSH CORGI, CARDIGAN** (1991)—*General Appearance—Low set with moderately heavy bone and deep chest. Overall silhouette long in proportion to height, culminating in a low tail set and fox-like brush.*
>
> **General Impression**—*A handsome, powerful, small dog, capable of both speed and endurance, intelligent, sturdily built but not coarse.*
>
> **Size, Proportion, Substance**—*Overall balance is more important than absolute size . . . Back length (from the base of neck to the base of the tail) should be approximately 1.5 times greater than the height . . .*
>
> **Neck, Topline, Body**—*Neck moderately long and muscular without throatiness. Well developed, especially in males, and in proportion to the dog's build. Neck well set on, fits into strong, well shaped shoulders. Topline level. Body long and strong. Chest moderately broad with prominent breastbone. Deep brisket, with well sprung ribs to allow for good lungs. Ribs extending well back. Loin short, strong, moderately tucked up. Waist well defined.* **Croup**—*Slightly downward slope to the tail set. Tail set fairly low on body line and reaching well below hock. Carried low when standing or moving slowly, streaming out parallel to the ground when at a dead run, lifted when excited, but never curled over the back. High tail set is a serious fault.*
>
> **Forequarters**—*The moderately broad chest tapers to a deep brisket, well let down between the forelegs. Shoulders slope downward and outward from the withers sufficiently to accommodate desired rib-spring. Shoulder blade (scapula) long and well-laid back, meeting upper arm (humerus) at close to a right angle. Humerus nearly as long as scapula. Elbows should fit close, being neither loose nor tied. The forearms*

(ulna and radius) should be curved to fit spring of ribs. The curve in the forearm makes the wrists (carpal joints) somewhat closer together than the elbows. The pasterns are strong and flexible. Dewclaws removed. The feet are relatively large and rounded, with well filled pads. They point slightly outward from a straight ahead position to balance the width of the shoulders. This outward point is not to be more than 30 degrees from center line; neither straight nor so crooked as to appear unsound. Overall, the bone should be heavy for a dog of this size, but not so heavy as to appear coarse or reduce agility . . .

Hindquarters—*Well muscled and strong, but slightly less wide than shoulders. Hipbone (pelvis) slopes downward with the croup, forming a right angle with the femur at the hip socket. There should be moderate angulation at stifle and hock. Hocks well let down. Metatarsi perpendicular to the ground and parallel to each other. Dewclaws removed. Feet point straight ahead and are slightly smaller and more oval than front. Toes arched. Pads well filled. Overall the hindquarters must denote sufficient power to propel this low, relatively heavy herding dog efficiently over rough terrain.*

Gait—*Free and smooth. Effortless . . . This is a herding dog which must have the agility, freedom of movement, and endurance to do the work for which he was developed.*

The crook in the front leg enables the dog to let the legs converge and approach single tracking. A tail set low on the body line improves agility.

Mastiff Type Dogs

These dogs, although greatly diversified, have many similarities. They originated in the mountains of Europe and Asia (Pyrenees, Massif Central of France, Alps, Himalayas and mountains of Tibet).

Muzzles are usually very short or medium short, and the head usually possesses pronounced stop, large drop ears, heavy coats, and an acute power of scent. The more common breeds are Mastiff, Great Pyrenees, St. Bernard, Newfoundland, Hycrancan (India), Molossian (Roman, extinct), Bullmastiff and Rottweiler. The Great Dane, having been crossed with the Greyhound, is modified in build compared to the others.

Herding dogs have two purposes: (1) to protect the herd from wild animals and marauders, and (2) to keep the herd together, drive the herd and cut out individuals. Protection, at one time, required a large massive dog that could drive off wolves, bears or big cats. Since the extinction of large predators in settled areas, the work of these dogs has diminished. The herding instinct is not related to the ability to protect; a Corgi has excellent herding ability but is hardly big enough to fight bears or wolves. Because the smaller dogs require less food, they are now more numerous.

Prior to the invention of gunpowder, the massive large dogs were used as war dogs; ferocity was in their nature. The Romans in traveling through the mountain regions of Europe left some of their massive Molossian dogs; these were bred to native dogs to produce some of the modern breeds.

The Mastiff is noted historically as a fighting dog, but today it is noted for both good nature and protectiveness. The Standard defines the differences between the dogs and bitches. (Refer to Figure 9-14.) The Standard (1991) states:

9-14. Mastiff. *Fox and Cook Photography.*

The Mastiff is a large, massive, symmetrical dog with a well-knit frame. The impression is one of grandeur and dignity. Dogs are more massive throughout. Bitches should not be faulted for being somewhat smaller in all dimensions while maintaining a proportionally powerful structure . . . Proportion—Rectangular, the length of the dog from forechest to rump is somewhat longer than the height at the withers. The height of the dog should come from depth of body rather than from length of leg. Substance—Massive, heavy boned, with a powerful muscle structure. Great depth and breadth desirable.

The index of a breed is found in the head—this is definitely true of the Mastiff. The Standard does an excellent job in defining what is proper for the Mastiff head; as with the body, the head has a massive appearance from any angle. The breed is moderately angulated and the proper rear is defined as: *"When the portion of the leg below the hock is correctly 'set back' and stands perpendicular to the ground a plumb line dropped from the rearmost point of the hindquarters will pass in front of the foot. This rules out straight hocks, and since stifle angulation varies with hock angulation, it also rules out insufficiently angulated stifles."*

The Bullmastiff (Figure 9-15), as stated in the Standard (1992), had foundation breeding of 60 percent Mastiff and 40 percent Bulldog. There is a tendency for a shortened foreface by reverting toward the Bulldog head. As stated, this is very undesirable. What is desired is a *"symmetrical animal, showing great strength, endurance, and alertness; powerfully built but active . . . The breed was developed in England by gamekeepers for protection against poachers."*

The points to look for in the Bullmastiff are: moderate angulation, head type, expression, proper bite, substance without coarseness, excellent muscle tone, moderate length neck, compact body and great power in movement.

The gait is described as follows: *"Free, smooth, and powerful. When viewed from the side, reach and drive indicate maximum use of the dog's moderate angulation. Back remains*

9-15. Bullmastiff. *Photo by Joan Ludwig.*

level and firm. Coming and going, the dog moves in a straight line. Feet tend to converge under the body, without crossing over, as speed increases. There is no twisting in or out at the joints."

The Great Pyrenees (Figure 9-16), a guard and herding dog of the Pyrenees Mountains, has its purpose clearly described in its Standard.

> **GREAT PYRENEES** (1990)—*General Appearance*—The Great Pyrenees dog conveys the distinct impression of elegance and unsurpassed beauty combined with great overall size and majesty. He has a white or principally white coat that may contain markings of badger, gray, or varying shades of tan. He possesses a keen intelligence and a kindly, while regal, expression. Exhibiting a unique elegance of bearing and movement, his soundness and coordination show unmistakably the purpose for which he has been bred, the strenuous work of guarding the flocks in all kinds of weather on the steep mountain slopes of the Pyrenees.
>
> *Temperament*—Character and temperament are of utmost importance. In nature, the Great Pyrenees is confident, gentle, and affectionate. While territorial and protective of his flock or family when necessary, his general demeanor is one of quiet composure, both patient and tolerant. He is strong willed, independent and somewhat reserved, yet attentive, fearless and loyal to his charges both human and animal.

Correct Great Pyrenees type is defined above under *General Appearance* and *temperament*. Additionally, correct head conformation consists of smooth, flowing lines with no apparent stop and proper eye expression. The eye expression is referred to as a far away, almost dreamy look or *elegant, intelligent and contemplative.* Unique characteristics are: "*Double dewclaws are located on each rear leg; rear feet have a structural tendency to toe out. This breed characteristic is not to be confused with cow hocks. When present, a 'shepherd's crook' at the end of the tail accentuates the plume.*"

9-16. Great Pyrenees..

(A) Stacked. *Photo by Rich Bergman.*

(B) Stride is well balanced with good reach and strong drive. *Photo by Kitten Rodwell.*

The thickness of the weather-resistant double coat requires that a hand examination confirm a visual examination of the dog. The tail is "*carried low in repose and may be carried over the back, 'making the wheel' when aroused . . . When gaiting, the tail may be carried either over the back or low. Both carriages are equally correct.*"

The Newfoundland is similar in some respects to the Great Pyrenees and may have been derived from it. Unlike the Pyrenees, it was developed as a superior water dog for icy conditions. Stonehenge in 1871 stated: "The speed with which the Newfoundland swims is very great, his large legs and feet enabling him to paddle himself with great force." Also, "From their great size and strength they are able to beat off most dogs when they are attacked, and their thick coats prevent the teeth of their assailants from doing much damage."

The Rottweiler (Figure 9-17) is closely related to the Roman war dogs, possibly a direct descendant. Its purpose in Roman times was to drive herds of cattle for the armies as well as guard or fight. Later the dog was used for cattle driving, pulling carts and

9-17. Rottweiler. *Photo by Stephen Klein.*

guarding. Cattlemen on buying trips often tied their purses around a Rottweiler's neck; few dared molest the dog.

Dog people characterize this group of similar dogs as having a Mastiff-like head and a massive body. A smaller version of the head is seen in the Bulldog, Pug and Boston Terrier. Today, the ability to bite people is not condoned at dog shows; a ferocious nature is unacceptable. Because of the origin of these breeds, constant care must be taken in breeding programs to prevent development of undesirable social traits.

Aesthetic Breeds

The art of judging dogs can be defined as the skill or the power of performing judging actions, acquired by experience, study or observation. Some breeds are judged more upon structural perfection, others more on aesthetic principles and others more on conformation to a narrowly defined type. Those breeds that are judged more by beauty than by structure depend upon the judge's application of skill and taste according to aesthetic principles; i.e., beauty of form, color and movement.

After meeting type requirements, which may or may not be stringent, many breeds of dogs, Toy dogs in particular, are to please people; beauty of form, color and graceful movement are the primary judging considerations. The Boston Terrier (Figure 9-18), Pomeranian, Chinese Crested (Figures 9-19 and 9-20), Maltese, Lhasa Apso (Figure 6-6), Pekingese, Poodle and Shih Tzu (Figure 7-14) are a few in this classification. For such breeds the student must study each by individual attention; no conformity to a group pattern exists. For many the quality, color and pattern of the coat is far more important than teeth or bone. To understand such breeds, prospective judges must devote much time talking to breeders and reading breed literature.

Breeds that please people more by their aesthetic qualities than by their structural qualities tend to cause a difference of opinion between breeder-judges and all-rounder judges. For example, there is the exact color pattern and shape of the Boston Terrier; the breeder-judge might tend to place considerable emphasis on the head, whereas

9-18. Boston Terrier. *Photo by Missy Yuhl.*

9-19. Chinese Crested. *Photo by Carl Lindemaier.*

the all-rounder judge might tend to place emphasis on soundness of the legs. It is our opinion that having both types of judges keeps aesthetic breeds from being too far out of line when establishing one point at the expense of another.

9-20. Chinese Crested in action.

Pointer

The shorthaired Sporting Dogs have their structure exposed. Qualities and faults are obvious and coat trims cannot hide deficiencies.

The Pointer's origin was English, although some Spanish Pointer infusion undoubtedly occurred. Also, it is apparent that the Foxhound, Setter, Greyhound and Bloodhound breeds were introduced in early crosses. The earliest reliable Pointer records in England date back to about 1650, to the time that Greyhounds were used for coursing. Pointers located and pointed hare; Greyhounds were brought up to chase the hare.

The Pointer (Figure 10-5) Standard (1975) states: "*Hound or Terrier characteristics are most undesirable.*" If the loose, soft hound skin had not made its appearance in Pointer offspring, the naming of the fault would have been unnecessary.

Comments on the Pointer Standard are in parentheses, with omission of Standard words pertaining more to type than to structure, are as follows:

POINTER (1975)—*Long, dry* (no loose skin; get rid of that hound character!) *muscular* (not thick), *and slightly arched* (to give strength), *springing cleanly from the shoulders.*

Shoulders—*Long, thin, and sloping* (to give smooth action with endurance). *The top of the blades close together* (thin muscle under the blade; not loaded which would produce out at the elbows).

Front—*Elbows well let down* (reaching to the keel), *directly under the withers and truly parallel so as to work just clear of the body. Forelegs straight* (as viewed from the front; pasterns are slightly slanted), *and with oval bone. Knee joints never to knuckle over* (straight fronts as on a Foxhound have a tendency to knuckle over). *Pasterns of moderate length, perceptibly finer in bone than the leg* (for faster movement of the leg), *and slightly slanting* (never knuckled over). *Chest, deep* *rather than wide* (a flat side gives better forequarter action), *must not hinder free action of forelegs. The breastbone bold, without being unduly prominent. The ribs well sprung* (coming out of the spine level, slanted towards the rear and turning into a chest deeper than wide), *descending as low as the elbow-point.*

Back—*Strong and solid* (Note: When a dog is well angulated and the back is pushed down, the rear legs will flex; the back is solid; the legs joints are flexible) *with only a slight rise from croup to top of shoulders. Loin of moderate length, powerful and slightly arched* (a retention of the Greyhound arch, not a roach). *Croup falling only slightly to base of tail* (to give a little more agility than found in a flat-crouped dog). *Tuck-up should be apparent, but not exaggerated.*

Tail—*Heavier at the root, tapering to a fine point. Length no greater than to hock* (the tail does not have to reach the hock; in fact, the desired "bee sting" tail is much shorter than to the hock). *A tail longer than this or docked must be penalized* (the long thick tail is a hound characteristic. Check for docked tails; they do not taper to a fine point) . . .

Hindquarters—*Muscular and powerful with great propelling leverage. Thighs long and well developed* (usually the longer the thigh, the shorter to hock; it can be expected that with long thigh bones there will probably be short hocks). *Stifles well bent. The hocks clean, the legs straight as viewed from behind. Decided angulation is the mark of power and endurance* (this is a statement of opinion and adds nothing to the required structure of the dog. Muscles generate power; the shape, size and condition of muscles are better criteria for power and endurance).

Feet—*Oval, with long, closely-set, arched toes, well-padded, and deep.*

Gait—*Smooth, frictionless, with a powerful hindquarters' drive. The head should be carried high* (for view of the terrain and to give better balance for quick changes in direction; head is carried high naturally, not strung up by the handler), *the nostrils wide, the tail moving from side to side rhythmically with the pace* (meaning gait; Pointers are judged at a trot not the pace), *giving the impression of a well-balanced, strongly-built hunting dog capable of speed combined with great stamina. Hackney gait must be faulted.* (The hackney gait is tiring and would reduce the stamina of a hunting dog. Sometimes the hackney gait is the result of the handler stringing the dog up. A Pointer should be shown on a loose lead.)

Balance and Size—*Balance and overall symmetry are more important in the Pointer than size. A smooth, balanced dog is to be more desired than a dog with strongly contrasting good points and faults. Hound or terrier characteristics are most undesirable. Because a sporting dog must have both endurance and power, great variations in size are undesirable* (bigger is not better in a hunting dog. The Pointer should give the impression of compact power and agile grace. Dogs or bitches that exceed the height limitations, 28 inches in dogs and 26 inches in bitches, are neither functional nor desirable) . . .

From the above it is obvious that in judging the Pointer, gait is important. This dog was designed for a utility purpose; fancy points are of lesser importance as compared to structural qualities.

German Shepherd Dog

The German Shepherd Dog (Figure 10-4) is the ultimate in structural design for a flying trot. Figure 8-4 shows the suspended phase of the flying trot. The German authors of the Standard must have been experts in dog engineering. Key passages from the Standard are as follows:

> **GERMAN SHEPHERD DOG** (1994)—*The first impression of a good German Shepherd Dog is that of a strong, agile, well muscled animal, alert and full of life. The German Shepherd Dog is longer than tall, with the most desirable proportion as 10 to 8½ .*
>
> **Neck, Topline and Body**—*The neck is strong and muscular, clean-cut and relatively long, proportionate in size to the head and without loose folds of skin. When the dog is at attention or excited, the head is raised and the neck carried high; otherwise typical carriage of the head is forward rather than up and but little higher than the top of the shoulders, particularly in motion.*
>
> **Topline**—*The withers are higher than and sloping into the level back. The back is straight, very strongly developed without sag or roach, but relatively short.*
>
> *The whole structure of the body gives an impression of depth and solidity without bulkiness.*
>
> **Chest**—*Commencing at the prosternum, it is well filled and carried well down between the legs. It is deep and capacious, never shallow, with ample room for lungs and heart, carried well forward, with the prosternum showing ahead of the shoulder in profile. Ribs well sprung and long, neither barrel-shaped nor too flat, and carried down to a sternum which reaches to the elbows. Correct ribbing allows the elbows to move back freely when the dog is at a trot. Too round causes interference and throws the elbows out; too flat or short causes pinched elbows. Ribbing is carried well back so that the loin is relatively short. Abdomen firmly held and not paunchy. The bottom line is only moderately tucked up in the loin. Loin—Viewed from the top, broad and strong. Undue length between the last rib and the thigh, when viewed from the side, is undesirable. Croup long and gradually sloping.*
>
> **Forequarters**—*The shoulder blades are long and obliquely angled, laid on flat and not placed forward. The upper arm joins the shoulder blade at about a right angle. Both the upper arm and the shoulder blade are well muscled. The forelegs, viewed from all sides, are straight and the bone oval rather than round. The pasterns are strong and springy and angulated at approximately a 25-degree angle from the vertical.*
>
> **Hindquarters**—*The whole assembly of the thigh, viewed from the side, is broad with both upper and lower thigh well muscled, forming as nearly as possible a right angle. The upper thigh bone parallels the shoulder blade while the lower thigh bone parallels the upper arm. The Metatarsus (the unit between the hock joint and the foot) is short, strong and tightly articulated.*
>
> **Gait**—*A German Shepherd Dog is a trotting dog, and its structure has been developed to meet the requirements of its work. General Impression—The gait is outreaching,*

*elastic, seemingly without effort, smooth and rhythmic, covering the maximum
amount of ground with the minimum number of steps. At a walk it covers a great deal
of ground, with long strides of both hind legs and forelegs. At a trot the dog covers still
more ground with even longer stride, and moves powerfully but easily, with coordination and balance so that the gait appears to be the steady motion of a well-lubricated
machine. The feet travel close to the ground on both forward reach and backward
push. In order to achieve ideal movement of this kind, there must be good muscular
development and ligamentation. The hindquarters deliver, through the back, a
powerful forward thrust which slightly lifts the whole animal and drives the body
forward. Reaching far under, and passing the imprint left by the front foot, the hind
foot takes hold of the ground; then hock, stifle and upper thigh come into play and
sweep back, the stroke of the hind leg finishing with the foot still close to the ground in
a smooth follow-through. The over-reach of the hindquarter usually necessitates one
hind foot passing outside and the other hind foot passing inside the track of the
forefeet, and such action is not faulty unless the locomotion is crabwise with the dog's
body sideways out of the normal straight line.*

Transmission*—The typical smooth, flowing gait is maintained with great strength
and firmness of back. The whole effort of the hindquarter is transmitted to the
forequarter through the loin, back and withers. At full trot, the back must remain
firm and level without sway, roll, whip or roach. Unlevel topline with withers lower
than the hip is a fault. To compensate for the forward motion imparted by the
hindquarters, the shoulder should open to its full extent. The forelegs should reach out
close to the ground in a long stride in harmony with that of the hindquarters. The dog
does not track on widely separated parallel lines, but brings the feet inward toward the
middle line of the body when trotting, in order to maintain balance. The feet track
closely but do not strike or cross over. Viewed from the front, the front legs function
from the shoulder joint to the pad in a straight line. Viewed from the rear, the hind legs
function from the hip joint to the pad in a straight line. Faults of gait, whether from
front, rear, or side, are to be considered very serious faults.*

The detailed word description of the German Shepherd Dog is far more revealing
than most other Standards. The long body allows longer strides without legs interfering
with one another. The well angulated joints allow long reach. Because of the extreme
angulation, sickle hock is more commonly found in this breed.

Bulldog

Bulldogs (Figure 10-3) are structurally designed to perfection for bullbaiting. Their low
center of gravity, wide front, great stability against overturning and unusual head and
jaw are unique among dogs. As a result of their build, they have an extreme roll in their
gait. Parts of the structural description include the following words:

BULLDOG (1990)—***Skull****—The skull should be very large, and in circumference,
in front of the ears, should measure at least the height of the dog at the shoulders.
Viewed from the front, it should appear very high from the corner of the lower jaw to
the apex of the skull, and also very broad and square. Viewed at the side, the head
should appear very high, and very short from the point of the nose to the occiput. The*

forehead should be flat (not rounded or domed), neither too prominent nor overhanging the face.

Cheeks—*The cheeks should be well rounded, protruding sideways and outward beyond the eyes.*

Stop—*The temples or frontal bones should be very well defined, broad, square and high, causing a hollow or groove between the eyes. This indentation, or stop, should be both broad and deep and extend up the middle of the forehead, dividing the head vertically, being traceable to the top of the skull.*

Eyes and Eyelids—*The eyes, seen from the front, should be situated low down on the skull, as far from the ears as possible, and their corners should be in a straight line at right angles with the stop.*

Jaws—*The jaws should be massive, very broad, square and "undershot," the lower jaw projecting considerably in front of the upper jaw and turning up.*

Neck—*The neck should be short, very thick, deep and strong and well arched at the back.*

Topline—*There should be a slight fall in the back, close behind the shoulders (its lowest part), whence the spine should rise to the loin (the top of which should be higher than the top of the shoulders), thence curving again more suddenly to the tail, forming an arch (a very distinctive feature of the breed), termed "roach back" or, more correctly, "wheel back."*

Body—*The brisket and body should be very capacious.*

Shoulders—*The shoulders should be muscular, very heavy, wide-spread and slanting outward, giving stability and great power.*

Forelegs—*The forelegs should be short, very stout, straight and muscular, set wide apart, with well developed calves, presenting a bowed outline, but the bones of the legs should not be curved or bandy, nor the feet brought too close together.*

Elbows—*The elbows should be low and stand well out and loose from the body.*

Feet—*The feet should be moderate in size, compact and firmly set. Toes compact, well split up, with high knuckles and very short stubby nails. The front feet may be straight or slightly out-turned.*

Skin—*The skin should be soft and loose, especially at the head, neck and shoulders.*

Gait—*The style and carriage are peculiar, his gait being a loose-jointed, shuffling, side-wise motion, giving the characteristic "roll." The action must, however, be unrestrained, free and vigorous.*

The hind legs (stifles turned out, hocks approaching each other, and hind feet turned outward) are built to attain quick stable action that prevents overturning. Perhaps more so than any other breed, the Bulldog Standard has more points described to set type.

The Bulldog has a wide, barrel chest with legs spread far apart to *prevent* overturning. The rear is narrower than the chest to give the body a pear shape. When moving,

9-21. Papillon.

the front legs move farther apart than the rear. As a result, the Bulldog walks with a four-track pattern. Failure to have the characteristic "roll" is a somewhat serious fault.

Papillon

This Toy dog was named after the genus of butterflies known as swallowtails; the breed's ears are butterfly-like ears. Without ever seeing this breed, a student of dogs should predict that the Papillon (Figure 9-21) does jump up on tables and desks with ease. Words from the Standard that form this picture are:

> **PAPILLON** (1991)—*General Appearance—The Papillon is a small, friendly, elegant Toy dog of fine-boned structure, light, dainty and of lively action; distinguished from other breeds by its beautiful butterfly-like ears.*
>
> **Neck** *of medium length.*
>
> **Topline**—*The backline is straight and level.*
>
> **Body**—*The chest is of medium depth with ribs well sprung. The belly is tucked up.*
>
> **Forequarters**—*Shoulders well developed and laid back to allow freedom of movement. Forelegs slender, fine-boned and must be straight . . . Front feet thin and elongated (hare-like), pointing neither in nor out.*

Hindquarters—*Well developed and well angulated. The hind legs are slender, fine-boned, and parallel when viewed from behind . . . Hind feet thin and elongated (hare-like), pointing neither in nor out.*

The Papillon defies the appearance of a fragile dog. They are little dogs that think and act big.

CHAPTER 10

Principles for Evaluating Dog Gaits

Training Your Eye to See the Dynamics of Motion

When Thelma and Curtis Brown first started exhibiting dogs in 1938, Curtis had trouble interpreting what he was seeing. The fault was not with his eyesight, but with incomplete knowledge of what to look for. After reading much, talking to many and learning what to look for, Curtis found he still had difficulty in analyzing motion, especially fast moving legs. He then took slow-motion pictures and studied the details of paw, pastern, back and head motions, over and over. After that and after again watching faster moving legs, his problems diminished. Viewing slow moving legs in movies enabled him to learn to see some things at faster speeds. If you look at artists' drawings of fast galloping horses made prior to the perfection of the camera, you will see many erroneous concepts of leg positions. Only with slow-motion pictures can you truly see exceptionally fast leg movement.

The difference between an expert and a novice is that the expert perceives instantly what the novice sees eventually.

If a prizefighter is in the ring and the opponent is delivering a straight right toward the chin, the fighter does not have time to think, "I must duck my head to the left." If he does take that time, he will have a short nap on the canvas. A fighter trains to the point that the subconscious will react to a situation without time-consuming conscious thinking.

When we say a judge has a good eye for a dog, what we are saying is that the judge's mind has been trained to take in the picture of the entire dog at once, without benefit of the conscious mind, and instantly recognize quality or lack of quality. The eye sees the dog and the results follow without analyzing each part one by one.

How do you train the eye? Or more properly, from what you are seeing, how do you train the mind to instantly recognize quality without stopping and thinking about each part? The process of training the eye can be compared to the training process involved in learning to type. Many students have a terrible time learning to strike the right lettered keys without looking at the keyboard. They have to think where each letter is located before they can hit the right key. Finally, after much practice, they can look at words and punch the right keys without thinking of each letter's location. Many are then able to gaze out the window, think up a sentence and type it without worrying or thinking about the spelling of each word. The subconscious does the routine work.

In selecting quality dogs, at first it is the slow process of correctly analyzing each part in detail. Later the whole dog is taken in at a glance and any asset or imperfection is recognized without conscious thinking. For some things, the hand must be used. There is no way of evaluating long-coated dogs except by getting the hands under the coat. The hands, like the eyes, can also be trained to utilize the subconscious mind to quickly recognize what is felt.

A Word of Caution

The subconscious mind can be trained to respond to poor yet *seemingly* correct specimens as well as those that are the best specimens. The importance of schooling the subconscious toward perfection, *not* imperfection, cannot be overemphasized.

In studying this book, you should aim for at least two objectives: First, *train the mind to know* what to look for in evaluating dogs. Second, *begin training the subconscious* mind to quickly recognize perfection, not imperfection, in the pictures before the eyes. This is called *positive judging rather than fault judging.*

Standard of Perfection

To evaluate the quality of a particular breed, there is a Standard of Perfection. If the Standard is clear and not ambiguous, judges are obligated to accept the words as written. However, most Standards are not precisely clear and do require interpretation. If the dog's eyes are described as large, but not too large, judgment must be used to select the best examples.

In Standards, omissions frequently occur. All judges move dogs at a trot, yet some Standards fail to mention gait. There is no Standard that says a dog must have four legs. *Omissions do not imply that all omitted subjects are unimportant*; the necessity of having four legs is important. Omissions place the responsibility on the judge without giving specific direction.

When judges are faced with an ambiguous Standard or one with omissions, in our opinion, they should select the dog with the structure best capable of performing the purpose of the breed. Some dogs run with endurance, others with speed. Some go to ground, others swim. Some need small size for ratting, others need large size for guarding. Each requires a different build. Our objective in this book is to point out which structure or structures best accomplish a particular purpose. Type and beauty, although important, are outside the focus of this book.

Deviations from Ideal Endurance Trot

Numerous writings, lectures, film presentations and slide shows are directed towards explaining how an ideal endurance trotting dog should trot. While this is a worthy subject, all too often the fact that perhaps the majority of breeds deviate from ideal endurance trotting style is not mentioned. For example, dogs designed for galloping should trot in a manner that indicates that they are efficient in the gallop; ideal endurance trotting is not of supreme importance. Only those breeds whose function demands endurance trotting (Collie, Shetland Sheepdog, Belgian breeds, and the like) need to trot with an endurance trotting style. Exceptions are in the Bull breeds, short-legged dogs, galloping breeds, Toy breeds and others.

Judges have been influenced by those describing ideal trotting style, and some have applied ideal trotting principles to breeds that should never display ideal trotting style. This chapter is in defense of those breeds that should have a trotting style different from the ideal. But first a few definitions need to be clarified.

GAIT. A gait is the manner of moving. Some gaits are: pace, amble, pace-like walk, walk, trot-like walk, trot, canter, diagonal or rotary gallops, half bound, full bound, pronk, etc. Although there are many gaits in show dog Standards, it is understood that the trot is normally described after the word "gait" or "movement."

TROT. The trot is a gait in that diagonal paws (left hind and right fore or right hind and left fore) move nearly in cadence. Although few exhibitors are aware of it, at dog shows paw cadence may be out of phase by 6 percent of the time of one stride, and yet be called a trot. For example, exhibits that speed around the ring with the appearance of drive, such as the Pointers, German Shepherd Dogs, Afghan Hounds and Poodles, often have one phase of the trot with only one rear paw on the ground (cadence out of phase).

PRINCIPLE 1. *Although no rule says so, at dog shows the quality of a dog's travel is usually judged at the trot. In a Standard, the description following the word "gait" is presumed to apply to the trot.*

Most dog Standards, when describing a dog's method of travel, use the word "gait" when the word "trot" is intended. The command "gait your dogs" actually means use any one of the many gaits, but in dog shows "trot your dog" is usually presumed to be the intended command.

PRINCIPLE 2. *Since the word "trot" only states that diagonal paws move in cadence, differences in the various trotting styles are due to animation.* Animation includes high paw lift (hackney trot), moving wide, single tracking, up-and-down motion of the backline, head carriage, tail carriage, attitude, follow-through, reach, extension, and others. Assuming a dog is trotting, then differences between the styles of trotting used by different breeds of dogs are due to animation.

PRINCIPLE 3. *If a Standard describes a breed's gait (trot), the quality of the trot is judged by how it conforms to the particular Standard, irrespective of efficiency or the violation of good trotting styles.*

The duty of the judge is to judge by the breed Standard. The description of the trot (gait) of breeds is not always based upon efficiency of energy consumption, as observed in the Miniature Pinscher's hackney trot, the high paw action of the Italian Greyhound, the rolling "trot" of the Bulldog and the side over-reaching of the German Shepherd Dog. It is not the office of the judge to impose personal beliefs. One of the major reasons why many breeds do not trot in a style believed to be ideal is because of a Standard's wording.

PRINCIPLE 4. *If a breed's gait (trot) is not described in the Standard or is only partially described, the quality of the trot is judged on the basis of (1) tradition, (2) what is functionally correct for the original purpose of the breed and (3) aesthetics.*

When a breed's gait is not described in its Standard, it can only be presumed that the quality of the trot is left to the opinion of the judge. In some breeds, over a period of time, tradition has established what breeders believe to be correct trotting style for the breed. While the Fox Terrier pendulum trot is described in the Standard, some other long-legged Terriers, by tradition, are judged on the same basis as the Fox Terrier. (Refer to Figure 10-1 for the Smooth Fox Terrier.) The Greyhound trot, while not described in its Standard, should be judged on the basis of: "How should a galloping dog trot in order to disclose that it is efficient in the gallop?" Some of the Toys and exotic breeds by tradition are judged on the basis of what is aesthetically pleasing.

10-1. Smooth Fox Terrier. *Ashbey Photography Inc.*

PRINCIPLE 5. *Very rarely does a given breed trot exactly the same as any other breed. It is the obligation of the judge to know the correct style of the trot for the breed being examined.*

In the trot the only factor common to all breeds is that legs move nearly in cadence. The style of movement, paw lift, bend of the joints, up and down movement of the backline, tail carriage, roll, single tracking, moving wide, reach, extension, backline and speed vary significantly from breed to breed. Knowledge of what the variations should be is knowledge required of the judge.

VARIATIONS. The following variations are discussed below: up and down motion, direction of spine's point, direction of leg motion, convergence of legs, nonconvergence of legs, flip-up of pastern, height of paw lift, reach and backline.

Up and Down Motion. The backline of all exhibits moves up and down, with maximum height occurring when the rearmost paw is leaving the ground, or slightly thereafter. No exceptions exist. Variations occur in the magnitude of up and down motion. Breeds designed for maximum endurance at the trot should have a minimum up and down motion. Some breeds, especially those designed for galloping, will have greater up and down motion at the trot than those designed for trotting endurance.

Direction of Spine. In most breeds the spine points in the direction of travel. *Exceptions:* Those breeds that have a roll in the rear (mostly Bull breeds). The spine bends to the right and then to the left. Bulldogs should lead with one shoulder as does a cantering horse, and therefore travel with the spine a bit *off* the direction of travel.

Direction of Leg Motion. In most breeds the legs swing back and forth in the direction of travel and in a straight column (the column may slope inward) without paddling, weaving, cowhocks, etc. Exceptions: Cardigan and Pembroke Welsh Corgis and Basset Hounds have a crook, or curve, in the leg. (Refer to Figure 10-2 for the Cardigan Welsh Corgi, both stacked and working.) In some cases the Petit Basset Griffon Vendeen has a slight crook in the leg. The Bulldog's and French Bulldog's rear legs swing forward in an arc.

Convergence of Legs. Those breeds designed for endurance at the trot should have the legs converge towards the center line of travel. The Standard in the Bull breeds states otherwise. Tradition in some long-legged Terriers is also otherwise. Many of the short-legged breeds have the front leg assembly wrap around the body as nearly as may be, with the front legs slanting in as much as possible. However, in those short-legged breeds with the front legs slanting in, the rear legs travel parallel to one another.

Nonconvergence of Legs. Most of the Bull breeds (Bulldog, Bull Terrier, French Bulldog, Pug, Staffordshire Bull Terrier, and American Staffordshire Terrier) travel with the legs parallel. (Refer to Figure 10-3 for the Bulldog.) The rear legs of those breeds with a roll in the rear have the rear legs swing forward in an arc (Bulldog and French

10-2. Cardigan Welsh Corgi.

10-3. Bulldog. *Photo by Tauskey.*

Bulldog). Fox Terriers trot with the legs parallel because the Standard says so. Some long-legged Terriers (Airedale, Irish) do so because of tradition.

Flipping up of Pastern. Breeds designed for trotting endurance (Collie, Shetland Sheepdog, Belgian Tervuren, etc.) have the pastern, when leaving the ground, quickly flip up parallel with the ground. Most of the breeds designed for galloping (Greyhound, Doberman, etc.) bring the pastern forward at 45 degrees to the ground (they need strong tendons and ligaments). Because of the Fox Terrier Standard and tradition in some other long-legged Terriers, these breeds bring their pasterns forward with a minimum bend in the pastern joint.

Height of Paw Lift. Breeds of dogs designed for endurance at the trot should never bring the front paw forward higher than the pastern joint is from the ground in its posed position. Some breeds, for aesthetic reasons, lift the paw higher (Italian Greyhound, Miniature Pinscher, and a few Toy breeds because of tradition). Those breeds with 25 degree bend in the pastern joint (German Shepherd Dog, etc.) bring the paw forward close to the ground.

Reach. *Reach* is the distance a paw extends in front of the forechest while in the air. *Set down reach* is the distance a paw is in front of the forechest at the time it is set on the ground. The only time a paw can aid in forward push is when it is on the ground; set down reach is the important consideration.

Although long reach (the more the better, by the opinion of the average fancier) is looked upon favorably at dog shows, this excess reach is wasted energy. Some reach is necessary; the question is, what is optimum? When a paw is set on the ground, it must have a velocity towards the dog's body equal to the forward speed of the dog. Ground velocity of a paw must be zero; the ground is not moving. The ideal reach must be sufficient to give the dog time for its paw to accelerate towards the body and attain a speed equal to the dog's forward speed. In other words, the swifter the dog moves, the greater the amount of reach is needed to attain the correct paw speed towards the body. In the gallop the paw is about straight out in front of the nose. Because long reach is looked upon with favor, to attain it, handlers move the dog faster. Increase of reach is the main reason why exhibitors like to move the dog swiftly. Reach should always be judged relative to the speed of travel: faster speed, more reach; slow speed, little reach.

The set down reach is nearly the same for all breeds; the paw is set down a short distance in front of the chest, with little variation with respect to speed or gait. Pressure plate tests have shown that a paw on the ground in front of the shoulder blade or hip joint during the trot causes the dog to decrease speed (decelerate). Long set down reach is undesirable.

Backline. During the trot, backlines (toplines) vary from level, sloping towards the front, sloping towards the rear, and arched. Those breeds with a backline sloping towards the rear are the German Shepherd Dog (Figure 10-4), Pointer (Figure 10-5) and several other breeds. From an aesthetic point of view, sloping towards the rear is preferred. The Old English Sheepdog and the Dandie Dinmont Terrier have their toplines sloping towards the front. A number of breeds require a level backline, such as the Afghan Hound, Basenji, Golden Retriever, Poodle and others. Superimposed on

10-4. German Shepherd Dog. *COOK phoDOGraphy.*

10-5. Pointer. *Photo by The Standard Image, Chuck & Sandy Tatham.*

the level topline is usually a *small* arch over the loin. The spires on the loin vertebrae vary in height and are highest in the middle of the loin. The low point of the backline is at the eleventh vertebra, which is the third vertebra in from the end of the ribcage. Many breeds have muscle fill-in across this vertebra, and the backline is level. A few breeds require a fall-away arch in the dog's rear—Greyhound, Whippet (Figure 10-6), Bedlington Terrier and Italian Greyhound.

10-6. Whippet. *Photo by Rich Bergman.*

Basic Principles for Judging Gait in Review

PRINCIPLE 1. *Although no rule says so, at dog shows the quality of a dog's travel is judged at the trot. In a Standard the description following the word "gait" is presumed to apply to the trot.*

PRINCIPLE 2. *Since the word "trot" only states that diagonal paws move in cadence, differences in the various trotting styles are due to animation.*

PRINCIPLE 3. *If a Standard describes a breed's gait (trot), the quality of the trot is judged by how it conforms to the particular Standard, irrespective of efficiency or the violation of good trotting styles.*

PRINCIPLE 4. *If a breed's gait (trot) is not described in its Standard or is only partially described, the quality of the trot is judged on the basis of (1) tradition, (2) what is functionally correct for the original purpose of the breed, and (3) aesthetics.*

PRINCIPLE 5. *Very rarely does a given breed trot exactly the same way as any other breed. It is the obligation of the judge to know the correct style of the trot for the breed being examined.*

Summary

Trotting styles vary. Each breed of dog has a particular style of trotting, though at times the variation from other breeds is slight. No two breeds trot exactly alike, with the possible exception of the three Belgian Herding breeds. It is the responsibility of the judge to know the different styles of trotting. When judges take on the task of judging a new breed, they should be particularly careful not to judge the new breed's trotting style based upon the other breeds they have judged. Using the gait of a Collie as the basis for judging the gait of a long-legged Terrier can be a disaster.

A-1. Alaskan Malamute all champion sled team.

APPENDIX

Technical Data
in Summary

Introduction

This chapter contains a summary of technical information pertaining to locomotion and structure of dogs. This information has been derived from technical writings in the scientific press and from personal measurements. Immaterial details, such as "the dog has two nostrils instead of one," have been omitted.

It was only at the end of the nineteenth century, with the development of photographic techniques, that it became possible to clearly define gait movements. Today comparative biomechanical research has barely begun. Many of the principles needed to determine optimum structure or form for a particular function have not been defined; meaningful tests have not been run. Today no one can pick out the fastest dog or the dog with the greatest endurance by merely looking or feeling. The best that can be done is to select an exhibit with external characteristics found in the better performing dogs. The following technical information can only be considered as an aid towards selecting individuals that might give superior performance for a specific purpose.

General Technical Information

1. Mammals can be divided into two locomotion groups:

   a. The relatively rigid-spine galloping types called **dorsostable,** including horses and deer

   b. The flexible-backed galloping types called **dorsomobile,** including dogs and cats

   Structures of each of these types have many differences.

185

2. The flexible-backed, galloping mammals can be divided into two locomotion groups:

    a. The spurt runners, such as cats

    b. The sustained runners, including wild dogs (wolf, coyote, jackal and Cape hunting dog)

3. The structural differences between the flexible-backed groups are:

    a. *Cats* have a *white* type of muscle (glycolysis type). *Dogs* have a *dark* type of muscle (oxidative type). The white type of muscle is quicker reacting but has less endurance.

    b. The hindquarters of the cat are usually stronger than the forequarters, whereas in dogs each quarter tends to have equal capacity for work.

4. Domestic dogs were derived from an early type of sustained runner. After domestication, by selective breeding, man changed the function of some dogs to such purposes as hunting, speed, bull baiting, guarding, herding, etc. With a change in function came a change in structure and gait; many of the domestic breeds are no longer suited for sustained travel.

The Dog's Front

1. Actual measurements on the spine of a dog's shoulder blade have failed to discover a single sled dog with a 45 degree layback; 32 degrees off the vertical is well laid-back, as based on numerous measurements.

2. To date, all mathematical computations to show *45 degrees* to be superior to any other angle have been proven to be based on *incorrect* assumptions; the results are mathematical mirages.

3. To date no one has done sufficient pressure plate testing of trotting or galloping dogs to prove a relationship between shoulder blade layback and efficient forward push of the paw. However, the tests that have been done indicate that a 45 degree layback is probably counterproductive to forward propulsion.

4. The shoulder blade length varies in proportion to the upper arm depending upon the total leg length. In long-legged dogs (Saluki), the shoulder blade bone is 20 percent shorter than the upper arm; in the Golden Retriever, about 10 percent shorter; in the Basset Hound they are about equal.

5. The spine of the shoulder blade points between thoracic vertebrae 2 and 5 (T2 and T5) and usually points to T2 or T3.

6. Metacarpal bones (pastern) are shorter than the metatarsal bones (hock joint to paw).

The Dog's Rear

1. The PELVIS slopes at about 30 degrees in level-backed dogs. Dogs with a fallaway arch in the croup have a steeper angle. Too steep a croup restricts rearward extension of the rear paw but increases agility.

2. In dogs the FEMUR (upper thigh) and TIBIA (lower thigh) are about equal length for normal-legged dogs.

3. A long ISCHIUM (rear point of pelvis) increases the effectiveness of muscles of the thigh.

Odds and Ends

1. The largest ears are found in desert animals. Size may be partly for hearing, but is mostly for heat radiation. In cold areas short ears are desirable.

2. Ribs rotate to increase air intake; they should slant towards the rear, not be at 90 degrees to the spine.

3. For trotting dogs, the ribcage should be long in the fore part and short towards the rear.

4. PRONATOR MUSCLES (rotating the wrist without bending) are decadent in most speedy animals, though large in dogs.

5. The front foot is larger than the rear foot by about one and one-third times.

Gaits of Dogs

1. GAIT is a regularly repeating sequence and manner of moving legs in walking or running; the FOOTFALL PATTERN is an essential part of all gait definitions. Within a given footfall pattern many styles of motion and animation can occur.

2. The act of setting a foot on the ground is known as a FOOTFALL, and the sequence of footfalls means the order in which paws are set on the ground.

3. A STRIDE LENGTH is the distance covered in one cycle of a gait (after all paws have moved once).

4. Gaits are divided into SYMMETRICAL (walk, pace-like walk, amble, pace, trot, trot-like walk) and ASYMMETRICAL (canter, half bound and gallops). In symmetrical gaits the right side repeats as a mirror image what the left side did; failure to do so may indicate lameness, malformed structural parts, muscular or nervous system problems.

5. Domestic dogs commonly use the walk, pace-like walk, amble, pace, trot, canter and rotary gallop and rarely the half bound, transverse gallop and trot-like walk.

6. In the WALK each footfall occurs at about one-fourth of the time of one complete stride; in music it would be nearly or exactly 4-4 time. The sequence of footfall is LH, LF, RH, RF, LH, etc. (L—left, R—right, H—hind, F—fore). Usually the walk is performed at slow speeds; however, the elephant can do the running walk at nearly 20 miles per hour.

7. PACE-LIKE WALK is an intermediate gait between the walk and the pace; ALL long-legged dogs use it or the pace sequence in slow travel. The footfall sequence is the same as for the walk; the rhythm is different. The time interval between the LH and LF footfall in the walk is nearly 25 percent ($^1/_4$) of the time of one stride; in the pace-like walk the time interval between the LH and LF is between 10 percent and 17 percent of the time of one stride.

8. In the AMBLE, the footfall sequence is the same as for the walk; the *rhythm* is different. The time interval between the LH and LF footfalls is almost zero, but not quite.

9. In the PACE, the paws on one side set down together. Longer-legged dogs (Saluki, Great Dane, Doberman Pinscher, Golden Retriever, etc.) often use the pace footfall sequence in their slowest speeds. Speed is not a consideration in naming many gaits.

10. In the TROT, diagonal legs (LH with RF and RH with LF) move nearly or exactly in cadence. At dog shows, by custom, the trot is used to judge the quality of leg motion. Other gaits may be used at the option of the judge, even the gallop.

11. In the TROT-LIKE WALK, the time interval between footfalls on one side is about halfway between that of the trot and a walk.

12. In the GALLOP, both footfalls of one end (front or rear) occur before the footfalls of the other end. One side cannot repeat as a mirror image what the other side did; the gait is asymmetrical.

13. The footfall sequence in the ROTARY GALLOP is either LH, RH, RF, LF, LH, etc.—or RH, LH, LF, RF, RH, etc. The footfalls occur in a circle. Dogs normally use the rotary gallop, either clockwise or counterclockwise.

14. The footfall sequence in the TRANSVERSE (DIAGONAL) GALLOP is either LH, RH, LF, RF, LH, etc.—or RH, LH, RF, LF, RH, etc. A diagonal occurs between the rear and front footfalls. The transverse gallop is commonly used by horses, sometimes by dogs.

15. In the CANTER (sometimes called the lope in horse circles), a pair of diagonal feet land in unison; the other pair do not. The footfall sequence is LH and RF together, followed by LF, then RH. It is a rocking-horse gait with a lot of up-and-down motion in front and rear, but little in the middle.

Other Gait Features

1. For a given speed, mammals naturally select a gait that consumes a minimum of energy. As speed increases, when the energy it takes to trot exceeds that of the canter, the dog will shift to the canter. Domestic dogs can be trained to move at the trot at greater speeds than they would normally employ.

2. The trot is a nearly rigid spine gait. Though the body may move up and down, the spine moves as a unit without vertical bending or flexing.

3. At the trot, the spine *always* moves up and down some. In dogs proficient at the trot (not all breeds should be), the vertical motion should be minimal. Dogs designed for galloping have greater vertical motion during the trot than do good trotting dogs.

4. Breeds of dogs that roll during the trot move the rear back and forth horizontally; the withers move straight forward without roll.

5. Pacing dogs bend the body from side to side; the withers and top of pelvis do not roll.

6. Holding the head high during the trot causes the front paw to lift higher than it normally would with the head low.

7. Leg motion at all gaits is most efficient when confined to a single plane (sagittal). The legs move without paddling, weaving, etc., and without deformed joints such as cow hocks.

8. *Swing time* (the time it takes for a paw to lift off the ground and to set down on the ground) is nearly constant for all gaits of an individual. For horses and dogs it is about 0.32 seconds; for cheetahs it is about 0.23 seconds.

9. The *stance time* (the time the paw is on the ground) decreases as speed increases.

Efficient Endurance Trotters

1. Dogs efficient at the endurance trot must have the correct structure and must perform the trot in correct style of motion. In the trot it is assumed that wild dogs (wolf, coyote, jackal and Cape Hunting dog) have a structure and style of trotting that is near perfection for sustained travel.

2. The length of leg below the chest is about equal to the depth of chest.

3. The length of body from forechest to rump is 10 percent to 20 percent longer than the height of the dog at the withers.

4. Angulation, though present, is not excessive.

A-2. Alaskan Malamutes doing what they were bred for.

5. The shoulder layback measured from the point of the shoulder to a point on top of the shoulder blade where the spine intersects the top is in the range of 32 degrees to 39 degrees; as measured on the spine of the blade, 25 degrees to 32 degrees with all angles measured off the vertical. The optimum angle has never been determined by measurements.

6. The dog is on the lean side.

7. In trotting the following occurs:

   a. The length of step in front of the shoulder blade is about equal to the length of step behind the shoulder blade. Also the length of step in front of the hip joint is about equal to the length of step behind it.

   b. After the front paw leaves the ground, the pastern quickly flips up to a parallel with the ground position. The paw then moves forward at an elevation no higher than the pastern joint in the posed position. The paw does not have an ascending path.

   c. After the rear paw picks up it has sufficient follow-through to allow the paw to attain a height no higher than the pastern joint (carpus) in the posed position; usually the rear paw only attains half that height. The paw then moves forward on a descending path and sets down under the front paw just after the front paw has picked up.

   d. During the trot, paws converge, and the length of step is about equal to the height of the dog at the withers.

Efficient Gallopers

1. Galloping dogs come in two classes:

   a. Those designed for all-out speed, and

   b. Those designed for endurance as well as speed.

   The first class has a longer body than the second class.

2. Swift running requires great amounts of energy, which require enlarged lungs, heart and digestive system. All of this requires lengthening the spine. To increase the length of jumps and speed of running, it is advantageous to have the center of gravity nearer the hindquarters; this calls for a shortening of the spine. These two contradictory factors apparently control the length of the spine.

3. Square build (height at the withers equals the distance from forechest to rump). Arctic dogs of moderate weight apparently are the best long-distance running dogs.

4. The swiftest dogs are Sighthounds with flexible backs.

5. Flexing the back increases stride length and speed, but requires energy and decreases endurance.

6. Muscles of the back and lumbar region must be strong in mammals that arch their back while galloping; muscles of the pelvis must be very strong in all gallopers.

7. The arid plains habitat is the best environment for the development of swift animals (Saluki).

8. For speed, muscles are lightened in parts of limbs away from the main mass, and concentrated near the body. Tendons are lengthened with increased leg length, not muscles.

9. Slope of spinous processes of the back vertebrae denotes direction and degree of muscular stress. The eleventh thoracic (anticlinal) vertebra denotes the change in primary stress from front to rear; it is also the shortest and marks the beginning of the arch over the loin.

10. Speedy animals often have a small head (Whippet) or short neck or both (cheetah). A long neck does not increase speed; in most animals the length of neck is probably influenced chiefly by feeding or hunting habits in relation to length of leg.

11. Lengthening the leg *increases* stride length, but *decreases* power. For speed there is an optimum leg length for musculature and body weight; in dogs it is probably 1.2 to 1.35 times the depth of chest.

12. The length of leg is best expressed in relation to the depth of chest. The Saluki's front leg below the chest is 1.32 times the depth of chest; the giraffe 1.75; the Greyhound 1.17; the Fox Terrier 1.00 and the Basset Hound 0.28.

13. The smaller the foot, the greater the adaptation for speed; however, on soft surfaces, the foot must have a larger area of contact.

14. Most swift animals have steep shoulder blades as compared to trotting animals.

Pressure Plate Tests

1. Pressure plate tests prove that during the trot the front carries nearly three-fifths of the dog's vertical forces and the rear carries two-fifths.

2. When the paw is in front of the shoulder blade and in front of the hip joint, the paw acts as a brake and slows the dog (long forward reach during the trot is not desirable).

3. During the trot the front paw provides about the same forward propulsion as the rear paw.

4. During the trot, the front has the greater braking force, greater weight to support and almost the same forward propulsion as compared to the rear; the front does the greater amount of work.

A-3. German Shorthaired Pointer—form equals function.

Fancy Points

1. At dog shows breeds are often judged upon aesthetic appeal rather than functional efficiency. At times extremes are developed in the mistaken belief that if a little is good a lot is better, such as over-angulation in German Shepherd Dogs, and the trotting style and long neck in Afghan Hounds. The coat and sloping toplines of the Cocker Spaniel are another example. Boxers, Poodles and a few other square breeds of dogs have been developed to possess long forward reach of the front paw during the trot; it is very pleasing to the eye but very counterproductive to minimum energy consumption.

2. By authority of the Standard a judge is often asked to make decisions by criteria that can be proved to be functionally incorrect. The rules of the game are that the judge should judge by the Standard if possible. Judging is more an art than a science.

Breed Purpose

There is a specific conformation that provides superior performance for each particular breed. For instance, the Alaskan Malamute was developed for heavy freighting and tending trap lines in the Arctic. They are not as fast as the Siberian Husky, but were used as a sled dog where power and endurance were required. Figures A-1 and A-2 show the Alaskan Malamute performing its function. Those characteristics which contribute to a breed's purpose should be uppermost in mind when evaluating a dog.

The best exhibit of a functional breed should be selected on what is believed to be optimum form needed to efficiently execute that breed's function. (Refer to Figure A-3.) Thus, observable clues, either a dog's structure or its style of trotting, indicate that the exhibit is probably efficient in its function, and need discussion. That is the purpose of this book.

GLOSSARY

Note: Breed or breeds listed after a definition are for purposes of illustration and are not intended as an all-inclusive listing.

Abdomen. Lower portion of the body between the chest and the pelvis containing the stomach and most of the digestive system, along with the liver and a portion of the urinary system. Protected above by the lumbar portion of the spinal column and below by the belly. The belly is formed of muscle, tissue and skin.

Abdomen, slightly drawn up. Slight tuck-up. Dachshund.

Achilles tendon. Name of human tendon whose counterpart is the calcaneal tendon in the dog. Misapplied when referring to the dog. This large tendon (calcaneal) extends to the calcaneal process and is formed by uniting small tendons of the lower thigh; muscles pulling on the calcaneal tendon straighten the hock, thereby providing propulsive power.

Albinism. Deficiency of color pigment in skin, coat, nails, eyes, nose, eye rims; hereditary trait.

Albino. An animal born with deficiency of pigments in the skin, eyes and hair; eyes, nose and eye rims are pink (caused by blood showing); hair is always white.

Almond eyes. Eyes that appear shaped like almonds; the tissue (eyelids) surrounding the eyes creates the almond shape, i.e., almond-shaped tissue. The eyeball itself is always nearly round.

Angle. Used in reference to the junction of the throat and the lower jar. *"Throat clean cut at the angle."* Scottish Deerhound.

Angulation. The angle formed between the leg bones or pelvic girdle and spine, such as: forequarter angulation—shoulder blade and upper arm; pelvic angle—pelvic girdle and the spine; rearquarter angulation—upper and lower thigh; hock angulation—lower thigh and hock. Also see **overangulation.**

Ankylosis. Fusion and immobility of joints that are normally movable. A serious fault in a German Shepherd Dog whose tail has clumpy ends due to ankylosis.

Anus. The excretory opening for the digestive system; outlet at end of rectum.

Apple head. Roundness of topskull, humped toward center; shaped like an apple; the Chihuahua has a well rounded "apple dome" skull. Several breeds, such as the Keeshond, call apple head a fault.

Apron. The longer hair, or frill below underpart of the neck on the chest.

Arched. Applied to the neck, back, loin or toes when arched; rounded upwards. The arch may be formed by muscles or bones. Arched loin (caused by muscles); arched toes (caused by bones and muscles); arched back (camel back). A Greyhound or Whippet arched loin arches downward from a flat back, not like a roach.

Arm, lower. The region between the upper arm and the wrist or pastern. Consists of the radius and ulna and associated ligaments and muscles. Also referred to as forearm.

Arm, upper. The region between the shoulder and the forearm. Consists of the humerus and associated ligaments and muscles.

Arm, true. Upper arm. English Foxhound.

Articulation. Juncture of bones and the movement of one on the other at the juncture.

Back. On humans, from the neck to the end of the spine; on other animals the back is frequently used with the same meaning; on horses and some dog Standards, the five vertebrae between the withers and loin; the anatomical division of the spine is neck, withers, back, loin and croup; variable in meaning depending upon the context of the Standard.

Back, camel. Arched back like a single humped camel's back; convex curved back from neck to croup; usually describes a fault.

Back, hollow. Dip in the backline; sag in the backline; downward curved backline; concave curvature of backline.

Back, level. Back level (loin may be arched but the anatomical back is level).

Back, saddle. Too long a back with a dip behind the withers.

Back, wheel. Extreme form of roached back; line of back wheel-shaped; a slight fall in the back, close behind the shoulders (its lowest part), whence the spine should rise to the loins (the top of which should be higher than the top of the shoulders), thence curving again more suddenly to the tail, forming an arch (a very distinctive feature of the Bulldog) termed a "roach back", or more correctly a "wheel-back." Bulldog.

Backline. That portion of the topline from the tenth vertebra or just behind the withers through the croup to the set-on of the tail.

Backskull. Braincase; cranium; area of skull from stop to occiput.

Ball and socket. Joint that has a head or ball articulating in a socket; hip joint; rib articulation with spine.

Bandy legs. Bowed legs. Objectionable in a Dandie Dinmont Terrier.

Barrel-shaped. Rounded or well arched shape of the chest; cylindrical in form; barrel-chested; barrel ribs.

Beard. Profuse hair on the chin. Afghan Hound, Airedale Terrier, Bouvier des Flandres.

Beefy. Overly heavy muscled, especially the hindquarters.

Belly. Muscular floor of the abdomen.

Bilateral cryptorchid. A male dog with both testicles undescended.

Bitch. Female canine.

Bitchy dog. Male dog displaying feminine characteristics; overly refined dog.

Bite. Determined when the mouth is closed. The position of the upper and lower incisor teeth in relation to one another. *Level bite*, level mouth, or pincer bite: vise-like bite where upper and lower incisors meet edge to edge. *Scissors bite*: upper incisor teeth fit tightly over the lower incisors. *Reverse scissors bite*: lower incisor teeth fit tightly over the upper incisors. *Misaligned teeth* or irregular bite: one, some, or all incisors have erupted in abnormal fashion. Sometimes the misalignment is caused by an injury during development. *Overshot*: front teeth (incisors) of the upper jaw extend slightly beyond the front teeth of the lower jaw when the mouth is closed; upper jaw overhanging the lower jaw (overshot and undershot are relative to the lower jaw). *Pig jaw*: upper jaw extending far beyond the lower jaw; a fault in all breeds. *Undershot*: upper jaw does not extend as far as the lower jaw; lower jaw projects beyond the upper jaw. Bulldog.

Blade. Shoulder blade; scapula.

Blanket. A marking formed by a solid color on the back, shoulders and sides.

Blaze. A white stripe or line extending up the center of the face. Desirable in a Saint Bernard and required in the Bernese Mountain Dog.

Blocky. Applied to the head or body; square or cube like; a blocky head or blocky body.

Bobtail. Dog with tail bobbed (docked or natural); nickname of Old English Sheepdog. Australian Shepherd.

Body overhang. Prosternum or forechest, that portion of the breastbone that projects beyond the point of shoulder when viewed from the side. Australian Terrier.

Bone. Dense, semirigid, porous, calcified connective tissue of the skeleton; skeleton; also used to mean substance as "plenty of bone" or "well boned"; size (diameter) of bone; reverse of "light boned."

Bossy shoulders. Overdeveloped shoulder muscles.

Bow-legged. Bandy-legged; front legs bowed outward or hind legs bowed out at hock joints.

Bracelets. Long hair left on hind legs of Poodles, clipped or trimmed in the "Continental" clip.

Breast, pigeon. Narrow chest with short protruding breastbone.

Breastbone. The breastbone is composed of the brisket and forechest. The eight sternebrae, or the sternum, that encloses the bottom or floor of the chest. The first or forwardmost sternebra when it projects forward of the shoulder joint is referred to as the prosternum, point of forechest or point of breastbone. The Basset Hound, Bloodhound and Dachshund each have a prominent prosternum.

Breastbone strongly prominent. When viewed from in front the breastbone has a depression on either side. When viewed from the side it protrudes well beyond the point of shoulder. Dachshund.

Breech musculature. The muscles in the area of the inner upper thigh around the buttocks. Boxer.

Breeching/Britches. Culottes; trousers; long and thick hair on the rear of the thighs, not below. Alaskan Malamute, American Eskimo Dog, Australian Cattle Dog.

Brick-shaped head. Head, when viewed from above, with width of skull and muzzle of approximately equal width.

Bridge bones. Bones over the eyes, forward portion of the frontal bone; brows. Dachshund.

Bridge of nose. Nasal bone extending from nostrils to stop.

Brisket. Lower part of chest between and in front of legs; deep brisket or shallow brisket indicates the depth of the chest.

Brisket, shallow. Lack of depth of ribs; sternum well above elbow.

Brow. Superciliary arches or ridges; ridge formed above the eye by the frontal bone.

Brush. Moderately coated tail in the shape of a brush; has fringe of hair below the tail. Tail of a fox, Beagle or American Foxhound.

Bull neck. A heavy, short, well muscled neck.

Burr. Irregular inner area of the ear, partly exposed in a rose ear.

Buttocks. That portion of the body below the croup and above the upper thigh, or the muscular area around the ischium of the pelvic girdle.

Calcaneal process. Uppermost extension of the hock joint, called the point of the hock. The calcaneal tendon attaches to the calcaneal process; muscles pulling on the calcaneal tendon straighten the hock. Mistakenly referred to as os calcis (comparable process in humans).

Canines. Tusks; four fang-like teeth behind the incisors and in front of the premolars, one on each side of both the upper and lower jaws. They are the longest and strongest teeth in the mouth.

Cap. Face marking over the skull. Alaskan Malamute.

Cape. Long and thick hair that forms an additional distinct layer of hair that extends beyond the ruff and covers the shoulder region. Schipperke.

Carpi. Bones of the pastern joints; part of the front legs. Seven bones arranged in two rows, three bones in the upper row and four bones in the lower row. These bones are located between the radius and ulna and the metacarpal bones.

Carpus. Wrist; located between the forearm and the pastern or metacarpus.

Cartilage. A somewhat elastic tissue that often serves as bone in an embryo; it forms a bearing surface in joints; gristle.

Castrate. To remove the testicles of the male dog.

Caudal. Direction meaning toward or relatively near the tail.

Caudal vertebrae. Tail vertebrae; vary in number according to breed; average number is twenty; may vary from six to twenty-three vertebrae.

Center of gravity. A point in any body at which the entire weight can be considered as concentrated; the center of gravitational attraction.

Cheek. Fleshy part of side of head below eyes and behind and above mouth.

Cheek bumps. Cheeks bulgy; overdevelopment of the masseter muscles.

Cheeky. Cheeks prominently rounded. Well developed cheek or masseter muscles in retrievers are undesirable (retrievers are soft-mouthed and do not need well developed jaw muscles to gently pick up and carry birds). Desirable in the American Staffordshire Terrier and Staffordshire Bull Terrier.

Chest. The forepart of the body enclosed by ribs and breastbone. *Chest, deep.* Chest that reaches to at least the elbow. *Chest, oval.* Chest deeper than wide; usually a tapered oval chest (deeper than wide but wider at top than at bottom of chest). *Chest well let down.* Lower line of chest, keel, brisket or sternum; extends *below* the elbows.

Chicken-breasted. Protrusion of forechest below the point of shoulder.

Chiseled. Cut away below the eyes; Cocker Spaniel Standard: "*The bony structure beneath the eyes is well chiseled . . .* "

Chiseling. Veining on the muzzle. Afghan Hound.

Chops. Fleshy and pendulous upper lips. The Bulldog Standard defines it as follows: "*The chops or 'flews' should be very thick, broad, pendant and very deep, completely over-hanging the lower jaw on each side.*" The German Shorthaired Pointer Standard states: "*The chops fall away from a somewhat projecting nose. Lips are full and deep yet are never flewy.*"

Clean-cut. Head with smooth and trim features. German Shorthaired Pointer.

Cloddy. Of low stature and heavy set; clumsy gait; often used in a derogatory manner.

Close-coupled. Short between the last rib and the forward end of the pelvis; short-loined.

Coarse. Unrefined; too heavy or overdone with bone.

Coat. Hairy outer covering of the skin; can be single-coated or double-coated, outer coat and undercoat, depending upon breed.

Coat, broken. Wire-coated or hard-coated with undercoat; the hairs having a tendency to twist, and of dense, wiry texture, growing so closely and strongly together that, when parted with the fingers, the skin cannot be seen. At the base of these hairs is a shorter growth of finer and softer hair, termed the undercoat. Airedale Terrier.

Coat, brush. Natural short coat of less than an inch in length that is harsh, absolutely straight and offstanding on the main trunk of the body but generally lying somewhat flatter on the limbs. When coat is extremely short it is called a horse coat. Chinese Shar-Pei.

Coat, closely curled. Mass of thick tight curls. American Water Spaniel.

Coat, corded. See corded.

Coat, curly. Compact, cylindrical curls, somewhat lusterless. Portuguese Water Dog. Also a thick mass of small, tight, crisp curls lying close to the skin, resilient and water resistent. Curly Coated Retriever.

Coat, double. Two coats; two-ply; a soft undercoat for warmth and waterproofing along with a hard outer coat resistant to wear.

Coat, guard. Outer coat; guard hairs; longer hairs on double-coated dogs; stiffer hairs that protect the undercoat; coat of a single-coated dog.

Coat, harsh. Stiff, wiry coat.

Coat, horse. Natural coat of extremely short length, much less than one inch, that is harsh, absolutely straight and offstanding on the main trunk of the body but generally lies somewhat flatter on the limbs. Chinese Shar-Pei.

Coat, marcel. Coat pattern with deep regular waves. American Water Spaniel.

Coat, pily. Penciled coat; body coat is a mixture of about two-thirds hardish hair with about one-third soft hair, giving a sort of crisp texture. The hard hair is not wiry. The effect of the natural intermingling of the two types of hair is termed "pily" or "penciled," vaguely resembling quills. Dandie Dinmont Terrier.

Coat, smooth. A short, close, straight coat.

Coat, stand-off. Standing-off coat; undercoat of soft, short, thick, close wool with longer harsh hair growing through it to form the outer coat, which stands straight out from the body. Samoyed, Pomeranian, Keeshond.

Coat, wavy. Falling gently in waves, not curls, and with a slight sheen. Portuguese Water Dog.

Cobby. Compact; a cob (short-legged stocky horse). Scottish Terrier, Schipperke.

Collar. A coat color marking around the neck; a white collar. Alaskan Malamute.

Collarette. Neck coat, relatively short ruff, somewhat longer than regular coat. Belgian Malinois, Belgian Sheepdog, Belgian Tervuren.

Color, coat. Hairs containing rings of pigment in these colors: black, brown (tan) or yellow (white has no color pigment). All coat colors and patterns are due to the amount and varying arrangements of pigment rings, which produce different optical effects. The pigmentation may be uniform throughout the hair, or it may vary. The same coat color may be called different names in different breeds; as in "blue-ticked" (Coonhound) and "blue belton" (English Setter).

Corded. Coat that hangs naturally in tight, even strands of varying length. Cords are formed naturally and they are felt-like to the touch. Komondor, Poodle, Puli.

Corny feet. Horny, thick soles on feet.

Coupled, loosely. Long coupling; long loin and some tuck-in of loin.

Coupled, strongly. Well coupled; short loin and little tuck-in of loin.

Coupling. Lumbar area, loin, flank and abdominal muscles; the area between the last rib and the forward end of the pelvis; couples.

Covering ground. The distance between front and rear legs and the ratio of the distance between the ground and brisket. Daylight under a dog is also the same ratio; shows too little daylight (too close to the ground). Also refers to a smooth, efficient gait.

Cow-hocked. Hocks similar to the hock of most cows; hocks turned inward toward one another; a fault for most dogs; Bulldogs may be slightly cow-hocked.

Cranial. Directional term meaning toward or relatively near the head or braincase.

Cranium. See backskull.

Crest. Crest of neck; the upper rear arched portion of the neck, just below the occiput; hair on head of Hairless variety of Chinese Crested starts at the stop and tapers off between the base of the skull and the back of the neck. Also refers to the top of the shoulder blade.

Cropping. Cropped ears. Surgically removing the outer part of ears to make them stand erect and provide a specific shape to the ear.

Crotch. Region at the junction of the two hind legs.

Crouch. Hindquarters pulled up such that first and second thigh are at a near 90 degree angle. Fault in Smooth or Wire Fox Terrier and Kerry Blue Terrier.

Croup. That portion of the body above the hind legs and extending from the loin to the set-on of tail and buttocks area. Used interchangeably with the term "rump." The pelvis is a part of the croup; but the pelvic angle and the croup angle are not necessarily the same.

Croup, flat. Croup level with topline; croup not steep; sometimes used to mean less than desirable for the breed, as "too flat a croup for an Afghan Hound." A flat croup has a high tailset and no fall-off of the backline.

Crown. Topskull; highest part of the head, also called dome; crown of a tooth is the exposed portion above the gum line; the ridge of the Rhodesian Ridgeback contains two identical crowns or whorls located directly opposite each other.

Cryptorchid. An adult male in which one or both testicles have not descended into the scrotum. Only one testicle descended is referred to as "unilateral cryptorchid," while two testicles undescended is referred to as "bilateral cryptorchid." A castrated dog has had testicles surgically removed.

Cuffs. Area of the pastern on the foreleg and the hock on the rear leg. Can have short hair on cuffs of the Afghan Hound.

Culotte. Breeching; trousers; long and thick hair on the rear of the thighs, not below. Schipperke.

Cushion. Exceptionally thick lips or flews; thick pads of feet; muzzle with rounded cushion (Basenji); area well filled out under eyes (English Toy Spaniel).

Dentition. Arrangement, kind and number of teeth. For a description of dentition see: Teeth, deciduous; Teeth, permanent.

Dewclaw. Unused digit (fifth toe) on the inside of both the front and rear legs. Dewclaws are usually removed at birth. Double rear dewclaws are *required* on the Briard and the Great Pyrenees.

Dewlap. Loose, pendulous folds of skin about the neck. Bloodhound, Basset Hound, Clumber Spaniel, Bulldog.

Diamond. Black diamond-shaped marking on the forehead. Pug.

Diaphragm. The muscular tissue separating the thorax and the abdomen; the breathing diaphragm.

Digits. Bones of the toes (first three bones of each toe, or phalanges).

Dimple. Small depression on either side of forechest.

Dish-faced. The nose curves upward like a dish; topline of muzzle is concave; nose is higher than stop. Proper in Pointers, a fault in most other breeds.

Distal. A position far away from the main part of a structure.

Distemper teeth. Pitting of the tooth enamel; often caused by distemper or other illness occurring at the time of teething.

Distichiasis. Extra row of eyelashes on the inner surface of the eyelid, causing irritation and possible damage to the eye. It can range from one hair to a large number of stiff, irritating lashes. Cause for excusal in Golden Retrievers.

Dock. To surgically remove the tail or a portion of the tail; a docked tail; stumped tail.

Dog. Male canine or any member of the genus *Canis familiaris*.

Doggy bitch. Female dog displaying masculine characteristics.

Domed. Domed skull; rounded in topskull; convex topskull.

Dorsal. Directional term meaning toward or relatively near the back.

Down-faced. Muzzle inclining downwards as on Bull Terrier and Miniature Bull Terrier. Less pronounced and not desirable in other breeds.

Down in pastern. The metacarpus (pastern) set at a greater angle from the vertical than that called for in the Standard. A German Shepherd Dog is supposed to have a 25 degree angle from the vertical; a German Shepherd is "down in pasterns" if the angle is substantially more than 25 degrees. The term is usually a fault. Many breed Standards call for vertical pasterns; others "slightly inclined."

Droop. Hindquarters bending downward. Fault in Smooth and Wire Fox Terrier and Kerry Blue Terrier.

Drooping. Loin is well arched and the line of the arch is followed to the set of the tail. Scottish Deerhound.

Dry. Dry skin (not loose). As applied to the Pointer: Neck—Long, dry (this means *no loose skin*; skin taut). Dry head. Australian Shepherd.

Dry, moderately. Not showing an excess of loose skin. Neck of Mastiff.

Ear. Auditory organ for sense of hearing; external part often called lobe, leather, flap or pinna. *Ear flap.* Ear leather. *Ear flat.* Ear where the ear leather is flat against the head.

Ear fringes. Long silky hair on the edges of the ear leather.

Ear set. Junction of the ear lobe base to the backskull. Ears joining the backskull below eye level are called "low set," while those that join above eye level are called "high set." Ears set wide on the backskull are called "set on wide."

Ear tassel. Hair on tip of ear resembling a tassel. Bedlington Terrier.

Ears, bat. Ears standing erect, like those of a bat. The ear is broad at the base, elongated, with round top, set high on the head but not too closely together, and carried erect with the orifice to the front. French Bulldog.

Ears, bear. Small and very round-tipped ear; fault in the Samoyed.

Ears, broken. Breakdown of ear cartilage. Fault in the Akita, disqualification in the Chow Chow.

Ears, butterfly. Large erect ears with rounded tips, carried obliquely and moving like the spread wings of a butterfly; when alert, each ear forms an angle of approximately 45 degrees to the head. Papillon.

Ears, button. Top of ear folded forward; topline of the folded ear should be above the level of the skull, so as to close the ear opening (orifice) with the tip near the skull; tip of ear is generally pointed toward the outside corner of the eye.

Ears, cropped. See cropping.

Ears, dead. Hound-like in appearance. Severely penalized fault in Irish Terrier and very undesirable in Kerry Blue Terrier.

Ears, drop. Not erect or prick; any deviation from erect, from full drop to tips of ears dropping or folding forward.

Ears, erect. Pricked; upright; stiff upstanding ear leather open toward the front. Pomeranian, Belgian Malinois, Belgian Sheepdog, Belgian Tervuren, German Shepherd Dog.

Ears, folded. Drop or pendent ears in which the lobes are folded vertically. Black and Tan Coonhound, Bloodhound, Otterhound.

Ears, flying. Ears that show excessive rectile power are said to "fly." A dog that is supposed to have semi-prick ears which instead stand up has "flying ears." Ears pricked up more than is correct for the breed.

Ears, heart-shaped. Ear leather shaped like a heart. Portugese Water Dog, Pekingese.

Ears, hooded. Strongly erect with outer edges of lobes curving forward, carried slightly forward in line with back of neck. Basenji, Akita.

Ears, hound. See ears, folded. American Foxhound.

Ears, lobe-shaped. Lobular ears. American Water Spaniel, Cocker Spaniel, Irish Water Spaniel, Sussex Spaniel.

Ears, low-set. Set or attached to side of head rather than to top of head.

Ears, mobile. Ears that can move, such as the Saluki, such that the ears in repose can be set on the side of the head and when alert are pulled upwards to set on the top of the skull.

Ears, natural. Uncropped ears.

Ears, Phalene. Papillon drop ears that are carried drooping and completely down.

Ears, prick. Erect ears; usually pointed and erect. Ibizan Hound.

Ears, rose. A drop ear where the lobes fold inward at the back lower edge, the upper front edge curving over, outward and backward, showing part of the inside of the burr. Seen in the Bulldog, Greyhound, Irish Wolfhound, Whippet and in some Australian Shepherds and Pugs.

Ears, "rounded." English Foxhound ears may be "rounded," which means about $1\frac{1}{2}$ inches is taken off the end of the ear. This often designates membership in a hunting pack.

Ears, semi-prick. Ear that is approximately three-fourths erect and the top one-fourth tips or breaks naturally forward.

Ears, spoon. Variation of bat ears.

Ears, tulip. Ear breaking much above the midpoint of the leather; stands upright from base for about one-half to two-thirds of its length; top half or third of the leather bent forward, parallel with or slightly toward the head; the tip clearly visible well above the level of the skull.

Ears, vine leaf. Shaped like a vine leaf. Welsh Springer Spaniel.

Ectropion. Loose eyelid sagging and turning outward (everted). Exposed tissues are subject to irritation and injury.

Egg-shaped head. Full face oval in outline when viewed head on, and filled completely up, giving the impression of fullness with a surface devoid of hollows or indentations. Bull Terrier.

Elbow. The joint between the upper arm (humerus) and forearm (radius and ulna).

Elbows, out at. Elbows protruding from the body or from a straight line from shoulder joint to foot when viewed from the front; most easily seen during movement; loose elbows; elbows not close to body.

Elbows, pinched. Elbows closer together than pasterns when viewed from the front. Generally associated with lack of depth of brisket.

Elbows, tied-in. Elbows pulled in too tightly against chest wall, generally causing toeing out and/or feet further apart than the elbows.

Entire. An adult male with both testicles normally descended into the scrotum.

Entropion. Eyelid rolled inward (inverted), causing irritation due to hair contacting the surface of the eye. Generally only the lower lid is affected; less frequently the upper lid may be affected as well.

Estrus. See **oestrus.**

Expression. Appearance of eyes, mouth, ears and general head appearance; outward head appearance of disposition; expression of the face as Terrier expression; foxy expression.

Extensor. A muscle that straightens or extends a limb.

Eye. Similar to human eye. Size—most dogs' eyeballs (orbits) are round and approximately the same size for similarly sized dogs. *Apparent* size is a function of depth of orbit in socket and eyelid shape; shape of the surrounding tissue and eyelid determines the apparent eye shape as called for in Standards; placement of the eye on the skull determines the field of vision (directly forward, or to the side).

Eye, circular. Non-protruding round eye. Smooth Fox Terrier.

Eye, full. Round, slightly protruding eye; popeye. Pug.

Eye, hazel. Light brown eye.

Eye, light. Yellowish or light in color.

Eye, pig. Unusually small, squinty eyes.

Eye, pop. See eye, full.

Eye shapes. Shape of the area exposed by the eye rim or opening. Some of the shapes are: almond, circular, diamond, globular, lozenge, oval, round, triangular eye. *Almond eye*—eyelids shaped like an almond; eyeballs are round or globular; the surrounding tissue is almond-shaped. Afghan Hound, Doberman Pinscher, Kuvasz, Chinese Crested. *Circular*—Smooth and Wire Fox Terrier. *Diamond*—four equal sides with two inner obtuse angles and two inner acute angles, or with a "V" at the bottom. Clumber Spaniel. *Diamond or lozenge*—Bloodhound. *Globular*—Pug. *Oval*—Lakeland Terrier, Miniature Schnauzer, Australian Cattle Dog. *Round*—Affenpinscher, Japanese Chin, Maltese, Pekingese. *Triangular*—Somewhat three-cornered–appearing eye; the tissue surrounding the eye has a triangular shape. Bull Terrier, Miniature Bull Terrier.

Eyelid. There are three eyelids: upper, lower and third eyelid (also called "haw" or "nictitating membrane"). Eyelashes are located along the edge of the upper eyelid. The haw can be pigmented or unpigmented and prevents foreign objects from injuring the eye.

Eyelid, everted. Eyelid that turns outward, or away from the eye.

Eyelid, inverted. Eyelid turned inward towards the eye.

Eyes, bird of prey. Yellow eyes, harsh, hard and staring. Fault in the Rottweiler.

Eyes, china. A clear blue eye.

Eyes, Mongolian. Obliquely set eyes; outer corners of the eyes set higher than the inner corners; slanted eyes.

Eyes, obliquely set. Eyes set on an angle in the skull; outer corner of eye higher in skull than the inner corner. Basenji, Finnish Spitz.

Eyes, prominent. Protruding eyes.

Eyes, sunken. Eyes deep in sockets.

Eyes, terrierlike. Moderately small, rather deep-set, full of fire and nearly circular in shape. Fault in a Beagle.

Fall. Hair falling over face.

Fangs. Canine teeth. Four large teeth behind the incisors and in front of the premolars. One on each side of both the upper and lower jaws. They are the longest and strongest teeth in the mouth.

Feathering. Long hair on ears, back of legs, chest, belly or underside of tail. Fringes.

Feet, cat. Round, compact foot with well arched toes; center toes approximately as long as the outer and inner toes; close-cupped feet.

Feet, close-cupped. Cat feet.

Feet, east and west. Toes turned out.

Feet, ferrety. Long, narrow, flat thin feet, lack of knuckling in toes. Fault in Cairn Terrier.

Feet, flat. Toes straight or flat when viewed from the side; toes not well arched.

Feet, foxlike. Feet similar to those of the red fox or the grey fox: feet close and compact, toes well arched; center toes are longer than outer and inner toes, but not as long as on the hare foot. American Foxhound.

Feet, hare. Center toes are considerably longer than outer and inner toes.

Feet, open. Splay feet.

Feet, oval. Spoon-shaped feet; compact foot in oval shape with well arched toes; center toes slightly longer than outer and inner toes.

Feet, paper. A thin pad usually associated with a flat foot.

Feet, slew. Feet turned out.

Feet, snowshoe. Feet that are large, tight and deep, with well-cushioned, thick and tough pads, toes tight fitting and well arched with a protective growth of hair between the toes and a firm, compact appearance. Alaskan Malamute.

Feet, splay. Spreading feet; toes set far apart from each other; toes not tightly knit; toes spread out; open feet; usually with a lack of knuckling.

Feet, spoon-shaped. See feet, oval.

Feet, tightly knit. Toes set firmly next to each other.

Feet, well arched. Toes well knuckled up.

Femur. Upper thigh bone; bone located below pelvis; heaviest bone in skeleton; bone between pelvis and stifle or knee joint.

Fetlocks, overbent. Based on comparative anatomy, this horse term has been wrongly applied to the Irish Wolfhound. Refers to the wrist or pastern joint and means *down in pasterns*. Fault in the Irish Wolfhound.

Fibula. Smallest of two bones between stifle joint and hock joint; located in lower thigh.

Field condition. Dog in prime physical condition with firm, supple muscle tone. German Shorthaired Pointer.

Fill. Fullness of bone.

Flag. Tail with long feathering; a feathered tail as seen on an Irish Setter.

Flank. Area below the loin between last rib and thigh; the area thinly covered with flesh and skin between last rib and hindquarters; groin flap.

Flanks, deep. Little or no tuck-up.

Flap. Ear leather; flank.

Flare. A blaze that flares (widens) out near top of skull.

Flashings. White markings on the neck (either in part or as a collar), chest, legs, muzzle, underparts, tip of tail and as a blaze on the head. Cardigan Welsh Corgi.

Flat back. Back that is straight from the withers to the set-on of the tail. Severely penalized fault in Manchester Terrier.

Flat bone. Leg bone elliptical; not rounded. Borzoi have somewhat flattened shoulder blades and foreleg bone.

Flat-sided. Variable in meaning depending upon the breed. Flatter than called for in the Standard. A Bulldog has well rounded ribs; a flat-sided Bulldog would have well rounded ribs as compared to a Greyhound. Usually derogatory.

Flew. The corner rear portion of the upper lip when it hangs loose, not tight and closed. Basset Hound, Bloodhound. Flews, which hang loose, are a fault in the Brittany. Also in some Standards refers to the corner of the mouth; *"flews are tight and dry fleshed"* (Ibizan Hound). In some Standards it refers to the fleshy, sometimes pendulous upper lips. *"Flews squared and fairly pendent"* (English Setter).

Flexors. A muscle that bends or flexes a limb.

Folds. Folds in the skin running downward from the lower edge of the stop on both sides of the muzzle. Boxer.

Forearm. The region between the upper arm and the wrist or pastern. Consists of the radius and ulna and associated ligaments and muscles. Also referred to as "lower arm."

Forechest. The area between the points of shoulder and down to the upper arm and forearm junction.

Foreface. All of the portion of the head in front of the eyes; muzzle.

Foreface depth. Distance downward from the stop to the lowest portion of the jaw.

Forehand. A horse term; forequarters and associated body.

Forelegs. Front legs.

Forequarter. Shoulder, upper arm, lower arm, pastern and forefoot. The combined front assembly including the bone, muscle, tendons, ligaments and associated nervous and circulatory systems.

Foxy. Expression of face that looks like a fox's; pointed nose with short foreface; a sharp face; head shape and expression of Pembroke Welsh Corgi.

Frill. Long hair on forechest; apron. Papillon, Pekingese, Pomeranian. Fine line hair pattern on each side of neck extending almost to the corner of the ear. Irish Terrier.

Fringes. Feathering.

Frogface. A face with a frog-like expression; extended nose and receding lower jaw, usually overshot; found in Bostons, Boxers, Bulldogs; caused by lack of depth of foreface.

Front. Front legs, chest, brisket and withers but not the neck and head.

Front, Chippendale. Front shaped like a Chippendale chair.

Front, fiddle. Front, when viewed straight on, shaped like a fiddle (violin); out at elbows, pasterns close, feet pointing out (east and west); often with excessive curvature in lower arm; Chippendale front; French front. Objectionable in Dandie Dinmont Terrier.

Front, pinched. Narrow front; elbows and pasterns close together when viewed from the front. Generally associated with poor spring of ribs and lack of depth of brisket.

Front, straight. Lower arm, pastern and forefoot when looked at straight on, i.e., a straight front. Afghan Hound.

Frontal bone. The skull bones over the eyes, containing the frontal sinus. Temple. Location of the stop. The size of the frontal sinus determines the depth of the stop.

Frost. White or grey on chin or muzzle, sometimes due to age.

Furnishings. Dense and wiry hair on muzzle, legs, and quarters. Welsh Terrier. Long softer hair that covers the legs and chest and appears on the face as whiskers and eyebrows. Miniature and Standard Schnauzer.

Furrow. Groove; fluting; median line or indentation: depending upon the breed, a depression in the skull that runs between the eyes and up through the center of the skull. Boxer, Bulldog, Clumber Spaniel, Chow Chow, etc.

Gaskin. Second or lower thigh; horse term applied to the dog. Bloodhound.

Girth. To measure the circumference.

Goose rump. Croup (pelvis) sloping too steeply toward the rear; low tail set.

Grossness. Excessive development of either muscle or bone or both; over developed; generally musclebound and restricted in movement.

Gun-barrel front. Straight front legs.

Hackles. Raised hackles; in anger a dog that involuntarily raises the hair on the neck, withers and top of the backline is said to have its hackles up.

Halos. Black or very dark brown skin surrounding the eyes. Bichon Frise.

Ham. The part of the dog corresponding to the ham on a pig; muscular development of the upper thigh (above stifle). Boxer.

Harefoot. Foot as on a rabbit (hare); an elongated foot; a narrow long foot; both center toes are longer than outer and inner toes, with good arch to toes.

Haunch bone. Rearmost bone of the pelvic girdle, ischiac tuber. Pharaoh Hound.

Haunches. Hip, buttock and upper thigh; German Shorthaired Pointer Standard—"*hair . . . somewhat longer on . . . back edges of the haunches.*"

Haw. A third eyelid, the conjunctival lining visible with a loose lower eyelid. A membrane in the inside corner of the eye (a third eyelid). Clumber Spaniels, Sussex Spaniels, Basset Hounds, and Otterhounds should show some haw; in most other breeds haw showing is a fault.

Head. Skull, associated muscles and the sense organs—eyes, ears, nasal cavity and the organ of taste; attaches to the first or axis vertebra of the neck.

Head, apple. Domed head; roof of braincase or backskull rounded. Chihuahua.

Head, "one piece." The characteristic head of the Flat-Coated Retriever; impression of the backskull and muzzle being "cast in one piece" is created by the fairly flat backskull of moderate breadth and flat, clean cheeks, combined with the long, strong, deep muzzle which is well filled in before, between and beneath the eyes. Viewed from above, the muzzle is nearly equal in length and breadth to the backskull.

Head, otter. Characteristic head shape similar to an otter's head; Border Terrier head shape.

Head planes. Top of muzzle, top of backskull and bottom of lower jaw. Many Standards only refer to the top of muzzle and top of backskull.

Head, Ram's. Profile of head from occiput to nose is a convex curve, an unbroken arc with the high point at the crown. Bedlington Terrier.

Heat. Oestrus; breeding cycle of bitches.

Heel. Rear pad on feet.

Height. Height of a dog is measured from withers to ground.

Herring gut. Bottom line of dog sweeps up excessively from brisket to loin due to improper depth of ribcage; ribs rapidly slope upward from keel to floating rib; a fault that decreases heart and lung room.

High on leg. Leggy; appears high off the ground; high stationed; up on leg. Basenji.

Hindquarters. Pelvic girdle, upper thigh, stifle joint and patella, lower thigh, hock joint, hock and rear foot. The combined rear assembly including the bone, muscle, tendons, ligaments and associated nervous and circulatory systems.

Hindquarters, bowed. Bowed hocks; hocks that turn outwards resulting in bowed hindquarters; barrel hocks.

Hip bones. Iliac crest of pelvic girdle; hucklebones.

Hip joint. Ball and socket joint located in the pelvic girdle that provides the attachment for the upper thigh or rear leg.

Hippopotamus muzzle. Shape of muzzle, broad and full with lips and top of muzzle well padded and may cause a slight bulge at base of nose. Chinese Shar-Pei.

Hock. The hock joint, lower joint on rear leg; joint between lower thigh and rear pastern; often used incorrectly in many Standards to mean the area from the hock joint to the foot; in a normal stance the hocks are perpendicular to the ground and parallel to each other.

Hocks, barrel. See hocks, bow. Pembroke Welsh Corgi.

Hocks, bow. When viewed from the rear, the points of the hocks are further apart than the feet; spraddle hocks.

Hocks, cow. When viewed from the rear, the points of the hocks are closer together than the feet.

Hocks, high in. Hock joints far from ground; long hocks. High in hocks provides jumping power.

Hocks, low. Hock joints close to the ground; short hocks. Low hocks provide endurance.

Hocks, open. When viewed from the side, angle between the second thigh and rear pastern is greater than desirable; straight hocks.

Hocks, set back. With hocks perpendicular to the ground, a plumb line dropped from the rearmost point of the hindquarters will pass in front of the hind foot. Mastiff.

Hocks, sickle. Inability to straighten the hock joint on the back reach of the hind leg; dog moves with a fixed angle in hock joint; dog stands with back of rear foot forward of point of hock.

Hocks, spread. Opposite of cow hocks; when viewed from the rear, hock joints further apart than feet; hocks pointing outward when standing or in motion.

Hocks, straight. Insufficient bend in the hock joint for the breed; correct for Chow Chow—"*hock joint . . . appears almost straight.*"

Hocks, well let-down. Hock joints close to the ground. Short hocks improve endurance.

Hollowness between the front legs. Lack of prosternum and forechest development causes hollowness between the front legs.

Hucklebones. Hip bones; iliac crest of the pelvic girdle. Very pronounced in the Afghan Hound.

Humerus. Bone between elbow and shoulder blade; upper arm.

Hunter. A class of horse developed to follow the hounds. The German Shorthaired Pointer is like a proper hunter—"*with a short back, but standing over plenty of ground.*"

In shoulder. Fault found in dogs with shoulder blade too far forward on chest; shoulders point in, not parallel with the spine; more commonly found on short-legged dogs; in shoulders and out at the elbows normally go together.

Incisors. Front teeth between canines: six front teeth in both upper and lower jaw between the fangs (canines).

Incisors, dropped lower central. The two lower central incisors set a little deeper than the other incisors. Great Pyrenees.

Ischial tuberosity. Point of ischium; rear edge of pelvis. Sometimes described as "dog behind the tail."

Jabot. Long and thick hair that extends across the chest and down between the front legs. Schipperke.

Jacket. Outer coat on the body; normally a hard, wiry, dense and close-fitting outer coat. Airedale Terrier, Welsh Terrier.

Jaw, pig. Exaggerated overshot jaw, with weak underjaw; upper jaw extending well beyond lower jaw; pig mouth.

Jaws. The jaw bones carry the teeth; upper and lower jaws border the mouth; see **dentition, complete.**

Jowls. Flesh of the cheeks and lower jaw, especially when plump or flaccid; dewlap.

Keel. Portion of breastbone running between the forelegs and extending backward to the line of the abdomen. Dachshund, Australian Terrier.

Keel, deep. Where the keel reaches to, or below the level of the elbows.

Kinetic balance. A dog in balance when in motion; a bicycle and rider are in balance when in motion (the rider falls off when out of balance).

Kiss marks. Spots over eyes and on cheeks.

Knee. Stifle joint in rear leg (pastern joint on the front leg is not a knee).

Knee joint. See knee.

Knuckling over. Pastern joint bent forward; instead of being vertical or sloped as required by the Standard; the front leg has a forward bend at the pastern joint. The Harrier is inclined to knuckle over very slightly; a fault in most other breeds.

Lachrymal glands. Glands that produce tears or lacrimal fluid. They are located above the eye and produce 70 percent of the tears, while the superficial gland of the third eyelid produces 30 percent of the tears.

Lateral displacement. Lateral instability; the force that causes side sway in a pacing dog (to a lesser degree in a trotting dog).

Layback. Layback of shoulder blade, nose (English Toy Spaniel), muzzle (Boxer) or ribs. The angle that the shoulder blade deviates from the horizontal; laid back. Nose layback, sometimes referred to as muzzle layback, describes the manner in which the nose recedes from the vertical. When looking from above, angle that ribs incline or slant toward the rear (angle between backbone and rib) is rib layback.

Lay in, Lay on. Slope of shoulder blade toward the spine. It is a function of shoulder placement on the ribcage, shape of ribcage in the area of the shoulder, and shoulder muscle condition.

Leather. Leather of a hound's ear; soft portion of the ear that provides external protection; flap of an ear.

Leggy. Legs too long for proper balance of the dog.

Lippy. Lips that do not fit tightly; excess lip; more lip than described in the Standard for the breed.

Lips, fluttering. Excessively pendulous lips overhanging the lower jaw. Undesirable in the Great Dane.

Lips, pendulous. Lips that do not fit tightly, fall square in front and, toward the back, in loose hanging flews. Basset Hound.

Lips, tight and clean. Lips fitting close to jaw without any flew. Australian Cattle Dog.

Loin. Area between the back or end of ribcage and the croup or pelvic girdle; lumbar area.

Lumber. More flesh or bone than needed.

Lumbering. Lumbering along; not graceful; awkward gait; heavy cumbersome gait.

Malocclusion. Faulty closure of teeth.

Mandible. Lower jaw bones.

Mane. Mane as on a lion or horse; long hair on top of neck and at times including the side of neck and onto shoulders. Scottish Deerhound, Kuvasz, Norfolk and Norwich Terriers, Japanese Chin, Pekingese, Keeshond, Tibetan Spaniel, Collie, Shetland Sheepdog.

Mantle. On the Saint Bernard, the dark shaded portion of the coat on neck, back, shoulders and sides. Alaskan Malamute.

Mask. Dark shading on the muzzle.

Metacarpus. Bones of front leg from pastern to front foot; bones of pastern.

Metatarsus. Bones of rear leg from hock joint to rear foot; bones of hock.

Molars. Located at back or upper and lower jaws; two true molars on each side of the upper jaw and three on each side of the lower jaw.

Molera. Incomplete closing (ossification) of bones in center of skull, between frontal and parietal bones. Found in young puppies and some adult Chihuahuas.

Moles. Cheek markings on a Pug.

Monorchid. A male dog with one testicle descended into the scrotum (the other may be in the abdominal cavity); correctly known as unilateral cryptorchid.

Multum in parvo. Translation: "Much in little." Pug.

Muscle. Tissue composed of fibers capable of contracting and relaxing to effect movement; provides the power for circulation, respiration, digestion, secretion, excretion, locomotion and many minor functions.

Muscle tone. Quality or health condition of muscle tissue; firm, supple muscles are both healthy and good quality muscle.

Mustache. Thick and long hair on the upper lip. Bouvier des Flandres.

Mute. To track silently; to run mute while trailing.

Muzzle. Foreface; forward portion of the upper and lower jaw and nose portion of the head; the head in front of the eyes. Also a device fitting over a dog's mouth to prevent biting or eating.

Muzzle band. The white marking around the muzzle in the Boston Terrier and Bernese Mountain Dog.

Muzzle, conical. Variation of the tapering muzzle; muzzle is cone-shaped. Ibizan Hound.

Muzzle, pinched. When viewed from above, the muzzle at the junction of the backskull is narrower than the muzzle at the nose.

Muzzle, short. Muzzle that is less than half the length of the backskull.

Muzzle, snipy. When viewed from above, the muzzle at the junction of the backskull is pinched the entire length of the muzzle. Incisors or front teeth are crowded.

Muzzle, square cut. Blunt and cut off square, forming a right angle with the upper line of the muzzle; blunt muzzle. Beagle.

Muzzle, tapering. From the junction with the backskull, the muzzle tapers to the nose.

Muzzle, truncated. Form of a square-cut muzzle; muzzle appearing to be shortened and cut off square, forming a right angle with the upper line of the muzzle. Komondor, Mastiff.

Muzzle, wedge-shaped. Variation of a tapering muzzle; sides of muzzle are flat.

Nape. Area of junction of base of skull with top of neck.

Neck. The area between the head and the shoulders; included are the first seven cervical vertebrae of the spinal column.

Neck, cloddy. Short, thick neck. A fault in Beagles.

Neck, concave. Backline of neck has a concave shape.

Neck, ewe. Concave neck; like the neck of a sheep; a ewe neck does not have an arch.

Neutered. An animal whose reproductive ability has been surgically altered.

Nose. External nose, associated cartilage and the nasal cavity. Most Standards refer to just the external nose; some Standards refer to the entire muzzle.

Nose, butterfly. Two-tone nose; nose with flesh-colored spots; usually undesirable or faulty.

Nose, crusty. A granular build-up of skin on the nose.

Nose, Dudley. Unpigmented nose. Correspondingly, usually eye rims are also unpigmented.

Nose, ram's. Arched muzzle; slightly convex from stop to nose tip.

Nose, Roman. Bridge of nose near tip bends downward; convex curvature of nose near tip. Afghan Hound, Borzoi, Dachshund.

Nose, slightly aquiline. Shape of external nose is curved or hooked like an eagle's beak. Scottish Deerhound.

Nose, snow. Winter nose; nose that is normally deep black or liver, which fades to light pink, sometimes streaked, in winter. Alaskan Malamute, Samoyed, Siberian Husky.

Nose, split. A line that extends from the lip and continues between nostrils, going up over the top of the nose (naso-labial line). Disqualification in the Great Dane.

Nostrils. The two external openings of the nose serving as an air-breathing nasal passage.

Nostrils, spread flat. Nose broad, flattened in profile. Mastiff.

Nuchal crest. Top of occiput.

Occipital protuberance (occiput, peak). Some hounds and gun dogs have the occiput well developed and called the occipital protuberance. Irish Setter, Irish Water Spaniel, Clumber Spaniel, Field Spaniel, Afghan Hound, Basset Hound, Bloodhound, Petit Basset Griffon Vendéen.

Occiput. Back part of the head or skull; the high point of the back part of the head.

Oestrus (also **estrus**). Period of time during which a bitch is ready to accept a dog for mating.

Off-square. Slightly longer from point of shoulder to point of buttocks, than height at withers. Chihuahua.

Os calcis. Properly called the calcaneal process, uppermost extension of the hock joint, called the point of the hock.

Outline. Line from crest of neck to tip of the tail. Dandie Dinmont Terrier.

Overangulation. Having more bend of stifle (or front angulation) than called for in the Standard. For most breeds, when in a stacked position with the rear hocks perpendicular to the ground, the rear toes are well behind the point of the rump.

Overdone. Caricature; extreme in one or more breed attributes.

Overhand. Forechest extends well in front of the legs and drops well down into the brisket.

Overhang. Heavy, pronounced brow.

Pad, stop. Carpal pad; small pad at the back of the hock joint which provides cushioning to joint when dog is in a gallop.

Padding. Flapping; the front feet flap up (opposite of hackney action, where the toe points downward); more common in short-legged breeds such as Dachshunds; lifting the front feet higher than normal in the forward stride in order to prevent pounding.

Paddling. Moving the front legs like a canoe paddle motion; a rotary motion; when the front feet move forward, they have a somewhat circular motion.

Pads. Tough soft material on underside of dog's feet; pads absorb shock; soles of feet, composed of a roughened outer surface, papillae, which provides traction, then a thickened epidermal and dermal part and a deeper fat pad.

Pads, deep. Pads of feet thick.

Pads, horny. Tough pads.

Pads, stands well over. Pads of forefeet are directly under the withers. Alaskan Malamute.

Palate. Consists of a partly bony or hard palate and partly membranous or soft palate partition in the roof of the mouth, which separates the nasal and oral cavities, or respiratory and digestive passages of the head.

Palate, cleft. Congenital defect in some breeds in which the two bony halves of the hard palate between the upper teeth fail to unite along their center boundary, leaving a gap between them.

Pants. Thick hair on the back of thighs. Cardigan Welsh Corgi, Keeshond.

Pantaloon effect. Feathering along the back of the thighs. Great Pyrenees.

Pastern. The region between the wrist or carpus and the forefoot. Consists of the five metacarpal bones and associated ligaments and muscles.

Pastern, down in. Pastern with too much slope for the breed. Generally means pastern at or in excess of 45 degrees to the vertical.

Pastern, rear. Area from the hock joint to the paw; in normal stance the rear pasterns, called hocks in many Standards, are perpendicular to the ground and parallel to each other.

Pastern, straight. Upright pastern; erect pastern; pastern with no noticeable slope when viewed from the side; pastern perpendicular to the ground.

Patella. Kneecap.

Paw. Foot.

Paw, ball of hind. Situated to the rear of the four active hind toes is a large pad called the metatarsal pad or ball of hind paw. Dachshund.

Peak. Back of occipital protuberance; topknot *coat pattern* of Irish Water Spaniel providing a well defined peak between the eyes.

Pear-shaped. Shaped like a pear; the Pekingese and Bulldog have pear-shaped bodies.

Pelvic shelf. Buttocks extending beyond tail; tail set well up on back provides a pelvic shelf. Lakeland Terrier. (See Ischial tuberosity.)

Pelvic slope. Angle between the horizontal and the axis of the pelvic girdle; pelvic angle.

Pelvis. Pelvic girdle; bones fused to spinal column at rear of dog between the loin and tail which provide sockets for attachment of rear legs.

Penciling. Distinct black or pencil-mark line running lengthwise on the top of each toe. Gordon Setter, Black and Tan Coonhound, Rottweiler, Manchester Terrier (Standard and Toy). See also coat, pily.

Pendulous. Hanging loosely; suspended so as to swing or sway; Bloodhound has loose skin on the head that has pendulous ridges and folds.

Pigeon-toed. Toes turned in; toes pointing toward one another; toes turned in from the line of progress.

Pigmentation. Dark pigmentation of nose, eye rims, lips, toenails, pads and skin; color of pigment generally follows coat color; in most breeds the pigment should be completely filled in and it should not show any sign of spots; lacking pigment is indicated by flesh or light color.

Pile. Dense, soft undercoat.

Pisiform. The bone at the front pastern joint (carpal assembly) that gives action to the pastern and foot; a tendon pulling on the pisiform moves the pastern and foot.

Pliant. Skin in healthy condition; supple skin; flexible skin. Akita, Basenji.

Points. Shoulder blade upper tips. English Foxhound, Smooth and Wire Fox Terrier.

Point of buttocks. Rearmost projection of the buttocks in the area of the tuber ischium.

Point of forechest. Point of breastbone; forward point of first sternum bone; when the manubrium projects in front of the points of the shoulder blades when viewed from the side, this is referred to as the prosternum.

Point of shoulder. Forward point of shoulder and upper arm joint.

Pole. The joint between the second and third cervical vertebrae of neck; joint in spine near occiput.

Pompon. Pertains to Poodles; a round tuft of hair on the end of the tail produced by trimming.

"Pot-casse" ring. The ring of the Old English Sheepdog's bark.

Pot-gutted. An overlarge abdomen; distended stomach.

Propellers. Hindquarters. English Foxhound.

Prosternum. The part of the dog in front of the point of shoulder, when viewed from the side.

Proximal. Position near the main part of a structure.

Puffs. Long hair left on forelegs of Poodles, clipped or trimmed in the "English Saddle" or "Continental" clip.

Quarters. Usually used as hindquarters or forequarters; one rear leg forms a hindquarter.

Quicksilver movement. Movement where the dog makes abrupt turns, springing starts and sudden stops while herding. Briard.

Racy. Tall and thin, as a Greyhound; looks racy; looks like a speedster; too light in structure.

Radius. Radius and ulna bones form the foreleg or forearm; weight-bearing bone of the foreleg.

Ragged. Muscles do not appear smooth; from a ragged cloth as opposed to a smooth-cut cloth. English Foxhound.

Rangy body. Long and lightly built and high on leg. Serious fault in the Akita.

Rearhand. Horse term; rearquarters and associated body (pelvic girdle, croup, rump) and tail.

Rib, floating. Last or thirteenth rib, which is unattached to other ribs.

Ribbed back. Long ribcage and short loin. Australian Cattle Dog.

Ribbed-up. Ribs angling rearward at approximately 45 degrees in respect to the spinal column; well ribbed-up; in some Standards this refers to a long rib cage and short loin. Angle of the floating rib in respect to the spine indicates the angle of the other twelve ribs. When ribs at 45 degrees rotate to the 90 degree position, as in a barrel chest, they provide the maximum increase in chest cavity size, which increases breathing capacity. The ability to change chest cavity size determines stamina. A true barrel chest has the ribs at 90 degrees to the spine and cannot provide any change in the size of the chest cavity.

Ribs. Thirteen ribs form the sides of the chest cavity; bones whose shape determines the depth, length and width of the chest cavity and that provide protection to the lungs and the heart and various other organs. The first nine ribs are called the true ribs; the tenth, eleventh and twelfth are the false ribs and the thirteenth rib is the floating rib.

Ribs, flanged. A ridge at or near the bottom on one or both sides, resulting from an inward curve in the downward slope, resulting in a ridge or flange in all or part of the ribcage; fault in the Basset Hound.

Ribs, flat. Ribs spring out from spine and then arch downward; they are relatively flat, then turn in to connect with the sternum. Bedlington Terrier, Bearded Collie.

Ribs, well sprung. Ribs that spring out from the spine nearly level forming a broad back, arch downward and at the lower end curve in to connect with the breastbone; shape of chest (arch and lower end curve) can be round, oval or flat. The Black and Tan Coonhound has full, round, well sprung ribs; the Otterhound has a well sprung oval ribcage; the Whippet has ribs well sprung but with no suggestion of barrel shape; Bearded Collie ribs are well sprung from the spine but are flat at the sides.

Ridge. 1. Characteristic feature of the Rhodesian Ridgeback. The ridge on the back is formed by the hair growing in the opposite direction to the rest of the coat. The ridge is clearly defined, tapering and symmetrical; it starts immediately behind the shoulders and continues to a point between the prominence of the hips and should contain two identical crowns (whorls) directly opposite each other, located in the upper third of the ridge. 2. Frontal bones above eyes. See supra-orbital ridge.

Roach. Usually a roached back; an upward curved backline; backline humped; convex curvature of backline.

Ropey. Overly heavy facial wrinkles.

Rosettes. Tan spots on each side of the chest above the front legs. Manchester Terrier.

Rounded. Trimming about $1^1/_2$ inches off the ends of ear leather. Sometimes done on English Foxhounds to prevent tearing of ears while hunting and to denote dogs in a pack.

Rudder. Tail.

Ruff. Long and thick hair growth beginning in back of the ears and extending completely around the entire neck; the mane is on top of the neck. Golden Retriever, Norfolk Terrier, Japanese Chin, Schipperke, American Eskimo Dog. Preferred on Smooth Coat Chihuahua, Finnish Spitz, Keeshond, Shiba Inu.

Saddle. A dark (usually black) marking over the back; from location of a saddle as placed on a horse. The Afghan Hound saddle is short and close hair starting at the shoulders and continuing along the back from the ribs and flanks upwards forming a smooth back in mature dogs.

Samoyed smile. Mouth slightly curved up at the corners.

Scapula. Shoulder blade.

Scrotum. A paired pouch containing one testicle in each pouch, located on the abdominal floor between the hind legs.

Septum. Vertical line between the nostrils.

Set on. Tail set; sometimes used to refer to how head is set on neck joint; rarely used to refer to the set of neck into the shoulders.

Shaggy. Coat that is rough, coarse and rugged. Bearded Collie.

Shanks. Thighs; upper and lower shanks or upper and lower thighs. Doberman Pinscher.

Shelly. Narrow body with little spring to ribs and lack of depth to brisket.

Short-bodied. Short between front of chest and rear of dog.

Short-coupled. Short space between last rib and pelvis; short in loin.

Shoulder. Shoulder blade or scapula and associated muscles.

Shoulder height. Height of a dog measured from withers to ground.

Shoulder, point of. Foremost point of shoulder where scapula and humerus join.

Shoulder, sloping. Shoulder blade laid back.

Shoulders, closely set. Tops (or points) of the shoulder blades close to spine; in most breeds less than two fingers' spacing between the tops of the shoulder blades.

Shoulders, loaded. Excessively muscled shoulders; overdevelopment of shoulder muscles; loaded under the shoulder blade (causes out at the elbow).

Shoulders, loose. Shoulder not firmly attached to the side; normally caused by a lack of proper condition.

Shoulders, moderately well knit. Tops (or points) of shoulder blades moderately close to spine but well into the ribcage. Scottish Terrier.

Shoulders, oblique. Shoulder blade well laid back; a shoulder blade laid back at about 50 to 60 degrees from the vertical is "well laid back." A steep shoulder blade, 70 degrees or more, approaches the vertical and is not "well laid back."

Shoulders, out at. Tops (or points) of shoulder blades too far apart at the withers for a given breed (causes out at the elbow).

Shoulders, straight. Shoulder blades nearly vertical as opposed to well laid back; upright shoulder.

Sine qua non. Literal translation: "Without which not." An *essential* element or condition that has no equivalent. "*Elbows set quite straight . . . are a sine qua non*" (English Foxhound).

Sinew. A tendon; that which transmits strength or power from muscle to bone.

Sinewy. Having sinews of marked development; strong; tough; firm.

Skull. Bone components that make up the head; composed of a braincase (area from stop to occiput) and foreface or muzzle. Many Standards use term to refer to the braincase, topskull or backskull.

Skull, flat. Flat topskull.

Skull, well domed. Rounded in topskull; convex topskull.

Skully. Thick and coarse through skull.

Slab-sided. Flat ribs with too little spring from the spinal column for the given breed.

Snipy. Muzzle pointed and weak; no fill under the eyes, with narrow, thin jaws.

Socks. Hair on the feet from the front toes to the pasterns and from the rear toes to the hock joint on the Hairless variety of Chinese Crested.

Sound. Free from flaw, defect or decay; perfect for the kind; undamaged or unimpaired; healthy; robust; not diseased; dog with all its breed physical and temperament characteristics functioning properly.

Spayed. Female whose ovaries have been surgically removed.

Spectacles. Combination of markings and shadings in the orbital (eye) area that includes a delicate, dark line slanting from the outer corner of each eye toward the lower corner of each ear, coupled with expressive eyebrows. Keeshond.

Spinal column. Vertebrae from neck to end of tail; composed of cervical (seven), thoracic (thirteen), lumbar (seven), sacrum (three fused), and coccygeal (six to twenty-three) vertebrae.

Square or **square in profile.** Height at the withers equals the length of the body. Height is measured from the withers to the ground, and length is usually measured from the point of the forechest or breastbone to the point of the rump.

Stationed. Comparative ground to brisket height versus withers to brisket height; a high-stationed dog has ground to brisket height *greater* than withers to brisket. A low-stationed dog has a ground to brisket height *less* than withers to brisket. Basenjis are a high-stationed breed.

Stern. Rear end; tail; to the rear.

Sternum. Breastbone; brisket.

Stifle. Knee joint; stifle joint; located between the upper and lower thigh; the stifle includes the area on each side of the stifle joint. A well bent stifle has a marked angle at the stifle joint (German Shepherd Dog). Chow Chow stifles show little angulation.

Stilted. Without bend at the rear leg joints; usually used as in "stilted gait"; or moving without flexing the joints. (See Stifle.)

Stop. Dividing point between muzzle and skull. The change in profile line between the muzzle and skull; the step up at the junction of the nasal (maxilla) bone and frontal bone of the skull; Cocker Spaniel has a pronounced stop, Bull Terrier has none.

Substance. Plenty of bone; refers to heaviness of bone rather than fat. A well muscled dog also has substance, but a well muscled, small-boned dog is not referred to as having substance.

Superciliary ridge. Supra-orbital ridge; superciliary arch; region of the frontal bones forming the brows. Moderately raised in the Mastiff. Very strongly developed and forms nearly a right angle with the axis of the head in the Saint Bernard.

Supra-orbital ridge. See Superciliary ridge.

Swayback. Back with downward bow in it; concave curvature of back from withers to pelvis.

Tail. Caudal or coccygeal vertebrae; six to twenty-three vertebrae which attach to the sacral vertebrae; last part of spinal column.

Tail carried gaily in hound fashion. Tail carried at approximately 90 degrees to backline when dog is in motion. Basset Hound.

Tail, carrot. Relatively short, with good substance, as straight as possible, shaped like a carrot, standing erect, set on high, covered with hard hair and without feather. West Highland White Terrier.

Tail, corkscrew. Tail with a twist in the end. Very serious fault in Bichon Frise.

Tail, crank. Pump handle tail; tail resembling a crank or old-fashioned pump handle in shape. Staffordshire Bull Terrier.

Tail, crook in. Crook at extremity, terminal crook, similar to the printed letter "J" when viewed from dog's right side. Briard.

Tail, curled. Tail which curls over back; can be three-quarter or full, single or double curl. Akita, Basenji, Norwegian Elkhound, Pug, Finnish Spitz, Keeshond. Pug tail is curled as tightly as possible over hip; double curl is perfect.

Tail, flag. Hair on tail hangs down and forms a flag. Longhaired Dachshund. A fault in the Wirehaired Dachshund.

Tail, flagpole. Thin long tail carried up.

Tail, fox brush. Well-furred tail, covered all around with medium-length, bushy, stand-off, brush-like coat. Siberian Husky.

Tail, gay. A tail carried higher than desirable for the breed; usually the tail is held over the back.

Tail, hooked. Tail with an upward hook at the tip. Serious fault in Great Dane.

Tail, kink. A sharply angulated tail; a tail sharply bent because of a joint defect.

Tail, low-set. Tail base below level of backline.

Tail, "making the wheel." When excited, tail is carried high in a full circle above the back with the tip just touching either side of the loin. Great Pyrenees.

Tail, otter. Thick towards the base, gradually tapering towards the tip, of medium length, free from any feathering, clothed thickly with a short, dense coat, thus giving a rounded appearance. Labrador Retriever.

Tail, pipestopper. Tail that is too thin, lacking in substance and usually indicating lack of bone. Especially objectionable in Smooth Fox Terrier.

Tail, plumed. Long, flowing feathering on tail; hair on the tail as on Setters; long fringe of hair hanging from tail; a heavy coated tail carried over back. Maltese, Papillon, Pekingese, Pomeranian, Bichon Frise, Hairless variety of Chinese Crested.

Tail, pot-handle. Tail carried up and over the back, raised high above the topline in an arc, never touching or lying flat against back.

Tail, rat. Thick at the root and covered for two or three inches with short curls, tapers to a fine point at the end and from the root curls is covered with short, smooth hair so as to look as if it had been clipped. Irish Water Spaniel. Also a tail with entire absence of brush; fault in the American Foxhound.

Tail, ring. Tail that curves in a circular fashion; varies from the ring on the end of the Afghan Hound tail to the large circular ring of the Ibizan Hound.

Tail, rocker. Tail that curves like the rocker of a rocking chair. American Water Spaniel.

Tail, saber. Tail with a slight curve in the shape of a saber. At rest the German Shepherd Dog's tail hangs like a saber. The Petit Basset Griffon Vendéen carries the tail like the blade of a saber about 20 degrees to the aft of the vertical.

Tail, scimitar. A curved tail shaped like an Oriental sword. Bedlington Terrier.

Tail, screw. Short, hung low, with downward carriage, thick root and fine tip, with bends or kinks well defined—they may be abrupt or knotty, but no portion of the tail should be elevated above the base or root. Bulldog.

Tail, screw, carried well over the back. Tail set on high enough so that it is carried well over the back in a screw or tight or spiral curl, the end of which falls to the loin area and may have a kink at the end; not a pot-handle tail. Lhasa Apso.

Tail, shepherd's crook at end of. End of the tail is shaped like a U or kink called a shepherd's crook. Great Pyrenees.

Tail, sickle. Tail carried out and up in a loose semicircle (shaped like a sickle), but not touching the back. Siberian Husky.

Tail, snap. Similar to a sickle tail, but curves over the back with the tip in direct contact with the back.

Tail, spike. Straight short tail that tapers rapidly .

Tail, squirrel. Tail carried up and curved forward.

Tail, straight. Short, hung low, with downward carriage, thick root and fine tip, cylindrical and of uniform taper. Bulldog.

Tail, taper. Tail thicker where it joins the body, tapers to a point, and reaches no further than the hock joint. Manchester Terrier.

Tail, teapot curve. See tail, pot-handle.

Tail, tight. Tail that cannot be lifted from the body.

Tail, well curled. Tail that is tightly curled and rests entirely on either side. Basenji.

Tail, whip. Carried straight, stiff and pointed.

Tail set. How the base of the tail sets on the rump; level tail set (level with the back), low tail set (goose rump; dip at base of tail).

Teeth, deciduous. Milk teeth; puppy teeth. Twenty-eight properly placed teeth, fourteen in lower jaw and fourteen in upper jaw. Lower jaw—six incisors, two canines, six premolars; upper jaw—six incisors, two canines, six premolars. There are no teeth until three weeks of age; the twenty-eight teeth emerge between three and six weeks of age. The deciduous teeth are replaced with permanent teeth between two and seven months of age.

Teeth, eye. Upper canines.

Teeth, permanent. Adult teeth; forty-two properly placed teeth, twenty-two in lower jaw and twenty in upper jaw; lower jaw—six incisors, two canines, eight premolars, six molars; upper jaw—six incisors, two canines, eight premolars, four molars; full complement; full dentition.

Temple. Trumpet; region of the dog that is comparable to the temple in man; area behind eye socket on outside of skull; slight depression on each side of skull behind eye socket. See trumpet.

Tendons. Tissue fiber forming tough cords which in many cases attach muscle to bone.

Terrier front. Straight front as found on Fox Terriers; shoulder *well laid back* and upper arm relatively short and upright.

Testicles. Male gonads; the testes' two main functions are the production and storage of the male sperm cells and the secretion of the male sex hormone, testosterone; male dogs entered in dog shows are required to have two normal testicles properly descended into the scrotum.

Thigh. Portion of rear leg called *upper and lower* thigh, which is located between the hip joint and the hock joint; upper thigh is the area between the hip joint and the stifle joint; lower thigh is the area between the stifle joint and the hock joint.

Thorax. Portion of the body encased by the ribs; the thoracic cavity contains the lungs and heart.

Throat. Part of the neck below the lower jaw, containing pharynx, esophagus, larynx, trachea and gullet.

Throatiness. Excessive or loose skin under the throat.

Thumb mark. Black patch in the shape of a thumbprint on the forehead. Pug.

Thumbprint. Black patch surrounded by rust on the front of each foreleg at the pastern; on chocolate dog the patch is chocolate. Manchester Terrier. This is a disqualification in the Miniature Pinscher.

Tibia. Largest of two bones between stifle joint and hock joint; located in lower thigh.

Timber. Heavy bone, especially of legs.

Toenail. Claw; horn; cutaneous structure; the upper portion is called the wall and the bottom surface the sole. When the toenail is clipped too close, the nerves and blood vessels of the dermis respond by producing pain and bleeding.

Toes. There are four active toes or digits and in some cases one relatively functionless toe or dewclaw. A toe consists of three phalanges, with the toenail covering the third phalange. The active toes are joined by tissue or membrane called webbing. Each toe is cushioned by a digital pad. Situated to the rear of the four active toes is a large pad; the forefoot pad is called the metacarpal pad and the hind foot pad is called the metatarsal pad.

Toes, fused. Toes that are fused, or joined, together. Acceptable in the English Toy Spaniel.

Toes, well arched. Toes well knuckled up. Australian Cattle Dog.

Topknot. Hair on skull, from stop to occiput—Poodle; Profuse topknot highest at the crown, and tapering gradually to just back of nose—Bedlington Terrier; covering only top of skull—Australian Terrier; long, loose curls growing down into a well-defined peak between the eyes and falling like a shawl over the tops of ears and occiput—Irish Water Spaniel; head surmounted with a topknot of long, silky hair—Afghan Hound; head covered with long, silky hair that extends to cover the upper portion of the ears—Dandie Dinmont Terrier.

Topline. The line formed from the back of the ears, over the neck, withers, back, and croup to set-on of the tail. Often used in many Standards to mean the backline—from the rear of the withers to the tail set. A level topline refers to the backline being level. A sag in the topline refers to the backline being concave or sagging in the middle, with the low point just forward of the loin. A roach in the topline is a convex curve in the backline.

Topskull. Upper portion of backskull.

Trace. A black line extending from the occiput to the tail. Pug.

Trichiasis. One or more regular eyelashes positioned abnormally so that they can irritate the surface of the eye. Exudate and tear stain may be evident at the corner of the eye.

Trousers. Breeching; culotte; pants; profuse feathering on the rear leg down to the hocks—not below. Keeshond.

Trumpet. Region of the dog that is comparable to the temple on man; area behind eye socket on outside of skull; slight depression on each side of skull behind eye socket. Weimaraner.

Truncated. Muzzle blunt, cut off, square. Mastiff, Old English Sheepdog.

Tuck-in. Looking down on the loin, the sides are as wide as the ribcage and rearquarters and there is a smooth transition between the ribcage and the rearquarters.

Tuck-up. Narrow-waisted in the loin; rise in bottom line at loin area; ribs are normal, not herring-gutted, and tuck-up begins at the end of the ribs; area of the lower stomach line or belly.

Turned-upward. Muzzle or foreface turned up; uptilted foreface; upsweep of underjaw; turning up of lower jaw. Bulldog.

Ulna. Non–weight bearing bone of the foreleg. Radius and ulna form the foreleg or forearm.

Undercoat. At the base of the outer coat is a shorter growth of finer and softer hair, the undercoat.

Underline. Bottom line; the line formed from behind the elbows along the brisket and belly or abdominal floor to the hindquarters; lower line of brisket and loin; underbody—Miniature Schnauzer.

Up on leg. Leggy; appears high off the ground; high-stationed. Basenji.

Upper arm. The region between the shoulder joint and the lower arm. Consists of the humerus and associated ligaments and muscles.

Upsweep. Lower jaw turns up and out.

Varmity. Typical of Terrier's expression; a piercing expression; the expression of varmints.

Veil. Head hair which screens the forehead and eyes. Skye Terrier.

Vent. Opening of lower intestine; area around the anus of the dog; area around the anus and vulva of the bitch. Manchester Terrier.

Ventral. Directional term meaning toward or relatively near the belly.

Walleye. Merle eye; eye with whitish iris; associated with merle coat color in Collies, Shelties, Australian Shepherds, Old English Sheepdogs and Harlequin Great Danes; either or both eyes can be walleyed.

Weaselness. Long and slender body with short legs. Old English Sheepdog should be absolutely free of weaselness.

Webbing. Membrane between the toes. Especially useful for traveling over marshy or soft ground, sand and snow and for swimming. The extent of the webbing varies with the breed; Arctic breeds, retrievers, Otterhounds and Salukis have well developed and strong webbing that approaches the end of the toe. Webbing reaches the toe tips in the Portuguese Water Dog.

Wedge, well-blunted lean. Head shape; head is smooth and clean in outline; on the sides it tapers gradually and smoothly from the ears to the end of the nose; muzzle is well rounded and blunt with strong underjaw. Collie.

Weedy. Light-boned, lacking substance.

Well filled-in under eyes. Foreface and braincase juncture under the eye showing strength and substance. Australian Cattle Dog.

Whiskers. Specialized type of hairs; tactile hairs; sometimes mistakenly referred to as vibrissae; large single hairs which are surrounded by many nerves that are responsive to touch; functional part of a hunting dog; tactile hairs can be located grouped along the orbital crest (eyebrows), on the zygomatic arch, down and directly below the outer corner of the eye, below the nose and above the upper lip, on the lower jaw, under the forward portion of the lower jaw, and under the rear portion of the lower jaw. The location and extent vary by breed; in some cases complete mustache and beard develop.

Wiry jacket. Outer wire coat with dense undercoat. Border Terrier.

Withers. First nine dorsal or thoracic vertebrae; bony projections of vertebrae in the vicinity of shoulder blades; highest point of the shoulders behind the neck.

Withers spot. White mark varying in size, but centered on the withers or at the base of the neck. Alaskan Malamute.

Wrinkle. Wrinkled skin on foreface and forehead. Basenji, Bloodhound. Wrinkles typically appear on the forehead of the Boxer when the ears are erect. A fault in the Boxer when this wrinkle is either too deep (wet) or lacking (dry).

Wrist. The region between the forearm and the pastern, consisting of the seven carpal bones and associated ligaments and muscles.

Wry-jawed. Wry mouth; lower jaw area of foreface noticeably out of level.

Zygomatic arch. Forms the cheekbone, located below the eye. The (temporalis and masseter) muscles attach to the zygomatic arch and close the mouth by lifting the lower jaw. The stop and zygomatic arch are the major contributors to head shape. the Rottweiler has a well developed zygomatic arch.

INDEX

A

Aesthetic appearance, 1, 2, 8
Aesthetic breeds, 166–68
Afgan Hound, 6, 43, 44, 47, 48, 49, 51, 52, 71, 83, 104, 107, 114, 118, 131, 136, 137, 139, 151–52, 177, 181, 195
African Hunting Dog, 125–126
Agility, 39, 40, 46, 48, 51, 114
Airdale Terrier, 47, 87, 95, 111, 157
Akita, 87, 108, 145, 146, 147
Alaskan Malamute, 33, 51, 55, 66, 74, 105, 120, 144, 145, 146, 184, 190–91, 195
Amble, 7, 17, 19–21, 177, 188
American Eskimo, 145
American Foxhound, 107, 157
American Kennel Club, 2, 3, 17, 122–23, 143
American Staffordshire Terrier, 78, 179
American Water Spaniel, 122
Anatomy, 3, 12
Angulation, 46, 62–64, 105–6
excessive, 23, 52, 140
Antelope, 42, 44, 47, 67
pronged, 49, 50, 131, 132
Arch, fall of, 113, 182
Arched neck, 7, 103–4, 108
Arctic dogs, 12, 49, 73, 119, 136, 145–49, 192
Articular head, 62
Artist's point of view, 7–8
Australian Terrier, 79, 155

B

Back, 3, 108–12, 134–35
sideways movement, 135
Backline, 108–12, 178, 181, 182
Back reach, 39, 42, 44, 45–46, 57
Backskull, 3, 92
Balance, 99–100
Ball and socket, 35, 44–45, 49, 62, 115, 140, 143
Barrel chest, 115–16
Basenji, 44, 46, 70, 95, 96, 122–23, 136, 137, 181
Basset Hound, 79, 86, 87, 92, 98–99, 123, 132, 186, 193
Beagle, 8, 51, 57, 71, 76, 77, 78, 82, 83, 87, 90, 95, 97, 99, 107, 118, 119, 157
Bearded Collie, 66
Bedlington Terrier, 80, 89, 100, 111, 113, 182
Behavior, 3, 12, 124
Belgian Malinois, 66, 78, 114
Belgian Sheepdog, 48, 78
Belgian Tervuren, 51, 78, 105, 133, 180
Biceps, 30, 34
Bichon Frise, 83–84, 112
Bighorn sheep, 43, 44
Bite, 93
fixed, 93–94
Black wolf, 7
Bloodhound, 12, 86, 92, 95, 96, 101

Body
long, 23, 136–37
short, 70, 71, 136–37
Border Terrier, 100, 155
Borzoi, 48, 49, 78, 82, 83, 84, 87, 90, 94, 114, 118, 119, 136
Boston Terrier, 82, 83, 118, 166, 167
Bottom line, 114
Boxer, 48, 70, 133, 136, 195
Brachiocephalicus muscle, 31, 36, 38, 80, 103, 136
Brachycephalic head, 70, 82, 83–84
Briard, 21, 112
Brittany, 85, 86, 87, 89, 108, 112, 122
Brussels Griffon, 87, 90
Bulldog, 2, 10, 12, 13, 19, 23, 51, 73, 74, 78, 79, 83, 84, 90, 92, 93, 94, 96, 105, 109, 110, 116, 128, 129, 132, 133, 141, 166, 171–73, 177, 179
Bullmastiff, 114–15, 133, 162, 163–64
Bull Terrier, 48, 78, 87, 179
Bush dog, 6, 8, 125
Buttocks, 44

C

Cadence, 141, 177
Cairn Terrier, 33, 54, 56, 90, 91, 155
Calcaneal process, 39, 40, 50, 51

Camel, 20, 52, 55
Camouflage, 117, 120
Canine teeth, 85, 94, 95
Canter, 177
Carpals, 53, 58
Cat feet, 37, 52, 56
Center of gravity, 19, 24–26
Cervical ligament, 103, 106
Cheek muscles, 84, 93
Cheeky, 85, 93
Cheetah, 33, 37, 49, 67, 104,
    130–32, 150, 193
Chesapeake Bay Retriever, 6,
    52, 88, 110, 119, 130
Chest, 29, 31
    circular, 73–74
    flat, 74
    principles of, 72–74
Chihuahua, 87, 90, 92–93, 100
Chinese Crested, 166, 167, 168
Chinese Shar–Pei, 79, 110,
    113, 120
Chow Chow, 49, 51, 57, 90, 91,
    93, 112, 145, 148–49
Claw, 53
Coat, 6, 117–19
    curly, 121
    oily, 119, 120
    pattern, 88, 118
    regulation, 123
    stand off, 119
    summer, 121
    texture, 119–21
    winter, 121
    wire, 119, 120
Cocker Spaniel, 6, 13, 47, 85,
    90, 93, 97, 98, 99, 112,
    138, 195
Collie, 66, 83, 84, 87, 88, 89,
    90, 98, 105, 118, 177,
    180
Color, self, 118
Coonhound, 96
Cow-hocked, 67, 128, 129,
    179, 189
Coyote, 125, 128, 186, 189
Crabbing, 22–23, 128, 139–40
Crest, 3
Croup, 3, 42, 43, 44, 46–48,
    109, 117, 187
Cryptorchid, 97, 122–23
Curly–Coated Retriever, 121
Cursorial, 18, 48, 78, 113, 126,
    128, 136, 149–54

D

Dachshund, 2, 6, 10, 47, 49, 51,
    66–67, 71, 74, 75, 80,
    97, 105, 106, 118, 132,
    137, 141, 159
Daisy clipping, 133–36
Dalmatian, 10, 66, 112
Damara zebra, 43, 44
Dandie Dinmont Terrier, 100,
    105, 111, 155, 181
Depth of perception, 90
Diagonal, 188
Diaphragm, 116
Digging, 6, 54, 57, 66, 74, 75,
    93, 155, 157, 159
Doberman Pinscher, 26, 54,
    104, 180, 188
Dog terms, 4
Dolichocephalic head, 82, 83
Double suspension gallop, 17,
    26–28, 68, 104, 134,
    136, 137
Draft, 33, 46, 49, 51, 52, 66, 70,
    74, 132, 135, 145–46
Drooping ears, 95
Drop ears, 96

E

Ears, 95–96, 187
Elbow, 3, 35, 77
    out at, 62, 70, 105, 106,
        128, 129
Endurance, 2, 7, 23, 33, 38, 44,
    46, 50, 51, 64, 65, 74, 117,
    125–26, 128, 136, 189
English Foxhound, 76, 78, 119
English Setter, 78
English Springer Spaniel, 66,
    78, 87
English Water Spaniel, 2
Eskimo Dog, 145
Ewe neck, 7, 103, 104
Extensor, 34, 61
Eye color, 87–89
Eyelid, 92
Eye rim color, 89
Eyes
    dark, 10, 12, 87, 118
    placement, 89–91

sunken, 90, 91
wide-angle vision, 90

F

Faking, 89, 123–24
False ribs, 101, 103, 116
Fancy points, 3, 10, 12, 195
Feet
    cat, 52, 56, 150
    flat, 57
    hare, 52, 56, 150
    large, 6, 52, 55, 56, 130
    in motion, 52–57
    webbed, 6, 52, 56
Field Spaniel, 78
Finnish Spitz, 87, 108, 145,
    149
Flank, 3, 134–35
Flapping, 79, 80–81
Flat-Coated Retriever, 112,
    121, 139
Flat feet, 57
Flew, 3
Flexor, 34, 61
Flying trot, 23, 37, 49, 127,
    129
Follow-through, 39–40
Forechest, 3
Foreface, 3, 92
Forequarters, 58, 59–81
Foxes, 23, 136
Foxhound, 12, 71, 77, 95, 107,
    157
Fox Terrier, 11, 75, 76, 77, 84,
    89, 93, 98, 100, 107,
    117, 136, 157, 180,
    193
French Bulldog, 109, 179
Front, 75, 76–77, 157, 186

G

Gait, 17–28, 37, 64, 126–28,
    175–83, 187, 188
Gallop, 17, 26–28, 38, 40, 48,
    112, 177, 188, 192
Genes, 68–69, 118, 122
German Shepherd Dog, 21, 23,
    49, 50, 57, 78, 83, 107,

108, 112, 115, 127, 128, 129, 133, 138, 139, 170–71, 177, 180, 181, 195
German Shorthaired Pointer, 49, 73, 86, 194
German Wirehaired Pointer, 78, 111, 138
Giant Schnauzer, 21
Giraffe, 20, 69, 71, 72, 130, 135
Glenoid cavity, 62
Golden Retriever, 66, 74, 86, 111, 133, 139, 181, 186, 188
Goose rump, 44, 46
Gordon Setter, 106
Great Dane, 70, 88, 162, 188
Great Pyrenees, 162, 164–65
Greyhound, 5, 6, 7, 12, 17, 33, 38, 48, 49, 51, 52, 57, 78, 84, 85, 96, 113, 114, 117, 118, 119, 130, 131, 135, 136, 137, 180, 182, 193
Guard hairs, 119

H

Hackney gait, 6, 79, 133–34, 177
Hackney-like action, 79–80, 142
Hare feet, 52, 56
Harrier, 76, 77, 78, 107, 112, 157
Head, 100–101
    motion, 38, 103, 135
    narrow, 83, 84, 90, 94
Herring gut, 114, 117
Hindquarters, 39–58
Hipbone, 44, 101
Hip socket, 35, 44, 45, 49, 140, 143
Hock, 39, 50, 117
    angle, 51–52
    close, 5
    joint, 3, 39, 40, 41
    well-bent, 51–52
Hopping, 141
Horse terms, 17
Hucklebone, 44
Hycrancan, 162

I

Ibizan Hound, 112, 153–54
Incisors, 94–95, 104
Inheritance, 122
Interfering, 142
Iris, 87, 88
Irish Setter, 65, 80
Irish Terrier, 100, 157
Irish Water Spaniel, 52
Irish Wolfhound, 48
Ischium, 40, 48, 187
Italian Greyhound, 48, 90, 105, 114, 177, 180

J

Jackal, 67, 125, 136, 186, 189
Jaws, 6, 33, 85, 93, 104
Jimela Topi, 16, 18, 19, 44
Joint
    ankle, 39, 40
    elbow, 35, 59, 65, 77
    hinge, 35, 48, 62, 77
    hip, 35, 39, 40, 44, 45, 49
    hock, 3, 39, 40, 41, 50
    knee, 39, 40
    shoulder, 35, 36–38, 58, 62, 65
    socket, 35, 44–45, 49, 62, 115, 140, 143
    stifle, 49
    wrist, 53, 58, 59, 60

K

Keeshond, 9, 114, 145, 149
Kerry Blue Terrier, 21, 47, 98, 105, 158–59
Kinesiology, 32

L

Labrador Retriever, 20, 84, 89, 118
Lakeland Terrier, 93
Lame dogs, 125, 143

Large Water Dog, 2
Lateral instability, 19, 23–26, 132
Legs
    long, 6, 23, 44, 65, 130
    short, 6, 8, 66, 70, 71, 74, 75, 130, 132, 141, 159
    speed, 6
    trotting, 7, 128
Levers, 31, 34, 37, 39, 59, 131–32
Lhasa Apso, 86, 87, 166
Ligaments, 34, 61
    cervical, 34
Loin, 3, 69, 70, 78, 101, 102, 108, 109, 112–14
Loose skin, 92, 96

M

Maltese, 121, 166
Manchester Terrier, 112, 114
Mandible, 84, 85, 104
Maned wolf, 125
Mastiff, 162–63
Mastiff-type dogs, 162–66
Merle coat, 118
Mesaticephalic head, 82, 83
Metacarpals, 53, 59
Miniature Pinscher, 6, 47, 49, 80, 98, 142, 177, 180
Miniature Schnauzer, 21, 120
Molars, 94–95
Molossian, 162
Monorchid, 97, 122–23
Musclebound, 33
Muscles, 29–38
    biceps, 30, 34
    brachiocephalicus, 31, 36, 38, 80, 103, 136
    characteristics, 33–34
    dark, 33, 37, 186
    development, 35
    digastricus, 85
    extension, 34, 61
    flexor, 34, 61
    latissimus dorsi, 30, 36
    longissimus lumborum, 113
    longissimus thoracis, 115
    masseter, 30, 31, 85, 93
    omotransversarius, 30, 36
    pectineus, 41, 49

Muscles (*cont.*)
  pectoral, 36
    deep, 30, 31, 77
    superficial, 30, 31, 77
  pectoralis major, 115
  pectoralis minor, 115
  rearing, 48–49, 55, 110, 137
  rhomboideus, 36
  capitis, 31
    cervicis, 31
    thoracic, 31
  serratus ventralis, 32, 36
  temporal, 30, 84, 85, 93
  trapezius, 30, 36, 59, 62, 69
    cervical, 30
    thoracic, 30
  triceps, 30
  white, 33, 37, 186
Muzzle
  snipy, 93
  square, 93

N

Neck, 3, 29, 31, 102, 104
  long, 33, 68, 70, 103–4, 135
  short, 33, 68, 70, 103–4, 136
Newfoundland, 95, 162, 165
Newton, Sir Isaac, 132
Norfolk Terrier, 155
Norwegian Elkhound, 35, 49, 51, 137, 145, 148
Norwich Terrier, 155
Nose, 86–87
  color, 86, 118
  parti-colored, 86

O

Occiput, 3
Occipital protuberance, 83–85, 104
Old English Sheepdog, 20, 87, 136, 141, 142, 181
Optical illusions, 7, 21, 47, 138–39
Origin of dog, 125
Os calcis, 50
Otterhound, 95
Out at elbow, 62, 70, 105–6, 128–29

Overshot bite, 93–94
Oxen, 66

P

Pace, 17, 19–21, 177, 188
Padding, 80, 81
Paddling, 46, 62, 69, 71, 74, 77, 80, 81, 128, 129, 143, 179
Pads, showing, 57
Papillon, 50, 55, 173–74
Pasterns, 3, 39, 40, 41, 50, 58, 59, 60, 77, 79, 106, 180
Patella, 32, 39, 40, 44, 101
Paws, 37
Pekingese, 79–80, 83, 84, 90, 166
Pelvis, 39, 40, 41, 42, 44–46, 48, 101, 102, 187
Pendulum, 75, 76, 130, 134
Pendulums, 31
Petit Basset Griffon Vendeen, 179
Pharaoh Hound, 153–54
Pisiform bone, 53, 58, 77
Plume, 119, 136
Pocket Beagle, 2
Pointer, 19, 78, 87, 104, 113, 114, 130, 168–69, 177, 181
Point of
  breastbone, 32, 103
  buttocks, 3
  elbow, 58, 59
  forechest, 3
  hock, 3, 39, 40, 41, 50
  shoulder, 3, 58, 63, 105, 106
Polo pony, 44
Pomeranian, 108, 138, 145, 149, 166
Poodle, 80, 94, 95, 110, 115, 121, 136, 166, 177, 181, 195
Portuguese Water Dog, 56
Posed examination, 97–124
Prick ears, 95
Pronged antelope, 49–50, 131–32
Prosternum, 32, 60, 103
Pug, 8, 70, 83, 84, 90, 91, 115, 138, 166, 179
Puli, 137

Purpose of a breed, 2, 6, 8, 49, 51, 145, 195

R

Radius, 53, 58, 59, 60, 63, 77, 101
Rearing muscle, 48–49, 55, 110, 137
Rear leg assembly, 39–52
Rhythm defects, 22, 141
Rib
  false, 101, 103, 116
  floating, 101, 116–17
  well sprung, 114–15
Rib cage, 3, 59, 68–70, 71, 101, 102, 115, 187
Roach, 5, 113, 149
Rocking horse, 129, 188
Rocky Mountain bighorn sheep, 43, 44
Roll, 23, 79, 141, 177, 189
Rope walking, 143
Rose ears, 96
Rottweiler, 162, 165–66
Ruby eyes, 87, 88
Running uphill, 39, 42–44, 46, 137

S

Sagittal crest, 83–85
Saint Bernard, 162
Saluki, 13, 27, 28, 87, 112, 117, 120, 152–53, 186, 188, 193
Samoyed, 20, 51, 54, 87, 113, 117, 119–20, 130, 145, 146–48
Scapula, 63, 101
Scenthounds, 12, 149
Schipperke, 118, 145
Scientific principles, 2, 6, 7, 132, 145–74
Scissors bite, 93–94
Scottish Deerhound, 2, 13, 42, 48, 78, 106, 112, 113, 149, 153
Scottish Terriers, 70, 71, 106, 112, 132, 133, 155–56
Sealyham Terrier, 106, 155, 156
Setters, 83

Shetland Sheepdog, 20, 54, 66, 80, 88, 89, 133, 177, 180
Shiba Inu, 145
Shih Tzu, 121–22, 166
Short back, 70–71, 136–37
Short legs, 6, 8, 66, 70–71, 74, 75, 130, 132, 141, 159
Shoulder blades, 2, 35, 36–38, 58, 59, 60, 61, 62–72, 101, 103, 105–6, 186
Shoulder joint, 58, 59, 62
Shoulders loaded, 105–6
Showing pads, 57
Siberian Husky, 9, 66, 89, 139, 145, 149, 195
Sickle hocks, 52, 134
Side sway, 25–26
Sighthounds, 17, 26, 27, 48, 61, 67–68, 73, 78, 104, 126, 135, 145, 149–54, 192
Similarities, 145
Single plane, 126, 128, 129, 189
Single suspension gallop, 17, 26–27, 137
Single tracking, 7, 23, 26, 73, 128, 132
Size, 99
Skin, loose, 92, 96
Skull, 84–85, 92–93, 102, 104
Skye Terrier, 70, 100, 155
Smooth Fox Terrier, 76, 89, 108, 117, 157, 178
Soft mouth, 6, 85
Soundness, 3, 10
Spanish Pointer, 12
Sparring, 100
Speed, 39–40, 44, 46, 49, 50, 51, 66–68, 70, 73, 78, 114, 117, 128, 130–32, 150, 192, 193
Square body, 69, 136–37, 192
Square muzzle, 93
Staffordshire Bull Terrier, 48, 84, 85, 93, 179
Standard of perfection, 2, 3–6, 98–99, 176
Standard Poodle, 33, 60
Standard Schnauzer, 70, 80
Sternebrae, 101, 103
Stifles, 3, 39, 40, 41, 49–50, 117

Stop, 3, 53, 83–85, 104
Stringing up, 80, 135, 139
Structure, 1, 101–24, 185
Sunburn nose, 86
Sussex Spaniel, 115
Symmetry, 1, 99–100

T

Tail, 3, 43, 44, 46, 47, 48, 101, 102, 109, 119, 136
Talbot Hound, 2
Teeth, 85, 93–95
Tendons, 34, 38, 39, 50
Terriers, 12, 71, 74–75, 84, 85, 92, 97, 98, 100, 107, 120, 142, 145, 154–59
Testicles, 122–23
Thigh, 29, 32
  first, 3, 39, 41, 46
  second, 3, 39, 41
Topline, 65, 108–12, 181
Toy dogs, 89, 97, 100, 130, 166–67, 173, 178
Tradition, 3, 8–9
Trot, 7, 17, 20, 21–23, 25, 35, 40, 51, 61, 65, 74, 128, 139, 176–78, 177, 188, 189, 193
  flying, 23, 37, 49, 127, 129
  ordinary, 23, 37
  short, 23
Type, 3, 8, 10, 11, 98–99

U

Uganda kob, 42, 44
Ulna, 53, 58, 59, 60, 63, 77, 101
Undershot bite, 93–94
Upper arm, 3, 36, 58, 59, 60, 65, 66, 74, 75, 77

V

Vertebrae, 46, 68–69

atlas, 103, 104
axis, 104
caudal, 44, 101, 102
cervical, 36, 85, 101, 102, 103, 104
lumbar, 101, 102
thoracic, 36, 59, 60, 64, 101, 102
Vizsla, 70, 114

W

Walk, 17, 18–19, 61, 177, 188
Weaving, 62, 128, 129, 143, 179
Web feet, 6, 52, 56
Weimaraner, 56, 88, 122, 123
Welsh Corgi, Cardigan, 48, 88, 101, 106, 133, 138, 160–62, 179
Welsh Corgi, Pembroke, 160–61, 179
Welsh Terrier, 120, 157, 158
West Highland White Terrier, 112, 115, 155
Whippet, 48, 51, 78, 114, 115, 118, 119, 122, 130, 150, 182, 193
Wild dogs, 67, 125, 140, 186
Withers, 3, 58, 59, 62, 65, 78, 101, 106, 108
Wolves, 6, 7, 23, 42, 67, 88, 125, 128, 136, 186, 189
Wrist joint, 53, 58, 59, 60

Y

Yellow eyes, 10, 12, 87, 88, 118, 122
Yorkshire Terrier, 121

Z

Zebra, 43, 44
Zygomatic arch, 83–85